T0330051

Venture
Capital
Valuation

Founded in 1807, John Wiley & Sons is the oldest independent publishing company in the United States. With offices in North America, Europe, Australia, and Asia, Wiley is globally committed to developing and marketing print and electronic products and services for our customers' professional and personal knowledge and understanding.

The Wiley Finance series contains books written specifically for finance and investment professionals as well as sophisticated individual investors and their financial advisors. Book topics range from portfolio management to e-commerce, risk management, financial engineering, valuation, and financial instrument analysis, as well as much more.

For a list of available titles, visit our Web site at www.WileyFinance.com.

Venture Capital Valuation

Case Studies and Methodology

LORENZO CARVER

John Wiley & Sons, Inc.

Published by John Wiley & Sons, Inc., Hoboken, New Jersey.
Published simultaneously in Canada.

For general information on our other products and services or for technical support, please contact our Customer Care Department within the United States at (800) 762-2974, outside the United States at (317) 572-3993 or fax (317) 572-4002.

Wiley also publishes its books in a variety of electronic formats. Some content that appears in print may not be available in electronic books. For more information about Wiley products, visit our Web site at www.wiley.com.

Library of Congress Cataloging-in-Publication Data:

Carver, Lorenzo, 1968–
  Venture capital valuation : case studies and methodology / Lorenzo Carver. — 1
    p. cm. — (Wiley finance series)
  Includes index.
  ISBN 978-0-470-90828-0 (hardback); ISBN 978-1-118-18232-1 (ebk);
  ISBN 978-1-118-18233-8 (ebk); ISBN 978-1-118-18234-5 (ebk)
  1. Venture capital—Case studies.   2. Valuation—Case studies.   I. Title.
  HG4751.C367 2012
  658.15—dc23
                                                            2011037186

Printed in the United States of America

10 9 8 7 6 5 4 3 2 1

Contents

Acknowledgments

I'd like to thank God for giving me the time and wherewithal to write this book, John DeRemigis of John Wiley and Sons for suggesting I write it and making that happen, and my friends, family, clients, customers, and partners who put up with my efforts to get it done. Also, I'm grateful for Jennifer MacDonald's, of John Wiley and Sons, patience as I tested ways to communicate a complex topic to a broader pool of beneficiaries than just valuation professionals.

Thanks to my immediate family, Sandra Carver, Lorenzo Carver Sr., Lester and Vanessa Carver, and Sandra and Todd Welch, Kaila, Jasmine, Victor, Veronica, Charity, Aaron, Avery, and Rachel.

Many of my friends, and all of my business partners, helped me with these efforts just by being themselves and having a passion for entrepreneurs and entrepreneurial finance as much as I do. But some of those were particularly instrumental in keeping me focused on this task or otherwise allowing me to focus on it by picking up the slack elsewhere. This list includes, but is not limited to, my friend and valuation partner Connie Yi, Esq. of Carver Yi, LLP, all my friends, partners, and shareholders at Liquid Scenarios, Inc., but especially Sacha Millstone, Alan Kaplan, Chris Svarczkopf, Michael Edwards, David Jilke, Tony Jones, Henry Wright, Alexey Gavrilov, Alexander Vinogradov, Eugene Mymrin, Manoj Biswas, Susan Jarvis, Sue Perrault, Tim Barlow, Claudine Schneider, KG Charles-Harris, Manish Jindal and Peter Fusaro, and my friends and fellow shareholders at Free409A/TapMyBooks, David Berkus and Eric Woo.

I also wish to thank my customers and clients, who have effectively subsidized my continuous education in this area over the past 20 years, especially my friends Mark Freedle, Frank Maresca, Sina Simantob, Jason Mendelson of Foundry Group, Jeff Donnan and Stephen Pouge of First Round Capital, Jack Genest, Sarah Reed and the finance team at Charles River Ventures, Harry D'Andrea of Valhalla Partners, Matt Potter of Delphi, and all other Liquid Scenarios Users, the thousands of small companies that have purchased BallPark Business Valuation and the millions that visited BulletProof Business Plans over the years.

What You Don't Know About Valuation Will Cost You Money

How would you feel if you sold $2 million "worth" of Google stock and received $50 in cash instead of $2 million? This happens to venture-backed companies everyday and that's why understanding valuation is critical.

The terms "value" and "valuation" are used a lot for high-growth private companies and that's a bad thing. It's bad because when founders, VCs, angels, attorneys, CFOs, CEOs, and employees use these words and don't truly understand what they mean, those same people end up losing lots of money as a result.

Imagine you log in to your brokerage account. You see your 2,000 shares of Google valued at $2,000,000, place a market order to sell all 2,000 shares, and wait for it to clear. A few minutes later you get a confirmation that you sold 2,000 shares, received $0 in proceeds, and owe the brokerage firm $50.00 in commissions. A transaction you expected to put $2,000,000 in your pocket has instead effectively taken $2,000,050 out of your pocket. How would that make you feel? What would your spouse's reaction be? Most of us would experience a rapid increase in heart rate and an unpleasant feeling in our stomachs. The culmination of this fight-or-flight response would at least be a call to our broker to find out what happened to the other $2,000,000 (yours) and get it back.

Yet this same scenario plays out for real every day for VCs, founders, angels, limited partners, strategic investors, CEOs, CFOs and employees of high-growth companies and most people don't panic and don't feel the need to make a phone call. Why? Because they don't know what's happening to them until it's too late to do anything about it. This book represents an opportunity for those parties to stop losing money before it's too late to do anything about it, by understanding how "value" changes their rights to cash flow at every stage of a company's evolution.

WHAT THIS BOOK IS ABOUT AND WHOM IT IS FOR

In a broad sense, this book is for anyone who's involved with a venture capital- or angel-backed private company who wants to maximize his or her investment by controlling one of the few things you can when dealing with high-velocity, risky investments after you've committed: your understanding of valuation.

In many ways, valuing an early-stage venture-backed company (one that's received financing) is a lot easier than valuing a traditional privately held company. You would never know that by reading a 409A valuation report, looking at a certificate of incorporation, or viewing an investor rights agreement for a venture-funded company, though. While those venture deal complexities, which relate to rights and preferences for various securities and holders, are absent in the vast majority of traditional private companies, access to capital, networks, and long runways to the first meaningful customer are also absent in most traditional businesses. The result is that venture capital- and angel-backed company value is better measured in terms of volatility, as opposed to traditional private companies, which are generally more easily valued in terms of cash flow, or operating income benefit streams, in their early lives.

From a valuation perspective, this allows you to focus on the existing investors and capital structure (the known variables) more so than you could ever do with a traditional business. As these angel- and venture-backed companies evolve, faster and often more dramatically than would ever be acceptable for a traditional business, the one constant, in most cases, is the investors and, ideally, parts of the founding management team. These elements, and this pattern, can be reduced to simple math, and that simple math can produce useful indications and conclusions of value.

However, none of those conclusions, or indications of value, are of any use unless you understand how they were arrived at and what the limiting conditions and assumptions are. This book uses real-life cases where stakeholders in a given startup or high-growth company could have made out better simply by having better information about valuation. In other words, if the company had performed exactly as it did using misunderstood valuation inputs, parties in the know would have increased their profits without changing how the company operated in any way.

MY PERSPECTIVE ON VALUATION AND THIS BOOK'S SETUP

I've spent the better part of my adult life making it easier for those who want to understand high-growth company valuation to do so, primarily by creating software. But before I released my first valuation software in the late 1990s, I had spoken with hundreds of entrepreneurs, attorneys, investors, and other parties, who would always ask questions like:

- "What's this company worth?"
- "Is this a fair valuation?"
- "Are we leaving too much money on the table?"

The entrepreneurs I had the conversations with were some of the smartest people I've ever known, including award-winning PhDs, with patents to their name for products that have literally either saved or vastly improved the lives of millions around the world. Yet, explaining valuation to these sophisticated parties verbally or even with an interactive spreadsheet still didn't make it intuitive enough that they felt comfortable when the ink dried on their deals. That's when I decided to take six months off from consulting and write a software application that made it intuitive for almost anyone. I realized that software allowed people to get instant satisfaction and experiment with "what if" inputs that were hard to do on a scratch pad or on a spreadsheet. That software application, BallPark Business Valuation, focused on the discounted cash flow (DCF) and capitalization of earnings methods, which are both methods within the income approach to valuation mentioned in Chapters 3 and 4.

In the late 1990s, I created several hundred valuations as part of strategic planning for high-growth companies. These valuations were used to explain to management what a reasonable range of returns would be based on the capital they were seeking, the types of businesses they were starting (IT, Internet related, biotech, medical device, and so forth), and the time horizon to a liquidity event. In 1996 and 1997, the value indications I generated, both with respect to pre-money/post-money values and in terms of true "enterprise" values, tended to be close to what clients actually ended up realizing when raising funds. But when 1998 rolled around, almost all founders I built a valuation analysis for in conjunction with their finance strategy were quick to let me know that they were getting twice, or even four times, the "pre-money" valuations I suggested would be reasonable before they closed their financing. This trend increased, month after month, and by the time Red Herring had written an article on my strategic planning services, half the entrepreneurs I worked with would balk at the valuation estimates as being way too low. So who was right, me or my clients?

As you will see in the very first chapter of this book, "Using Facebook, Twitter, and LinkedIn to Explain VC Valuation Gains and Losses," my clients could be right with their higher assumed "valuations," and I could be right with my lower assumed "value indications," depending on what "standard" of value was used. Financial buyers, as discussed in Chapters 1,

3, 5, 6, 7, 8, and 9, are willing to pay for the cash flow, or benefits, a business is capable of producing as of the date of the transaction. If VCs and angels priced deals this way, they would effectively own almost 100% of each company they invested in, not including options reserved for future issuance. Instead, the expectation is that a series of subsequent financing rounds, ideally at increasing prices, should bring a venture-backed company closer to the point where financial buyers could foreseeably participate in either a financing of the company or an acquisition of the company.

Early in the process of building a valuation analysis as part of strategy engagements, I used to begin by trying to solve for the value of a client company to a financial buyer. I knew both experientially and from auditing VC funds before starting my consulting practice, BulletProof Business Plans, that most VCs, angels, and early-stage investors in general were not financial buyers. However, I also believed that once investment values and speculative values became "market values," there would be an opportunity to acquire any residual intellectual property once it was clear that little or no future cash flows would ever be realized for the vast majority of "overvalued" Internet companies, in the absence of restructuring. Based on that hypothesis, BulletProof Business Plans founded a publicly traded company to value and "harvest" the intellectual property from these companies as they went out of business. In exchange for investor rights to the IP, which a lot of parties were more or less walking away from at the time, investors in overpriced private companies about to fail would receive interests in a publicly traded, but restricted, stock, and the publicly traded company would redeploy the IP in new ventures or otherwise sell it.

That exercise taught me a lot about the concept of "fair value," which was just gaining more steam in the world of accounting, as well as emerging concepts concerning equity issued as compensation and transactions done using a company's own securities as currency, effectively. One of the biggest takeaways from that experience was that financial, strategic, investment, and even speculative "value" had everything to do with "who" was involved. Without analyzing and appreciating who, the most financially attractive opportunity could be destroyed by a single individual acting in concert with a small group. Examples of this include Enron, which we mention on page 35 of Chapter 1, "Facebook at $80 Billion Valuation versus Enron at $80 Billion Valuation," MCI Worldcom, and even the private mortgage securities that are impacting everyone's valuation today (ironically, in a positive manner at this time).

As you'll learn in Chapter 2, "Should Venture-Backed Companies Even Consider a DCF Model?" and Chapter 3, "Valuation Methods versus Allocation Methods," traditional income approaches to valuation do not generally work particularly well for most early-stage venture-backed companies without substantial modification, partly because market inputs are often better indications. Perhaps more importantly, how many VCs or angels do you suppose are pulling out a true DCF model when making a Series A investment?

Yet every investor, founder, and employee in these companies generally shares an expectation of future cash flow. They don't generally expect that cash flow to come from operations, although occasionally companies like Microsoft and Zynga will in fact produce enough free cash flow to theoretically be able to pay a dividend before going public (see Chapter 4, Exhibit 4.6 "Dividend History of Leading Venture-Backed Companies"). Instead, the majority of these companies will give a benefit stream to investors that is not directly from their operating cash flow but instead in the form of capital appreciation.

But after the VCs, or angels, purchase an interest in a company, how does that market input (supply and demand for the company's potential reduced to a preferred security) impact the founders? How does it impact the employees? How does it impact the limited partners of the venture funds? These may seem like complex questions to answer—and sometimes they are—but in other cases simply breaking down the motivations of the parties (generally their return requirements) within the context of a high-growth company's capital structure can produce superior results if, and only if, you understand the proper inputs. You can't get accurate value indications from a company's capital structure without creating an accurate waterfall of every likely scenario and time period.

Having personally looked at over 5,000 waterfalls in the past 10 years, I can assure you that 90% of the waterfalls you will ever see contain material errors. A lot of times very-early-stage investors assume that "a waterfall's a waterfall" for Series A investors, and doesn't really matter until Series B or later. It's true that it doesn't really matter, for certain investors. But it's also true that understanding it impacts value for every investor that plans to maximize return, as discussed in Chapter 6, "Why You Should D.O.W.T. (Doubt) Venture Capital Returns—Option Pool Reserve." In Chapter 6 we look at one of the simplest cap tables you'll probably ever see for a highly successful, venture-backed company, Microsoft. As simple as Microsoft's cap table was, when we apply the real techniques being used by VCs, analysts and CFOs, valuation professionals, and auditors you'll see how the varying methods used by these parties produce widely differing conclusions.

Before writing this book, I spent nearly a decade creating systems to enable financial information to be converted into actionable business intelligence for venture capital investors. The system was first released as a mobile application for Windows Smartphone (before the iPhone existed), then as a desktop application, and shortly thereafter as a Windows Server product. The first purchasers of the desktop system, to my surprise, were not VCs but valuation practices that needed to run waterfalls for 409A valuations that were expected to be required that year for venture-backed companies.

After around five months of sales, enough valuations (perhaps a few hundred) had been done with the system that we started to get requests from valuation professionals, CFAs, AVAs, ASAs, and so forth, to help them respond to auditor inquiries related to FAS123R (which is now known as Topic 718) and relates to accounting for employee stock options and equity compensation. Although this was very early in the life of 409A valuations being used for "dual purposes," I was, quite honestly, shocked at the conclusions audit teams from the leading (Big 4) accounting firms were drawing. This inspired me to create a course and webinar for the National Association of Certified Valuation Analysts entitled "Five Mistakes Your Auditor Made." Note, the title was not "Five Mistakes Your Auditor May Have Made" because, at that time, the firms were consistently generating payout calculations that materially overstated or materially understated the value of certain securities. Since the option grant prices effectively determined whether employees were being issued securities that had "zero value" or negative value, the auditor feedback influences people's lives in ways I'm guessing few personnel doing the calculations probably considered (and you'll read an example of this early on in Chapter 5's section "Did Auditors Drive Valuators to Overvalue Employee Stock Options?").

We address this topic of auditors, management, investors, and valuation professionals coming up with different conclusions throughout the book, but particularly in Chapter 5, "Enterprise Value + "Allocation Methods" = Value Destruction" and Chapters 8 and 9. A key thing I realized when teaching the course to valuation professionals is that, as with the auditors and VCs, there were techniques they were applying rather consistently that also had the impact of routinely changing value conclusions in ways that they may not have anticipated. In Chapter 9, "Don't Blame the Auditors (Blame the Practice Aid Instead)," I interview three valuation experts who have each done hundreds of 409A valuations and a number of Topic 820 valuations for venture funds. These interviews were conducted with a collection of CFOs and finance teams from venture funds listening in. As a group, these listeners represented well over $40 billion in capital. A few of the listeners sent me notes of appreciation for the session but told me "that was a lot of information and although I'm sure it's useful and accurate, I didn't understand most of what they [the valuation experts] were talking about." That's when I decided that the format of this book, which was originally intended to be a collection of cases analyzing payoff diagrams, such as the ones I have published on Sharespost over the past several years, had to be adjusted to focus on the most important pieces that these CFOs didn't seem to fully appreciate in the way it was being explained by top valuation professionals.

To address this, I started sending out analogies to both financial professionals and entrepreneurs with no financial backgrounds to see if I could find a way to communicate with examples the elements that would likely have the biggest impact on a venture-capital valuation. The most significant elements accounting for gaps in value conclusions were, of course, standards of value, discounts related to differences in standards (such as those for marketability and control), volatility, and the option pricing model as applied to venture-backed companies using Black-Scholes.

Using real-world examples such as Facebook and Twitter (Chapter 1) Yahoo! (Chapter 5), Microsoft (Chapter 6), Kayak.com (Chapter 7), and others, anyone with a true desire to understand valuation to maximize returns, as an employee, founder, VC, angel, or even a vendor, should be able to do so, or at least, that's the objective of this book.

And finally, because valuation is worth nothing to you if you can't make more money with it, Chapter 9 walks you through one of several cases I've created from popular venture-capital and angel-backed social media and Internet-related companies that went public. Using the techniques we explain, using cases from Chapters 1 through 8, Chapter 9 gives you the opportunity to see if you can reach a valuation conclusion that would make you more money as a founder, a VC, an angel, an advisor, or another party simply by having better tools to appraise rights to investment cash flows.

DID YOU KNOW EMPLOYEES LOSE $1 BILLION EACH MONTH DUE TO OVERVALUED (UNDERWATER) OPTIONS?

In 2003, 2004, 2005, and 2006 nearly one million employees at angel- and venture-backed companies were holding stock options they knew had a small possibility of increasing their personal wealth. In 2000 and 2001, a comparable number of employees were holding options they previously thought might be worth millions, but quickly realized might actually be worth absolutely nothing. During each of those periods, market movements, from booms to bubbles to busts, impacted not only those employees but anyone holding stock of public companies or companies with prospects of one day becoming public companies. No VC, angel, or employee associated with these high-growth public companies can escape this market, or systematic, risk. That, of course, is why "risk-free" securities, such as those issued by the U.S. Treasury, command a substantially lower rate of return than equity securities. This systematic risk is priced into every security, including options on privately held equities and employee options by publicly traded companies. However, this risk is more important to publicly traded

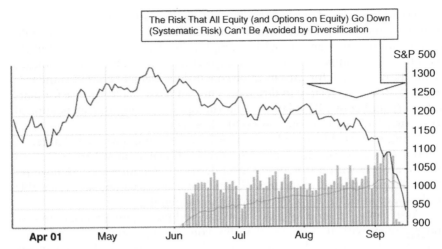

EXHIBIT I.1   Risk That Can't Be Avoided by Diversification (Systematic)
Source: Chart Liquid Scenarios, Inc. – Data Downloaded from Yahoo.com/Finance

companies and private companies in traditional industries than it is to angel-
and venture-backed companies for reasons we'll describe later in this book.
As a result, although the systematic risk of the public equity markets impacts
the stock options in venture-backed private companies to some degree, it has
very little to do with why employees today are losing tens of millions every
day due to mispriced employee options. (See Exhibit I.1.)

In 1996, 1997, 1998, and even 1999, tens of thousands of employees
were granted options that were underpriced, or issued below their fair market value. Most of those employees lost 100% of the value once inherent in
those options due to risks that were unique to their founders, their management teams, their key investors, their technologies, and other "idiosyncratic"
risks. Those are not the kind of daily losses we are focused on in this book.
(See Exhibits I.2 and I.3.)

VCs protect against idiosyncratic risks by having:

1. Portfolios of multiple investments.
2. Deal terms with embedded options that hedge company-specific risks.
3. A mechanism to allow investment decisions to be deferred as certain
   kinds of uncertainty dissipate.

Most employees, of course, don't share these advantages. Still, the mere
existence of company-specific risks, which most employees recognize prior

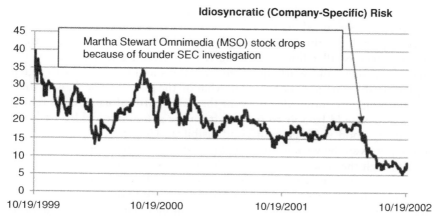

EXHIBIT I.2 Company-Specific (Idiosyncratic) Risk
Source: Chart Liquid Scenarios, Inc. – Data Downloaded from Finance.Yahoo.com

to accepting a job with a startup, does not account for the $1 billion per month being lost by employees at VC- and angel-backed companies due to mispriced options. The reason for the losses is due, in part, to a lack of access to information. But as we discuss more extensively in Chapter 5, the more significant reason for the losses is a lack of understanding about what to do with that information. Indeed, the only barrier to getting information

EXHIBIT I.3 Market Risk Compared to Martha Stewart Specific (Idiosyncratic) Risk
Source: Chart Liquid Scenarios, Inc. – Data Downloaded from Finance.Yahoo.com

from the company for certain venture-capital investors and other key parties with specific rights is asking for it.

As an analogy, think of an airplane dashboard. There are countless dials and meters all telling pilots the reality, terms, and logistics of the plane's machinery and workings. When the dials and meters start to signal the plane is about to go out of control, what do the pilots do? Well, with their basic training and knowledge of what the dashboard information is telling them, pilots should be able to recover from the situation quickly—at least, in relatively good weather with good visibility. However, a pilot with no training, or even the wrong training, will probably suffer a permanent loss.

Although the stakes are not as high with most venture investments, the relationship between what information is available versus what information is used to increase returns and offset losses is analogous. If access to information were the only barrier to losing money daily due to valuation, major investors in venture-backed companies who asked for the necessary information would never need to lose money for this purpose. The market risks and idiosyncratic risks would still be a very real threat, but knowing what you own on a given date and what its value is on that date would no longer be an issue. Naturally, both what a fund truly owns and what it is worth is not definitive to most VCs on any given date, even at the end of the year when estimates of value for the fund ultimately get sent to the limited partners who will make investment decisions and budgets as a result of those estimates.

As we discuss in Chapter 5, employees, VCs, angels, pension funds, and other LPs share this difficulty in quickly getting a reliable indication of value prior to something very good or something very bad happening. For anyone who's ever seen a VC or LP report, this reality can easily be proven without the use of a case study or a graph. If you've seen the term "market value," "residual value," or "net asset value" in an LP report, it was probably accompanied by a caveat disclosure noting the variety of ways funds come up with the residual values. In a world where most of the returns to venture fund investors are "unrealized" gains and many of the losses on any given date are offset by those estimates of unrealized appreciation in value, the need to know the proper inputs into a valuation is essential.

From the outset of this book, we will review three cases, in concert, to show examples where investors, employees, and other parties with a claim on equity in rapidly appreciating venture-backed companies lost rights to massive gains in value that could have been realized by applying basic math. In each of the three brief cases presented, all parties, with the exception of the employees, had access to all of the information needed to value the alternatives differently. Moreover, each of these companies represents some of the best-performing venture investments of the decade. Also, each of the cases involves extraordinarily competent and successful individuals. But as you will see, industry conventions they may have relied on in their decision-making processes may have created a lack of visibility into what they truly owned on a given date and what its value was. As a result, each may have transferred their rights to hundreds of millions in investment cash flow to other parties unintentionally.

ABOUT THE COMPANION WEB SITE

Please note, there is a companion Web site to this book featuring additional case study material as well as different valuation materials that will help you understand and use the techniques offered in this book. Please visit www.wiley.com/go/venturecapitalvaluation to access all of the materials mentioned throughout as available there for download.

CHAPTER 1

Using Facebook, Twitter, and LinkedIn to Explain VC Valuation Gains and Losses

How VCs, Angels, Founders, and Employees Give Up Investment Cash Flow Every Day

*"They engaged in discovery, which gave them access to a good deal of information about their opponents. They brought half-a-dozen lawyers to the mediation. Howard Winklevoss—father of Cameron and Tyler, former accounting professor at Wharton School of Business and **an expert in valuation**—also participated."*

—Excerpt United States Court of Appeals for the Ninth Circuit Opinion, *Facebook v. ConnectU*

H ow can someone realistically use the words "losses" in the same sentence as the names of three of the most successful venture-backed companies in recent history? Indeed, these three companies, along with three or four others, will likely account for 80% of IRRs reported by all U.S. venture-capital funds started after 9/11. So how could anyone lose on one of these transactions? The obvious answer would be the parties referenced in the quote preceding this chapter, the Plaintiffs in the Facebook ConnectU case. To put a face, or set of faces, with the parties, the ConnectU side includes the twin brothers portrayed in the movie *The Social Network*.

DID VALUATION IGNORANCE COST CONNECTU (AND THE WINKLEVOSSES) $50MM?

With half a dozen lawyers, and a father who was an "expert in valuation," how did the ConnectU team miss the obvious fact that it was receiving common shares that are, of course, worth less than preferred shares? To appreciate the answer, here's a brief summary of the lawsuits involved and what 409A is, for those not familiar.

The Facebook, ConnectU Related Lawsuits Timeline

- September 2004: Started with Facebook being sued for, basically, taking the "idea" away from ConnectU (Tyler and Cameron Winklevoss and Divya Narendra)
  - This happened about four months after Peter Thiel (founder of PayPal) invested $500,000 for around "10% of the company [Facebook]"
- April 2007: IRS issues final regulations for Section 409A, which among other things, effectively require venture-funded companies to have third-party appraisals done in order to get a safe harbor from potential penalties associated with mispriced options
- October 2007: Microsoft Invests $240 million in Facebook for 1.6% $240MM ÷ 1.6% = a $15 billion "valuation," according to press reports
- November 2007: Hong Kong billionaire Li Ka-shing invests $60 million in Facebook, apparently for the same Series D shares Microsoft received
- January 2008: 409A regulations become "effective"
- June 2008: Facebook settles with ConnectU founders for "$65 million" calculated (approximately) as follows—$20 million in Cash +$45 million in common stock = approximately $65 million
- August 2008: Press reports Facebook plans to allow employees to sell some of their shares at "internal" (409A) valuation of around $4 billion
- May 2009: DST invests $200MM in Facebook at a reported "valuation" of $10 billion
- July 2009: Michael Arrington reports that DST will offer employees $14.77 per share for their common stock, and they have 20 days to accept the offer
- July 2009: Sharespost "opens for business," with the sale of Tesla shares on a secondary market for private company shares, according to the *New York Times*
- December 2009: Zynga rumored (by Eric Eldon of Inside Social Games) to be offering exits to employees funded by DST at "$19 per share"

■ February 2010: Facebook investor Li Ka-shing Foundation invests in leading secondary market for Facebook shares, "secondmarket" at a reported $150 million valuation

■ January 2011: DST and Goldman invest in Facebook at a $50 billion "valuation"

As stated in the ConnectU Appeal Brief, "... it was a matter of simple math to conclude that each share of Facebook in February 2008 was worth approximately $35.90. ..." After negotiating a settlement with Facebook whereby ConnectU would essentially be acquired by Facebook in exchange for $20 million in cash and $45 million in common stock, the ConnectU plaintiffs discovered the existence of a 409A valuation report issued by Houlihan and Loukie that "valued" Facebook common stock at fair market value. Apparently, the ConnectU team believed their common stock was equal in value to the value of the preferred stock purchased by Microsoft months earlier. Considering the fact that nearly all 409A valuations undervalue the company and simultaneously overvalue the common stock, this mistake is not that uncommon. Millions of employees, tens of thousands of angels, thousands of founders, and even a few hundred VCs make the same mistake every year. However, few if any of those parties seek to rectify their mistakes through litigation, despite having substantially less access to information and fewer resources than the Winklevosses had according to court documents.

AN EXPERT DOESN'T NEED A 409A VALUATION WHEN HE OR SHE HAS A CERTIFICATE AND BASIC MATH

Despite the shortcomings of 409A valuations practices, today it takes only 3 to 15 minutes for a valuation expert familiar with venture-funded companies to give an approximate (rough) estimate of the value of common stock compared to the value of the last round of preferred financing. Even if the 409A valuation expert's conclusions are widely off the mark, the expert will still conclude that if Microsoft paid $35.90 per share for its preferred stock, and someone received common stock a few months later, that common stock is probably not worth more than 50% of what Microsoft paid for its preferred stock, unless an IPO is imminent.

This may sound like a simple rule, but there's real science behind it, and much of that science was initiated by the IRS in response to the economic devastation realized by those in the liquor business as a result of prohibition. Ironically, following the ConnectU settlement, many of the factors that would have caused a 409A valuator to arrive at a lower value for the common stock received by the ConnectU plaintiffs were superseded by a force that impacted each of the companies we mention here as well as the three other companies responsible for "80% of venture fund IRRs" produced by funds started after 9/11.

That superseding force essentially became the market maker in the world of social media investments and their name was DST, or Digital Sky Technologies. Without the bets they placed on Facebook, Zynga, and Groupon, it's unlikely that LinkedIn's IPO would ever spawn a $9 billion market cap so quickly or that Twitter would command a $10 billion "valuation." In fact, it's conceivable that without DST's primary and secondary investments in Facebook, venture capital, social media, and possibly a key part of the U.S. economy might look very different today.

VALUING FACEBOOK'S COMMON STOCK COMPARED TO PREFERRED STOCK IN MINUTES

The "trick" we are about to show applies to 90% or more of venture-funded companies in existence in the United States and around the globe as of the writing of this book. However, it no longer applies to Facebook, for reasons we will touch upon briefly later in the chapter. But in late 2007 and early 2008, when the ConnectU and Facebook dispute was about to reach a settlement, it was still applicable to Facebook's common stock. The Winklevosses could have determined that the "simple math" they were using to value the common stock based on the estimated Series D price paid by Microsoft was simply wrong.

Different Standards of "Value"

The first point concerning differences between the price Microsoft paid for preferred stock and the "value" of Facebook's common stock on the same date was evident to members of the press, which noted that the transaction was "strategic" in nature. However, what exactly does that mean from a valuation standpoint?

If you've ever read a valuation report, one of the first things you will see in the report is the "Standard of Value" being used to arrive at a conclusion. In the case of a 409A valuation, that standard is "Fair Market Value" as defined by the IRS, which is very different than the price a strategic investor or even an investing partner at a VC fund would be willing to pay.

Different Type of Ownership Interest Being Valued

A minority, or non-controlling, interest in a privately held company is generally worth less than a controlling interest. There have been lots of studies conducted to quantify the difference in value, but even if we were to conservatively say that the difference is 5% or 10% across the board, we would expect to get a lower value for a partial interest in common stock, versus an interest that gave us control of a class of preferred. Again, we will get into those details a little more in a moment, but for now, we have two widely accepted differences between the value of the Series D shares Microsoft purchased and the common shares that ConnectU was to have accepted in lieu of $45 million in cash.

Marketability, Liquidity, and Volatility

Perhaps the biggest difference between the price per share Microsoft paid for its preferred stock versus the fair market value of the shares of common stock ConnectU was negotiating is the applicable discount for lack of marketability, or DLOM. This area requires a somewhat more involved discussion, and also relates to the value of control. But as with the discount for lack of control we mentioned, an estimate of 40% to 45% is generally easy to support, assuming Facebook is not expected to go public or be acquired in the next three years or so. We can even quantify the 40% to 45% discount using a protective put, which we will discuss later, along with prevailing inputs for volatility. Although I don't agree with the prevailing volatility inputs for venture-funded company valuations, which routinely overvalue common stock and undervalue the total equity value of the company, the point here is that even if market volatilities for publicly traded "peers" were used, ConnectU would have ended up with a value per share for its common stock in Facebook that was 40% less than what Microsoft paid. Moreover, it wouldn't have had to do the calculation, because the studies supporting these discounts, which we will cover briefly, are well known. So, without any fancy math, applying basic valuation principals could have saved ConnectU, and their counsel, $45 million dollars and months of litigation as follows:

> Price ConnectU believed Microsoft paid per share: $35.90
>
> Back of napkin discount for lack of control: 10%
>
> Adjusted price reflecting lack of control: $32.31
>
> Back-of-napkin discount for lack of marketability: 40%

Adjusted price reflecting lack of marketability control: $19.39

Damages parties agreed would settle in stock: $45,000,000

Implied minimum shares of common issuable: 2,321,263 shares

Note that the discounts for lack of marketability and lack of control are applied in stages, as opposed to being simply added together. If we simply took a 40% discount for lack of marketability (DLOM), added that to a 10% discount for lack of control (DLOC), and multiplied $35.90 by 50%, we would have gotten a different (incorrect) answer of $17.95 per share. In this example we could still get an answer, but if instead the DLOM was 55% and the DLOC was 60%, you can see how it wouldn't work mathematically, which is an easy way to remember not to add the DLOM to the DLOC to get the total discount.

The valuation approach used by ConnectU, deliberately or by accident, is a "market approach." It's the most popular approach to valuing anything. We just demonstrated an application of the same approach, the market approach, using the same variables ConnectU used and got a fair market value indication that was 50% less than what it got. Facebook went on to become worth four times as much as the value "implied" by the Microsoft investment around the time of ConnectU's settlement negotiations, suggesting that the impact of basic math and basic valuation on the parties could grow to over half a billion someday very soon.

Granted, the reported "internal" 409A valuation for Facebook common stock at the time was 50% less than the estimate we just generated. But that official 409A estimate took a lot longer than two minutes to arrive at and involved multiple indications of value, a waterfall, allocations of calls on Facebook's total equity value and 50 to 100 hours of other work we can't fit into a single page, as we did with our estimate. However, a deeper understanding of how we can comfortably make an assertion that ConnectU's team could have come to a similar conclusion without the actual 409A report should be beneficial to anyone with an interest in valuing venture-capital-backed companies. Also, our value for common stock is more proportional to the firm we described as the "social media market maker," DST. DST apparently valued the common stock at around "$14.77" according to the Michael Arrington/Techcrunch reference cited earlier. That's still well within the range of our back-of-the-napkin discount math.

As of the writing of this book, ConnectU was never granted access to the 409A valuation of Facebook, and neither were we. However, any 409A valuation should have language and references similar to what we are about to present surrounding the standard of value, fair market value in accordance with revenue ruling 59-60, the interest being valued (a minority, non-marketable interest), and the process of applying appropriate discounts.

WHAT THE WINKLEVOSSES WOULD HAVE SEEN IN ANY 409A VALUATION REPORT

It's not an exaggeration to say that if I were to simply copy and paste comments from successful early-stage investors, founders, and CEOs I personally know concerning their dissatisfaction with 409A and the related valuation reports, it would easily exceed the 250 or so pages of this book. One of the complaints is that it appears that a lot of the information is "simply copied from one report to another." From the perspective of highly creative and unique founders and investors, I can see how this would be perceived as a bad thing. But I'm guessing that those parties would be scared if they found out that their tax attorney or CPA was completing their tax returns using a "unique" form he or she had created. I use the analogy because 409A is a tax regulation and, like more than 50% of all valuation work in the United States, these valuations would not exist without the IRS. So the redundancies can be beneficial, especially in the context of the details ConnectU's former shareholders felt they were missing in the absence of Facebook's 409A valuation. The typical 409A report elements that are of particular interest with respect to our back-of-the-napkin calculation are:

1. Standard of Value (Fair Market Value)
2. Non-Marketable, Minority Interest Being Valued
3. Revenue Ruling 59-60
4. Discount for Lack of Control Selected
5. Discount for Lack of Marketability Selected

Standard of Value

As we noted at the beginning of this book, the word "value" is used a lot of times without a context or specific definition as to what it is referring to. I like the example of the value of a massive penthouse apartment in New York City with multiple breathtaking views that you are approached by a buyer to offer versus the value for the same apartment the day after you are served divorce papers. While the buyer that approached may have offered you something "above" fair market value, you may need to accept something below fair market value in order to divide the proceeds for an estate or dissolution of marriage. Each of these can be, depending on the circumstances, separate standards of value. For a 409A valuation, the purpose of the valuation firms report would be to present an opinion of the fair market value of Facebook common stock.

The term "fair market value" is defined in Revenue Ruling 59-60 as follows:

> ...price at which the property (business) would change hands between a willing buyer and a willing seller when the former is not under any compulsion to buy and the latter is not under any compulsion to sell, both parties having reasonable knowledge of relevant facts. Court decisions frequently state in addition that the hypothetical buyer and seller are assumed to be able, as well as willing, to trade and to be well informed about the property and concerning the market for such property.

A key factor that can be confusing as you read a 409A valuation report, such as the one for Facebook, where the standard of value is fair market value, as defined in Revenue Ruling 59-60, is the definition of a "hypothetical buyer and seller."

In general, you might think of a hypothetical buyer as a party that has the willingness and ability to purchase a business or interest in a business on a given date (the valuation date) solely because of its ability to generate future cash flows as of a given date (the valuation date) without further material adjustments to the company (as is). Such a party is sometimes referred to as a "financial buyer" as opposed to a "strategic buyer." A strategic buyer, sometimes referred to as a "synergistic buyer," sees ways of enhancing the cash flows or advancing a strategy by purchasing a company and is often willing to pay far more than the current cash flow potential of a business. A strategic buyer of a fractional interest could acquire it to effectively block the acquisition of a firm by a competitor, gain access to an exclusive distribution channel, or otherwise make partnerships with competitors of the purchaser less attractive or commercially awkward. Each of these elements could have been additional motivations for Microsoft's Series D investment in Facebook, suggesting that Microsoft was not the hypothetical, financial buyer described in Revenue Ruling 59-60.

A hypothetical seller is similarly motivated by realizing the future cash flows of his or her business as of a given date (the valuation date), but as a single value due as of that date, solely because he or she receives a price that may produce better returns than his or her current business does. This theoretical party is not forced or otherwise unduly pressured into selling, as Revenue Ruling 59-60 indicates in the excerpt above, knows the market and his or her business, and is expected to act rationally based on these facts. This requirement also makes the Microsoft transaction problematic as a direct example of a fair market transaction. Clearly, the fair market value standard, in this context, is not similar to what VCs and "strategics" offer venture-backed issuers of preferred stock, as opposed to the motivations of a secondary seller and secondary purchaser of common stock already outstanding.

Non-Marketable, Minority Interest Being Valued

As discussed, the ConnectU founders contemplated receiving something far less than 1% of Facebook's fully diluted shares, and far less than 1% of Facebook's outstanding shares. Similarly, any employees of Facebook, with the exception of the founders, receiving options would potentially own non-controlling, or minority, interests in the company. Prior to the emergence of venues such as SecondMarket and Sharespost, employees desiring to convert their ownership interests in a venture-funded company into cash by selling the shares to a third-party purchaser was expensive. Even in the late 1990s when established investment banks were open to non-recourse restricted stock loans, there was a meaningful discount and some level of due diligence involved. This additional transaction time and cost still exists compared to a liquid public company and equals uncertainty. This uncertainty as to how long it will take to liquidate an ownership interest in the company has to be taken into consideration to properly reflect the fair market value of the interest being valued. Valuation professionals will often apply a discount to the interest being valued to reflect the cost, in time and money, of not being able to readily liquidate a position.

Along these same lines, an owner of less than 1%, which would include the ConnectU founders as well as most Facebook optionees, would not have the ability to direct a number of management actions that a VC, strategic investor, or controlling shareholder would have. This lack of control also has to be taken into consideration to properly reflect the fair market value of the interest being valued in a 409A valuation report. As with the discount for a lack of marketability, valuation professionals will often apply a discount to reflect the lack of control. By contrast, if a controlling interest were being valued, a valuation professional might apply a premium to reflect the increased economic benefits of having the option to direct management and other key decisions regarding the company being valued.

These relationships, between non-marketable, minority, and controlling interests, are sometimes referred to as levels of value. Exhibit 1.1 illustrates how the 409A valuation report for Facebook might have presented these

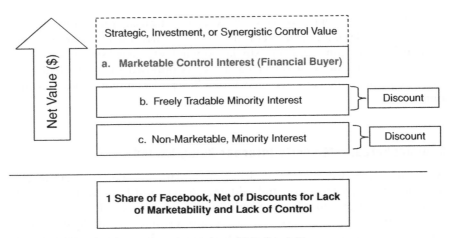

EXHIBIT 1.1   Levels of Value, Control, and Marketability
Source: Liquid Scenarios, Inc.

concepts to highlight where its valuation of common stock of Facebook falls on these three levels:

a. *Controlling interest value:* The equity value of the enterprise as a whole, when combined with debt, and net of cash; this is the "takeover" value of the company.
b. *Freely tradable minority interest value:* The value of a factional, minority interest that does not have control but does have the ability to quickly convert their interest into cash with the degree of certainty provided by market liquidity.
c. *Non-marketable, minority interest value:* The estimated value of a minority interest, net of a discount to reflect the lack of control and net an appropriate discount to reflect the lack of speed and uncertainty of costs with which the interest can be converted into cash at a fair market value (marketability).

Different valuation professionals address issues related to capturing discounts for lack of control based on their professional opinions as to the best approach in a given situation. Similarly, some valuation professionals differentiate discounts for lack of marketability from discounts from lack of liquidity. We will cover some of the differences later, but for now it's fair to assume that we view liquidity as a component of marketability and do not view "marketability" as a legal right to sell something, but rather as the commercial feasibility to sell something in a reasonable period of time for the item being sold.

Revenue Ruling 59-60

Exhibit 1.2 shows two columns, one column with the specific Revenue Ruling 59-60 valuation factor required to be at least considered for purposes of a 409A valuation and a second column where I note how that factor might have impacted Facebook's actual 409A valuation.

Discounts for Lack of Control and Discounts for Lack of Marketability

Discounts for lack of marketability (DLOM) and discounts for lack of control (DLOC), together, often have the largest single impact on many valuations of minority interests in private or closely held companies, as we illustrated at the beginning of this section of the chapter by cutting ConnectU's napkin math in half with a simple DLOM and DLOC. Unfortunately, as quickly as parties are to jump to a conclusion of value on a valuation report, they are not as quick to fully understand how the discounts were arrived at. This makes sense, in part, since you can easily assume that the discount was simply some kind of a "fudge" factor that allows a valuation analyst to arrive at a safe figure he or she believes. Indeed, this is often suspected with selected required rates of return, or "discount rates," where selecting a higher discount rate will reduce the value indication.

In reality, valuation professionals carefully consider the inputs to determine the appropriate discounts, the rationale behind sources of data, and the reasonableness of applying such discounts in each engagement. As a user of a valuation report, it's critical that you appreciate the relationship between these discounts and value conclusions reached.

Discounts for Lack of Marketability (Liquidity)

For purposes of this analogy in which we are valuing a minority interest for purposes of 409A FMV, the terms "marketability discount" and "liquidity discount" are used interchangeably. It is worth noting that different varying definitions exist and that an increasing number of business valuation professionals differentiate the terms. We've chosen not to do so here for several reasons, one of which is the inconsistencies in how parties choose to differentiate marketability from liquidity. Some parties regard marketability as the legal right to sale; others use marketability only when addressing the speed with which an entire firm can be sold and use liquidity when referring to the

EXHIBIT 1.2 Applicability of Revenue Ruling 59-60 to Venture-Backed Companies

Revenue Ruling 59-60 Factor	How It Applies to Facebook and VC Companies
(1) The nature of the business and the history of the enterprise from its inception.	For venture-backed companies, the history of the company is often better documented than it is for traditional private companies. However, the period of time covered is almost always shorter, since these companies are invested in by outside parties under the premise of high velocity and high trajectory growth.
(2) The economic outlook in general and the condition and outlook of the specific industry in particular.	The economy impacts everyone—as even Facebook and LinkedIn investors realized in Q4 of 2008. In a direct way these changes impact risk-free rates, return premiums for all equity securities, and volatility for peers.
(3) The book value of the stock and the financial condition of the business.	Book value is especially important for certain types of businesses, such as banks or oil companies, where the market value of their net assets is often closely reflected by what's on their balance sheets. Most of the value for venture backed companies is "intangible," largely because of how ongoing engineering and customer acquisition costs are accounted for. In light of the Enron analogy we spoke of earlier, most parties currently believe this practice is generally good for accounting, but it makes the balance sheet less relevant for valuation purposes.
(4) The earning capacity of the company.	This is the trillion-dollar question. What's the earnings capacity of a venture-funded company? You don't really know until it starts generating sustainable earnings, and that doesn't generally happen until long after the company has gone public. A more meaningful metric is what's the capacity to penetrate a market faster and more efficiently than rivals? Using common valuation techniques. this can be extended to represent a proxy for "earnings" capacity.
(5) The dividend-paying capacity.	The dividend-paying capacity is essentially an extension of earnings capacity, and therefore, in the context of a venture-funded company, the question is what's the ability to generate capital appreciation in the form of a liquidating dividend (M&A) or publicly traded security (IPO), as a multiple of invested equity capital?

EXHIBIT 1.2 (*Continued*)

Revenue Ruling 59-60 Factor	How It Applies to Facebook and VC Companies
(6) Whether the enterprise has goodwill or other intangible value.	Even the worst venture-funded company's value, and even the best venture-funded company's value, is composed of "intangibles," which for our purposes means something the creator or builder has successfully invested resources in but is unable to reflect at market value on the balance sheet due to accounting rules.
(7) Sales of the stock and the size of the block of stock to be valued.	Although the company's stock is not registered with the SEC for public trading, sales of preferred stock also have to be considered, since they are convertible into common, so there is no clear indicator of value. Second Market and Sharespost weren't venues for Facebook at this time. The size of the block of stock being valued is officially a minority interest in common shares.
(8) The market price of stocks of corporations engaged in the same or a similar line of business having their stocks actively traded in a free and open market, either on an exchange or over-the-counter.	When most people think of valuation, this is what they think of—comps, or market multiples. This would include other market inputs such as revenue multiples, price earnings ratios or price per user, page view, or other parameter. The missing element, or variable, that's hard to fit in most cases is growth prospects. Public company comps rarely reflect the comparable growth.

speed with which a minority interest in a firm can be sold. All of these efforts to refine the definitions are helpful in advancing this complex area of business valuation. However, these efforts also may make it difficult for outside parties to appreciate the various elements that support the use of DLOMs.

To simplify the explanation, we offer an analogy and some easily accessible, broadly used definitions of marketability. An analogy most people can relate to is the time it takes to sell one's home. Coincidentally, the acronym is similar, DOM, or days on market.

In a hot real estate market, such as the one experienced around the time of Facebook's Series C round, a high-end home would often sell within 30 days of being listed for sale. However, in a buyer's market, such as the one experienced during Facebook's Series E financing, that same home was taking four months to sell on average, or four times as long. The speed with which you can convert your home into cash, using an actual buyer, has an impact on the value of your home. This can be proven pretty easily, because if you decide that you simply don't want to wait four months to sell your home, what will you do to decrease the time required to find a buyer? In most cases, the obvious answer is to discount the price.

Although this is not a perfect analogy of each and every variable, it is an easily understood example of the concept of marketability and its effect on value as of a given date. Real estate is a hard asset, of course, whereas securities are not. But if you look at the popular definitions for "marketable securities" you can appreciate that the essence of marketability is very similar. Investopedia defines marketable securities as "very liquid securities that can be converted into cash quickly at a reasonable price." And the AICPA FAS 115 definition of marketable securities is

> *the fair value of an equity security is readily determinable if sales prices or bid-and-asked quotations are currently available on a securities exchange registered with the Securities and Exchange Commission (SEC) or in the over-the-counter market, provided that those prices or quotations for the over-the-counter market are publicly reported by the National Association of Securities Dealers Automated Quotations systems or by the National Quotation Bureau. Restricted stock does not meet that definition.*

Many publicly traded companies have sufficient volume to enable a minority shareholder to place an order with his or her broker at the most recently quoted market price and get a confirmation within a matter of minutes that the order has been filled at a price very close to the quote. Three days later, the proceeds from that sale will be in the seller's brokerage account, net of commissions, or selling costs. However, in thinly traded stocks, or bonds, of a company there's often a spread between the bid price and ask price for a security, making it more risky to simply place a market order, because if you do, the price you hope to get will likely be much lower than the price your order gets filled at. As a result, the time required to get the price you want may be longer than with a more "liquid" or actively traded security. As the time between when you decide you want to sell the stock and the time when the market can absorb your order at the price you want grows, uncertainty as to world events, economic events, news releases, company performance, political unrest, and myriad other potential factors can impact the price you are able to sell your security at. That uncertainty, as to when you will receive a fair market value, or when you will find a willing financial buyer based on the company's earnings, dividends, and potential for capital appreciation, must be reflected in the value of your security, compared to a similar security that is unencumbered by this uncertainty.

DERIVING A DISCOUNT FOR LACK OF MARKETABILITY FOR VALUATIONS

While there is virtually no debate about the reality that a discount for lack of marketability is applicable for private company shares where no secondary market, or known vehicle for liquidating on demand, exists, there's a fair amount of debate regarding how to measure the appropriate magnitude of such a discount. Valuation professionals generally cite five popular reference points they use in deriving a discount for lack of marketability for their valuations.

Restricted Stock Studies

Restricted stock studies, considered "empirical studies," refer to prices realized by sellers of shares that are not "free trading" stock, but are instead subject to regulatory restrictions by SEC regulations. When a company files a registration statement with the SEC, only the shares registered for sale can be freely traded, and even some of those shares can subsequently become subject to restrictions depending on who purchases them. These restrictions have changed over time, with respect to the holding period required prior to the ability to sell the shares and also with respect to other provisions. For instance, in 1997 Rule 144 shortened the holding period, and in 2008 it was shortened again.

Shares that are subject to these regulatory restrictions on resale typical have a notice, or "legend" on their back, similar to the following:

> *THE SECURITIES REPRESENTED BY THIS CERTIFICATE HAVE BEEN ACQUIRED FOR INVESTMENT AND HAVE NOT BEEN REGISTERED UNDER THE SECURITIES ACT OF 1933, AS AMENDED, OR ANY STATE SECURITIES LAW. THESE SECURITIES MAY NOT BE SOLD OR TRANSFERRED IN THE ABSENCE OF SUCH REGISTRATION OR ANY EXEMPTION THEREFROM UNDER THE SECURITIES ACT OF 1933, AS AMENDED, OR ANY APPLICABLE STATE SECURITIES LAW.*

Stock with this type of legend is sometimes referred to as "letter" stock, because in the absence of a letter from a securities attorney to the transfer agent, generally approved by the issuer's counsel, the legend will remain and the shares can't be offered for sale to the general public. This, of course, does not mean that the shares can't be sold, just that a holder can't deposit those shares in his oher brokerage account as free trading, place a sell order for those shares on the open market, and have the transaction settle (without violating securities laws). This limitation decreases the value to a purchaser. By observing the pricing behavior of those purchaces, insights into the appropriate discount rate for regulatory time restrictions enable an implied marketability discount to be estimated. The use of "marketability" by some valuation professionals to refer only to the "legal right" to market an interest is, in my view, at odds with this reality. However, there are also reasonable arguments for its use by other parties.

In addition to regulatory restrictions, private sales of securities, either in a private or publicly traded company, can be subject to additional restrictions, such as lockup agreements or restricted stock purchase agreement. An example of a legend related to such restrictions is as follows:

THE TRANSFER OF THESE SECURITIES IS SUBJECT TO THE TERMS AND CONDITIONS OF A RESTRICTED STOCK PURCHASE AGREEMENT EFFECTIVE AS OF (SOME DATE) BETWEEN THE COMPANY, INC. AND THE HOLDER OF RECORD OF THIS CERTIFICATE AND NO SALE, AS-SIGNMENT, TRANSFER, PLEDGE, HYPOTHECATION OR OTHER DISPOSITION OF SUCH SECURITIES SHALL BE VALID OR EFFECTIVE EXCEPT IN ACCORDANCE WITH SUCH AGREEMENT AND UNTIL SUCH TERMS AND CON-DITIONS HAVE BEEN FULFILLED. COPIES OF SUCH AGREEMENT MAY BE OBTAINED AT NO COST BY WRIT-TEN REQUEST MADE BY THE HOLDER OF RECORD OF THIS CERTIFICATE TO THE SECRETARY OF THE COM-PANY, INC.

Fortunately, there are a wide variety of restricted stock studies available to choose from. Unfortunately, the vast majority of these studies were conducted years or even decades ago. Also, after filtering out transactions, some of the more robust studies ended up with rather small samples. This is especially problematic when attempting to draw a direct conclusion about a unique, privately held company's appropriate DLOM from a small range of publicly held securities in a variety of industries, across a range of sizes and sampled as of a particular point in a given market cycle. Notwithstanding those limitations, these studies provide guideposts for comparisons, in general, to the lower range of reasonable discounts to apply. Exhibit 1.3 shows a summary of some of the studies that may have been reviewed and considered, as benchmarks or guideposts, in developing a DLOM for Facebook.

EXHIBIT 1.3 Sample of Mean DLOMs from Select Empirical Studies

Author/Publisher/Title	Mean Discount	Observations	Year Published
SEC Institutional Investors	26%	398	1971
Gelman	33%	89	1972
Moroney	35%	146	1976
Trout	35%	60	1977
Silber	34%	69	1991

Source: Adapted from NACVA.

The Silber study, conducted in 1991 on restricted stock sales to institutional investors by publicly traded firms, like many of the others listed, found a correlation between the size of the company, with respect to market capitalization (equity), revenue and earnings, and the applicable discount. However, this study also looked closely at the volume of the issuers' shares. As suggested earlier, liquidity is indeed a function of volume, so that one publicly traded company may have a less-developed market for its shares than another publicly traded company. This study, which applied a least-squares method to the data, found a median discount of 35% and a mean discount of 34%. This suggests that a minority interest in a private, untraded, unregistered company such as Facebook would command a discount of at least, likely greater than, 34%.

Although there are more recent studies available, most of the recently published studies either have (a) few observations or (b) reflect substantially shorter holding periods, due to the changes in Rule 144 noted previously. It's important to keep in mind that in most of these cases the implied DLOM exists where (a) all costs of going public have already been incurred by the issuer, other than ongoing costs, and (b) the ability to sell within a defined time period, albeit at an indefinite price, is known. Since a hypothetical buyer, and hypothetical seller, of Facebook minority would not have the advantage of either of these on the date in question, you might be able to argue that the relative size of Facebook's discount should be higher than those implied by these studies, all things being equal. On the other hand, venture-backed companies are generally operated and managed with an idea to one day going public if the IPO window is open and the company's traction can attract retail investors. This effectively suggests that the costs of going public for a later-stage venture-backed company are potentially comparable to the cost of being acquired, since the only remaining variables are additional legal, with fees/commissions and audit expense likely being comparable leading up to the exit.

Pre-IPO Studies

Pre-IPO studies, sometimes referred to simply as "IPO studies," are also considered "empirical studies" by the valuation profession. Whereas the restricted stock studies mentioned previously look at discounts implied by sales of restricted shares of publicly traded companies, the IPO studies look at private transactions in a company's shares prior to the company's registration statement becoming effective. In theory, these studies may reflect more of the uncertainty embedded in a private company's shares, since not every company that files a registration statement actually ends up trading, and the range of potential offering pricing is highly speculative prior to a new issue be priced for offering to the public. However, these studies also suffer from the bias of that speculation, as opposed to simply measuring the difference between being able to sell shares, with some certainty in the future.

In most of the studies I've looked at, base prices used for comparison are the private transaction purchase price and the initial offering price. It's worth noting that the closing first-day trading price can effectively be higher or lower than the IPO price, which would of course imply yet another data point to be considered. Still, it's most likely that including this data would suggest an even higher discount for venture-backed companies.

John Emory Studies at Robert W. Baird & Co.   Over 2200 transactions were examined as part of these studies for periods from 1980 to 1997. One key feature is the cutoff period of five months prior to the IPO. Out of that pool, only 310 transactions made it through the filtering process, which left 67 sales transactions and 239 option transactions. The median discount was 43% and the mean was 44%.

Other Emory Studies   John Emory conducted numerous other studies that are often references in valuation reports and, sometimes, in court cases. One of the broader studies covered a period from 1997 to 2000, with 1847 offering documents/registration statements. Based on various filtering criteria, the study concluded medians and means ranging from 44% and 48%, respectively, to 59% and 54%, respectively.

Quantitative Methods

There are a number of quantitative methods; one of these includes the QMDM, or Quantitative Marketability Discount Model, which looks at dividends, growth, an assumed holding period, earnings, and other factors in a manner similar to the discounted cash flow approach discussed later in Chapters 3 and 5. Unfortunately, this approach was challenged again by the courts about a year before Microsoft's financing of Facebook. Interestingly enough, the most popular method for valuing venture-backed company discounts, based on my observations, is the option-pricing methodology.

The option-pricing methodology, often in the form of a protective put, also require inputs with respect to holding periods and, as such, is ideally suited for venture-funded companies since it is the expectation of a liquidity event within a time horizon that's the foundation for an investment thesis in these companies. The key input, however, is volatility, and that, as we've touched upon, is routinely underestimated; thus, so is the resulting marketability discount estimate as a result.

Court Rulings

Given the use of a 409A valuation for tax purposes, the valuation analyst would have paid special attention to guidelines established in rulings by the tax courts with respect to applying discounts for lack of marketability. The most cited case in this area of valuation is perhaps Mandelbaum. In this case the court lists specific factors that valuation professionals should consider in determining a DLOM. They are the following:

1. Private versus public sales of the stock
2. An analysis of the financial statements of the company
3. The company's dividend policy (and capacity)
4. The nature of the company, its history, its position in the industry, and its economic outlook
5. The company's management
6. The amount of control in transferred shares
7. Restrictions on transferability of stock
8. Holding period for stock
9. The company's redemption policy
10. Costs associated with making a public offering

Starting from the bottom of the list up, we've discussed how, at the later stages of a venture-funded company, the costs of going public are already being reflected as a G&A (General and Administrative expenses) in the form of increased accounting and legal compliance expenses. Not all of these costs are specifically identifiable as being related to going public, but those that are will be disclosed in a registration statement and, in certain cases, accounted for differently.

This is different than the case for typical private companies, or for smaller venture-funded companies, or those at the earlier stages, for that matter. The direct costs of taking a small company public, as a percentage of proceeds, is higher than direct costs of taking a large company public. As noted, the pattern recognized in the most cited case illustrates a portion of the chasm between the two. However, what is not fully reflected in the numbers is the continuing lack of liquidity due to lower dollar volume, typically, for smaller capitalized companies, which tend to be thinly traded. A company like Facebook, which has tens of millions more "friends" than many Fortune 1000 companies, would not likely suffer from this weakness. As a result, the costs associated with taking Facebook public would probably not be considered a factor justifying an increased discount for lack of marketability by most valuation analysts.

Venture-funded companies do have formal redemption policies, but they do not function the same way as typical redemption policies at non-venture-backed privately held companies. The redemption policies with respect to common shares are often expressed as ROFRs (or rights of first refusal) and repurchase agreements. In both cases, these tend to support the appropriateness of a higher DLOM, whereas pure redemption policies in a privately held company's ESOP for instance would tend to do the opposite.

With respect to the holding period for the stock, this is an issue the courts have struggled with, as noted previously, concerning Quantitative Discounts for Lack of Marketabity (QDLM) methods. However, prior to the emergence of DST-type deals and secondary venues like Sharespost and SecondMarket, which weren't that active at the time of the ConnectU settlement, the holding period for common stocks was generally subject to the control of preferred stockholders. While these realities don't explicitly preclude a minority sale, they have historically reduced the likely pool of buyers for such an interest, implying that a higher discount would be applicable.

As noted, restrictions on transferability include some that relate to agreements employees execute, others that relate to shareholder agreements and/or the company's charter, and others that relate to federal and state securities regulations. As we noted early, there's typically a right of first refusal in place. I am of the opinion that these must always be examined and considered, especially if there's a specific price or pricing formula included in the ROFR, which is not uncommon in venture-funded deals. Federal securities laws, as noted, place restrictions on the sales of private company securities, as do state laws. The applicable exemptions to these regulations, while available to minority holders, still require legends on the stock, minimum holding periods, and additional limitations on shares acquired from "affiliates" and "control" persons. This also suggests a minimum holding period, which is of course directly related to nearly every study and quantitatively based approach to calculating marketability discounts for restricted shares in both private and public companies.

The amount of control in the transferred shares is another consideration. Most common stockholders, optionees, hold what are clearly a minority interests. When considering a company's management in the context of a DLOM, issues of both functional competence and ethics come in to play. Most venture-backed companies have stellar management teams, with strong cultures of fairness, which would be beneficial to a hypothetical buyer of a minority interest. However, at various times in history the perspective of controlling shareholders (VCs) has been primarily unfavorable to selling employees, which of course could offset this benefit.

IPO Offering-Cost Studies

IPO offering-cost studies, most often referred to as "Flotation Cost Studies," use the cost of taking a company public as an indication of the costs to achieve liquidity and, therefore, as the indication of a data point for a DLOM. Although the most cited study covering IPO costs was completed for the SEC in 1974, over three decades ago, the data is still very insightful and has use beyond simply extrapolating an appropriate DLOM rate or floor. Specifically, it confirms that the costs for smaller firms to achieve liquidity is substantially higher than for larger firms, as illustrated by a range of commissions or underwriting fees that, when combined with other costs, can exceed 25% for small issuers.

Discount for Lack of Control   As mentioned, minority shareholders can do few things in response to the actions of majority holders that they do not agree with. This, and a host of other factors, has long supported the notion that a minority interest in a private company is worth less than its proportionate share of a company's total equity, all things being equal. Some of the specific things a minority holder, acting alone, can't do, as opposed to a control interest holder, include the following:

- Change the capital structure of the company
- Declare dividends
- Appoint board members
- Sell the business
- Acquire another business (subsidiary)
- Direct management to consider or select a specific vendor

- Direct management to consider or select a specific employee or manager
- Repurchase shares through the company (treasury stock purchases)
- Change the company's bylaws, or articles, through the board of directors

This is not an exhaustive list, but it illustrates the vast difference in available options. The issue is, however, not if minority holders of securities have fewer effective rights than majority holders, but how and when do those differences in effective rights translate into quantifiable differences (discounts) in security values. The answer depends, in part, on what data is used to arrive at our primary indications of value used in our final conclusions.

Certain schools of thought concerning control discounts suggest that the interest rate used in the buildup process, in the case of the income approach, is generally a minority interest rate, since it's been obtained from an analysis of publicly traded equity returns. Similarly, others believe that if no control adjustments have been made to the benefit stream, then no control discount is warranted. I tend to be of the school of thought that says every situation and every company is unique, and all circumstances should be examined in light of the facts to determine if a control discount is appropriate.

One of the resources you will often see cited in a valuation report is the Mergerstat control premium data. In the case of traditional private companies, valuation professionals would look at discretionary earnings, which include things such as owner's compensation. But unlike most other early-stage privately held companies, venture capital–backed companies always have a formal, professional board of directors that's actively involved in approving management compensation plans. This means that founders and other owner/management compensation for Facebook would most likely already be at or around the industry averages for most periods, suggesting no control adjustment was warranted.

For traditional industries, Mergerstat can be a helpful input, listing the number of transactions in a given industry for a given year, along with an acquisition price "premium." The formula to translate a control premium into a minority discount is as follows:

$$\text{Minority Discount} = 1 - [1/(1 + \text{Mean Premium Paid})]$$

As you can see from the formula, the single input is in fact an estimated "Mean Premium Paid" or control premium. In the case of Mergerstat, this premium is calculated by determining a price that was not impacted by the acquisition offer versus the price after knowledge of the offer hits the market. The difference is a premium, and the formula simply converts that premium into an implied discount for lack of control. It's important to keep in mind that not 100% of the premium would be a function of "control" in the context of a fair market value standard. In fact, it's likely in many cases that the premium would also reflect the strategic value of the acquisition, depending on the circumstances.

As we've discussed, the inability to decide where to focus a company's efforts, who to hire, what strategy to pursue, and so forth represent a lack of control that, in many circumstances for private companies, can represent a reduction in fair market value. However, if the management team and owners charged with making these decisions have a proven track record of success and results substantially higher than the industry, this is actually accretive to minority holders. In some cases, those benefits exceed the detriments of not having control. In almost every case, the mix of control variables will be reflected, to one degree or another, in the financial results and position of a company as of the valuation date. Those variables will also be reflected, to a certain degree, in the DLOM. As such, care must be taken not to double count or undercount. It's my position that most of the threats of a minority interest in Facebook, beyond what one would find in a comparable public company, are offset by a management team that's delivering results that are hard to find in the marketplace. As a result, any control discount beyond the 10% rule we initially estimated would probably be excessive.

FACEBOOK AT $80 BILLION VALUATION VERSUS ENRON AT $80 BILLION VALUATION

What's the difference between Facebook being valued at $80 billion and Enron being "valued" at $80 billion? Most people would accurately include the fact that Facebook is not relying on off-balance sheet financing, questionable accounting practices, and outright fraud. However, I believe the real difference in value, as if a publicly traded company, is what I refer to as the Peter Lynch factor.

In this case, the Peter Lynch factor is 900 million people who had no idea how Enron worked or what it did for them, compared to over 900 million who know exactly what Facebook does for consumers. If and when Facebook goes public, some percentage of those users will be retail investors, unable to get in on the IPO pricing but knowing, intuitively and personally, the potential "value" to a user of Facebook's service. When they start putting orders in to buy shares of Facebook, any math you can apply to the fundamentals, or financials of the company, will appear conjured, juvenile, or both. The issue will no longer be demand for "financial returns" in the form of earnings per share or dividends, but instead demand for capital appreciation by those who know, personally, of the power of what the company offers and expect that to translate into growth in the values at which Facebook's shares trade in the public markets. Is that "irrational"? Lots of analysts, economists, and observers would say "yes," but I have to tell you that if there is an irony, that is largely how successful venture capitalists appear to sort through clutter and find the people that have an offering that will attract interest and then, later, find utility and fit in the marketplace. If you believe that ideas and opportunities evolve, that seems perfectly rational.

DEAL TERMS, WATERFALLS, AND THE PRE-MONEY MYTH

Whenever I use the expression "cash flow potential" in the context of a venture-backed company security, especially an early-stage investment, the first reaction I get from people is "there is no cash flow for most of these companies, so how can you value that?" We discuss this in more depth later, but for now I think it's safe to say that the ConnectU team failed to take into account the impact of volatility on investment cash flow potential, in the form of discounts for lack of marketability. They also appear to have not recognized that each security in a venture-backed company generally has a different investment cash flow potential until the value of the company is extraordinarily high, which ultimately was the case with both Facebook and Twitter, or the company goes public, which was the case with LinkedIn.

Cash Flow Potential, Volatility, and Deal Terms Are Driven by Time

Different classes of stock in the same company have different cash flow potential. A penthouse apartment at 15 Central Park sold for $7,800 per square foot, an $80-million sale. If you own a 600-square-foot basement unit in that same building, does that mean your unit is worth $4.68 million (600 X $7,800)? Most people would correctly say "probably not."

This is why simply taking the same price per share paid in the most recent round of venture financing and multiplying by the common stock held by a founder or the total number of shares outstanding rarely represents the "value" of the company. Each class of stock has different terms, rights, and privileges and therefore different investment cash flow potential.

A breakpoint chart (aka a payout diagram or waterfall analysis) is a graphic illustration of those cash flows at key values where the proportion of payouts to a class changes. We can use these charts to estimate the value of each class of stock.

Exhibit 1.4 illustrates how the implied optionality (OPM) value per share of Twitter's common stock in 2009 is different than the value of the Series E at almost every estimated company value listed until the estimated value of the company is 20 times greater than the amounts raised.

The first row in the exhibit shows the total company value, or enterprise value, estimated by each party (the column headings). This is assumed to equal the total equity value, since it's assumed that no substantial debt is outstanding for this company. The next row divides that amount by the estimated shares outstanding to come up with implied value per share. It's important to note that unlike many of the other cases in this book, Twitter is a private company so there's no official record publicly available of exactly how many shares of the company are outstanding. There are, however, official records of how many shares of each class of stock have been authorized. Using certain adjustments, which we illustrate on the pages that follow, we were able to adjust the authorized shares reported to estimate fully diluted shares outstanding. We used that data, along with information regarding the rights and preferences of different classes of securities from the company's restated articles of incorporation, to determine how much each share would be "worth" if we applied the Black-Scholes option-pricing method to the different types of shares versus simply treating all classes as equal.

The most capable parties for valuing a venture-funded company under the investment standard of value are the venture capitalists, entrepreneurs, angels, and management teams participating (bargaining) in each round of financing leading up to a liquidity event. However, when a liquidity event occurs, be it a merger, acquisition, or IPO, the bargaining power generally shifts to another market of buyers. It is absolutely impossible to forecast with any certainty exactly how those buyers will respond to the purchase opportunity, what market conditions will exist at the time of a purchase opportunity, and what competitive condition the company will be in compared to other acquisition or IPO candidates. What can be modeled with 100% certainty is how legal agreements governing the rights of securities, holders, employees, founders, and management impact investment cash flows across a range of potential exit scenarios.

If an assumed, or estimated, business enterprise value is plugged into an accurate model of payouts by security or holders, allocation of value becomes rather simple. This method of allocating enterprise value to different classes of securities is referred to by the *AICPA Private Company Valuation Practice Guide* as "the Current Method."

EXHIBIT 1.4 Various Twitter Value Estimates Converted to Option Values per Share

Sample Twitter Enterprise Values Estimates from Kim-Mai Cutler's 09/18/09 VentureBeat Post*

	Sharespost Low	Sharespost High	NextUp Bull	Insight	WSJ	TechCrunch	R. Scobble
In Millions *	$263	$385	$589	$1,000	$1,300	$1,700	$5,000
÷ By Est. Shares =	$3.89	$5.69	$8.70	$14.78	$19.21	$25.12	$73.88

Versus Value Per Share Based on Cash Flows to Each Type (Class) of Stock Using the Option-Pricing Method

Common	$2.96	$5.10	$8.65	$15.55	$20.44	$26.89	$78.34
Series E	$14.48	$15.35	$16.64	$20.31	$23.76	$28.97	$78.99

As the Enterprise Value Get Higher (from Left to Right), the Difference in Value Between Common and E Gets Smaller

Difference	389%	201%	92%	31%	16%	8%	1%

Source: Option Values per Liquid Scenarios, Inc.

In reality, any fair market valuation of a venture-funded company with more than one round of financing is only as good as the payout model and breakpoint (or waterfall) analysis.

If a company is worth $1 billion, but common stock is not entitled to any proceeds below $1.5 billion, is the common stock therefore worth $0? Is it worth something less than $0? Without an objective and forward looking means of allocating the $1 billion in value to different classes of stock, getting a meaningful answer to this question can be difficult and unreliable.

The SEC, FASB, AICPA, NACVA, and many other organizations that have studied the matter believe that the options-pricing method helps to solve this problem of allocating value where rights to proceeds vary by class of security. However, the AICPA also believes weaknesses of the options-pricing method include the sensitivity to the volatility input used and the complexity involved. There's little that can be done with respect to the sensitivity to volatility assumptions. However, with technology the issue of complexity can be eliminated, as is the case with the automated models herein.

The following Black-Scholes formula can be automatically applied to each of the breakpoints generated to allocate an associated "option value" to each preferred stock series, common stock, and employee option participating at a given breakpoint.

$$SN(d1) - Ke^{\wedge}(-rt)N(d2)$$

For our analysis purposes here, assuming Twitter has no debt and excluding any cash on the books: S = Enterprise (Company) Value Estimate, K = Strike price (which is each breakpoint), t = expected time horizon for an exit (sale of the company) to occur, r = risk free rate (generally the rate of a US Treasury),

$$d1 = (\ln(S/K) + (r + \sigma^{\wedge}2/2)t)/\sigma \sqrt{t}$$
$$d2 = d1 - \sigma \sqrt{t}$$

Throughout this book we provide additional representations and explanations of the Black-Scholes formula. Not all elements of Black-Scholes, or option pricing for that matter, are intuitive. However, there are analogies that make it easier to understand how some of the inputs to the model influence conclusions reached by an investor. A basic understanding of these relationships is important when determining whether the Black-Scholes model enhances an indicated value, contradicts a more reliable measure of value, or is simply not applicable within the context of an option-pricing model.

You can see from the previous formula for d2 that we must first solve for d1. Also in the d1 formula, you will notice that d1 is reduced by the product of sigma (volatility) times the square root of the expected time between the valuation date and a liquidity event (t). Without further analysis, it's fair to deduct that d2 can be sensitive to increases or decreases in volatility (sigma) input and to differences in the time horizon for a liquidity event (t). What's not so obvious without looking at the breakpoints and the formula inputs at the same time is that when d2 is derived from a breakpoint (strike price K) that's higher than the estimated company value (S), increasing volatility or increasing time tends to increase the indicated value for that breakpoint. These out-of-the-money breakpoints, breakpoints where the estimated company value is higher than the exit value being modeled, can play a key role in conclusions reached for venture-backed companies. This is due, in part, to both how d2 is calculated and how it is often interpreted.

Sometimes the standard normal distribution of d2, N(d2) in the preceding formula, is described as giving the probability that the call option will be struck or, put another way, the chances that the exercise price for the call option will be lower than company value by the time the option expires (t) for a given volatility (sigma). This can be a useful way to interpret N(d2) in some instances, but must be done with a couple of key caveats and considerations.

- A "risk-free" rate of return assumes a risk-neutral world
- Each breakpoint is a separate call option
- Higher volatility can hurt in the money breakpoints
- Higher volatility can help out of the money breakpoints
- Longer times to exit, t, help out of the money breakpoints

In the Twitter example in Exhibit 1.4, increasing the volatility input or the estimated time to liquidity would increase (help) the indicated value of common stock under the Sharespost Low case, since the estimated company value (S) was so much lower than the exit values where common stock starts to participate. These out-of-the-money breakpoints, or out-of-the-money options, are worth more if there's either more time for the value of Twitter to increase prior to an exit or if there's a greater dispersion (volatility) of possible values of Twitter between the valuation date and the date Twitter gets purchased or goes public. On the other hand, if the estimated value of Twitter is Robert Scobble's $5 billion shown in Exhibit 1.4, then increasing volatility could potentially decrease the value of common stock, since volatility works in both directions and could result in a lower future enterprise value between the valuation date and the date of an exit or IPO.

We will continue to introduce additional explanations and relationships between volatility, time, and values indicated by BlackScholes throughout this book.

Estimated Payout Diagrams: The Anchor for Applying Value   In most cases, the stated ownership percentage for a class is different than the percent proceeds that class would get if the company was sold. For instance, our analysis estimates that common stockholders owning 14.69% of Twitter's "fully diluted shares" on 9/09 would be get $0, 0%, if the company was sold for less than $172 million; $5.5 million, 3.2%, if the company sells for $172 million; 8.9% at a $216 million sale price; 9.7% at $227 million; and 13.6% at $357 million (each payout less than 14.69% of proceeds).

But at an acquisition price of $1 billion on 9/25/2009, based on our automated analysis generated estimates, common stockholders owning 14.69% of Twitter's fully diluted shares could be entitled to up to 16.74% of proceeds, or nearly 14% more than their fully diluted ownership percentage would imply. Exhibit 1.5 illustrates these relationships at a given date. If we push the date forward, the payoffs (or payouts) will change.

Pushing the hypothetical acquisition date out by two years decreases payouts to common stock at every point where a preferred series converts to common stock. These points, where slopes of any given payout line change, are sometimes referred to as "breakpoints." In certain companies, breakpoints change over time because of cumulative dividends, expirations of warrants, or expirations of uncapped participating preferred provisions. However, in this model, as in almost every other, the biggest impact on the change in payouts over time is the granting and vesting of options.

Because of changes in option pool activity, the Series E converts at $1.06 billion instead of $0.987 billion. This means Twitter has to sell for around $70 million more two years later for common holders to get payouts comparable to 2009.

Based on press reports and filings, Twitter's pre-money/post-money valuations increased from approximately $130K near its Series A round to around $80 million in 2008, a 615X step-up in value. And within a year of that to a $1 billion valuation, a 7,692X step-up in value from the Series A. Without any knowledge of high school statistics or the stock market, most people would say that the variability in the total equity value of Twitter is greater than 100% based on any one of those price moves. If that's correct, how reasonable is an estimate of 65% volatility as an input for a Black-Scholes option pricing model? What would happen if we simply doubled the volatility input? What would have happened if we "built up" the volatility

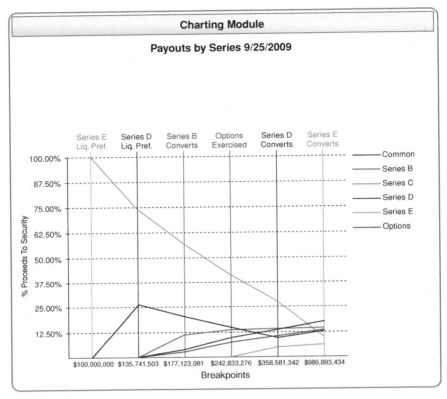

EXHIBIT 1.5   Payouts by Series 9/25/09

estimate similar to the way valuation professionals build up a discount rate or capitalization rate? We will address these critical issues later in the book, but for now you can see that the most substantial market data for the value of Twitter is the round-to-round pricing. However, the key to valuation of an ongoing business is to look at the future benefit stream to owners.

In the case of a venture-backed company, that future benefit stream is in the form of capital appreciation. Of the various Twitter value estimates arrayed in Exhibit 1.4 from Kim Mai Cutler's articles, Robert Scobble's estimate of $5 billion, which was the highest on the list, turned out to be closest to the next round of financing for the company, which "valued" Twitter at almost $4 billion. So does that $4 billion include discounts for lack of marketability? With thousands of investors willing to purchase junior equity securities of Twitter without access to financial information and at the same price or higher as the preferred investors that have control and information access, should $4 billion be the "value"? It all depends on the standard of value, as we've discussed previously.

Going back to the 2009 valuation estimates, to utilize that pre-money valuation of $1 billion as an enterprise value, it could be rationalized that the price paid for by VCs includes a discount for lack of marketability (or DLOM), since the purchasers in that round knew that their shares would be subject to transfer restrictions (not free trading shares, without a registration statement, and subject to other restrictions as a function of shareholder rights agreements).

Other possible enterprise values include the bull ($589 million) and bear ($441 million) valuation scenarios estimated by Michael Moe in his 7/17/09 Nextup Twitter report on Sharespost. Exhibit 1.6 from the Liquid Scenarios OPM module shows some of the variables that would be used to convert breakpoints into call option strike prices (K), apply the total equity value based on the pre-money value of $1 billion as the current stock price (S), and other Black-Scholes variables to allocate the call values at each breakpoint to common stock, Series A, Series B, Series C, Series D, Series E, and employee stock options.

In the previous example we applied a single average grant price to employee stock options. Using the same business enterprise example as in that example, Michael Moe's $441 million bear case scenario from 7/17/09, but with more detailed option prices used, you can see how breakpoints change and therefore values for each call on Twitter equity change accordingly. As a result, the value of common stock, Series A, Series B, Series C, Series D, Series E, and employee stock options also changes. See Exhibit 1.7.

In Exhibit 1.7, each of the column labels indicates what security behavior corresponds with a change in the slope of the payout line. Each breakpoint becomes a call value floor, or minimum strike price k. The business enterprise value (BEV) is the equivalent of the current stock price (S) variable in the traditional Black-Scholes formula. Each of the breakpoints represents changes in proceeds to certain securities. In cases where those changes increase the total proceeds as compared to a previous breakpoint, a proportional share of that breakpoint's call value (C) will be attributed to that security.

Using just a handful of variables for one case, on several hypothetical valuations, we've proven hundreds of cash flow implications not reflected in the value estimates of any of the experts that follow this one private company. If you can't determine the cash flow implications of an investment, any investment, then you will give that cash flow up daily to others that take the time to understand the terms embodied in the securities they purchased. This reality applies to founders, key employees, angels, and venture capitalists. Although the first example may seem a little complicated for some,

EXHIBIT 1.6   Option Pricing Model Based on 2009 Pre-Money Value of Twitter

	Total	Series E Liq. Pref.	Series D Liq. Pref.	Series B, Series C Liq. Pref.	Series A Liq. Pref.
Breakpoints		Breakpoint 1	Breakpoint 2	Breakpoint 3	Breakpoint 4
Strike Price (K)		$0	$110,000,000	$145,741,503	$165,806,503
BEV Estimate (S)	$1,000,000,000	$1,000,000,000	$1,000,000,000	$1,000,000,000	$1,000,000,000
Breakpoint Call Value	$1,000,000,000	$102,991,710	$32,552,021	$17,917,897	$86,371
Call Value at Floor		$1,000,000,000	$897,008,290	$864,456,268	$846,538,371
Term in Years (t)		2.00	2.00	2.00	2.00
Risk-Free Rate (r)		3.00%	3.00%	3.00%	3.00%
Volatility		65.00%	65.00%	65.00%	65.00%
d1		33.09	2.93	2.62	2.48
d2		32.17	2.01	1.70	1.56
N(d1)		1.00	1.00	1.00	0.99
N(d2)		1.00	0.98	0.96	0.94
S * N(d1)		$1,000,000,000	$998,283,671	$995,603,686	$993,425,288
K * e^-rt		$0	$103,594,099	$137,254,179	$156,150,684
Times N(d2)		$0	$101,275,381	$131,147,418	$146,886,916
C Value at Ceiling		$897,008,290	$864,456,268	$846,538,371	$846,452,000
Common	$161,633,397	$0	$0	$0	$0
Series A	$238,343,900	$0	$0	$0	$86,371
Series B	$128,294,740	$0	$0	$4,523,008	$0
Series C	$123,998,264	$0	$0	$13,394,889	$0
Series D	$118,506,987	$0	$32,552,021	$0	$0
Series E	$162,716,122	$102,991,710	$0	$0	$0
Options	$66,506,591	$0	$0	$0	$0

our introductory premise that cash flow is being sacrificed daily by these parties can be further proven using even more basic techniques. Comparing the way that venture capitalists typically expressed express value, pre-money or post-money value, to basic math reveals opportunities for all parties to improve their results. This can be accomplished by replacing the current definition of pre-money value used by VCs with simple valuation techniques such as waterfalls.

THE PRE-MONEY MYTH

Pre-money value is the most widely misused and misunderstood term quoted when speaking of the value of a venture-backed company. Simply adjusting the most popular definitions and interpretations for pre-money/post-money valuation is an easy, inexpensive way to achieve more transparency and

Common Participates	Options Exercised	Series D Converts	Series C Caps	Series C Converts	Series E Converts
Breakpoint 5	Breakpoint 6	Breakpoint 7	Breakpoint 8	Breakpoint 9	Breakpoint 10
$165,904,003	$258,063,693	$387,972,056	$443,809,171	$533,358,062	$1,017,409,997
$1,000,000,000	$1,000,000,000	$1,000,000,000	$1,000,000,000	$1,000,000,000	$1,000,000,000
$78,236,190	$97,667,798	$37,461,388	$54,829,126	$210,188,186	$368,069,313
$846,452,000	$768,215,811	$670,548,012	$633,086,624	$578,257,499	$368,069,313
2.00	2.00	2.00	2.00	2.00	2.00
3.00%	3.00%	3.00%	3.00%	3.00%	3.00%
65.00%	65.00%	65.00%	65.00%	65.00%	65.00%
2.48	2.00	1.55	1.41	1.21	0.51
1.56	1.08	0.64	0.49	0.29	−0.41
0.99	0.98	0.94	0.92	0.89	0.69
0.94	0.86	0.74	0.69	0.61	0.34
$993,413,488	$977,165,889	$940,014,725	$920,526,559	$886,606,348	$693,611,769
$156,242,506	$243,035,233	$365,378,322	$417,963,737	$502,297,706	$958,160,652
$146,961,487	$208,950,079	$269,466,713	$287,439,934	$308,348,849	$325,542,457
$768,215,811	$670,548,012	$633,086,624	$578,257,499	$368,069,313	$0
$19,652,772	$21,951,055	$7,252,286	$12,392,577	$36,238,438	$64,146,268
$28,969,390	$32,357,200	$10,690,314	$18,267,417	$53,417,678	$94,555,529
$15,049,227	$16,809,151	$5,553,481	$9,489,689	$27,749,799	$49,120,385
$14,564,801	$16,268,075	$5,374,718	$0	$26,856,550	$47,539,230
$0	$0	$5,193,470	$8,874,509	$25,950,886	$45,936,100
$0	$0	$0	$0	$23,000,018	$36,724,393
$0	$10,282,317	$3,397,117	$5,804,933	$16,974,816	$30,047,407

better communication between founders, venture funds, limited partners, angels, employees, journalists, and even potential acquirers.

"The Pre-Money Myth" uses widely disseminated quotes on the "value" of Facebook at different times, along with 2010 VC-backed IPO value disclosures to show how venture-funded company use of the term "pre-money value" is hurting venture-capital funds, founders, limited partners, employees, and innovation. It also provides some simple techniques anyone can use to immediately get a better grasp of the true company value implied by a recent round of preferred equity.

Highlights include:

1. Pre-money value for a VC-backed company is almost never equal to "the value of a company prior to receiving the latest round of financing" as most people believe it is and most definitions explicitly say it is.

EXHIBIT 1.7 Option Pricing Model Based on 2009 NextUp Bear Estimated Value of Twitter

	Total	Series E Liq. Pref.	Series D Liq. Pref.	Series B, Series C Liq. Pref.	Series A Liq. Pref.
Breakpoints		Breakpoint 1	Breakpoint 2	Breakpoint 3	Breakpoint 4
Strike Price (K)		$0	$110,000,000	$145,741,503	$165,806,503
BEV Estimate (S)	$441,000,000	$441,000,000	$441,000,000	$441,000,000	$441,000,000
Breakpoint Call					
Value	$441,000,000	$99,120,597	$27,922,038	$14,544,696	$68,721
Call Value at					
Floor		$441,000,000	$341,879,403	$313,957,365	$299,412,669
Term in Years (t)		2.00	2.00	2.00	2.00
Risk-Free Rate (r)		3.00%	3.00%	3.00%	3.00%
Volatility		65.00%	65.00%	65.00%	65.00%
d1		32.20	2.04	1.73	1.59
d2		31.28	1.12	0.81	0.67
N(d1)		1.00	0.98	0.96	0.94
N(d2)		1.00	0.87	0.79	0.75
S * N(d1)		$441,000,000	$431,781,889	$422,534,980	$416,293,549
K * e^-rt		$0	$103,594,099	$137,254,179	$156,150,684
Times N(d2)		$0	$89,902,486	$108,577,615	$116,880,881
C Value at					
Ceiling		$341,879,403	$313,957,365	$299,412,669	$299,343,948
Common	$61,108,769	$0	$0	$0	$0
Series A	$90,146,791	$0	$0	$0	$68,721
Series B	$50,465,914	$0	$0	$3,671,512	$0
Series C	$51,819,922	$0	$0	$10,873,184	$0
Series D	$51,938,680	$0	$27,922,038	$0	$0
Series E	$113,616,286	$99,120,597	$0	$0	$0
Options	$21,903,638	$0	$0	$0	$0

2. VC pre-money and post-money values, which are based largely on market capitalization–style calculations used for companies going public, always include substantially more shares in the pre-money and post-money calculations than companies going public include in the same calculation. This means that even on a basic math basis every VC-based "pre-money value" is overstated if you accept the current prevailing definitions and interpretations of the term.

3. For almost every company, the expected value of potential cash-on-cash returns for prior round investors, founders, and employees is lower than the value of potential cash-on-cash returns for investors in the current round (the new money). Stated another way, in almost every case the probability is that the last money in (the newest preferred shares issued)

Common Participates	Options Exercised	Series D Converts	Series C Caps	Series C Converts	Series E Converts
Breakpoint 5	Breakpoint 6	Breakpoint 7	Breakpoint 8	Breakpoint 9	Breakpoint 10
$165,904,003	$258,063,693	$387,972,056	$443,809,171	$533,358,062	$1,017,409,997
$441,000,000	$441,000,000	$441,000,000	$441,000,000	$441,000,000	$441,000,000
$57,118,727	$58,834,775	$19,504,086	$25,917,728	$75,622,628	$62,346,004
$299,343,948	$242,225,221	$183,390,445	$163,886,359	$137,968,631	$62,346,004
2.00	2.00	2.00	2.00	2.00	2.00
3.00%	3.00%	3.00%	3.00%	3.00%	3.00%
65.00%	65.00%	65.00%	65.00%	65.00%	65.00%
1.59	1.11	0.66	0.52	0.32	−0.38
0.67	0.19	−0.25	−0.40	−0.60	−1.30
0.94	0.87	0.75	0.70	0.62	0.35
0.75	0.57	0.40	0.34	0.27	0.10
$416,261,700	$381,917,993	$329,311,198	$307,714,363	$275,524,220	$154,479,929
$156,242,506	$243,035,233	$365,378,322	$417,963,737	$502,297,706	$958,160,652
$116,917,752	$139,692,772	$145,920,752	$143,828,004	$137,555,589	$92,133,925
$242,225,221	$183,390,445	$163,886,359	$137,968,631	$62,346,004	$0
$14,348,108	$13,223,247	$3,775,867	$5,857,971	$13,038,059	$10,865,517
$21,149,991	$19,491,876	$5,565,859	$8,635,008	$19,218,897	$16,016,438
$10,987,149	$10,125,780	$2,891,393	$4,485,776	$9,983,971	$8,320,334
$10,633,479	$9,799,837	$2,798,320	$0	$9,662,593	$8,052,508
$0	$0	$2,703,955	$4,194,981	$9,336,748	$7,780,959
$0	$0	$0	$0	$8,275,069	$6,220,620
$0	$6,194,036	$1,768,692	$2,743,992	$6,107,290	$5,089,628

has a higher present value and option value, on a per share basis than previously issued preferred shares. In the case of common stock, every class of preferred generally has a greater expected value.

What's the Cost of a Flawed Definition of Pre-Money/Post-Money Valuation?

Just a few of the implications of the widely held misunderstanding that pre-money value equals "the value of a company prior to receiving the latest round of financing" are as follows:

1. It suggests that venture capitalists routinely pay too much for (overvalue) the securities they purchase. If this were true, the assets class would not

outperform most conventional equity investments, as it has done for much of the past several decades.

2. It suggests that founders, employees, and management in a company hold stakes that are worth significantly more than what they actually own.

a. This leads to unrealistic expectations for investor behavior, which can create a lack of trust between investors, founders, management, and employees.

b. It also makes it more difficult for management to fairly view the options being used to recruit and retain employees and key management.

c. This also has the potential to turn an otherwise virtuous source of liquidity, such as secondary markets and secondary sales, into a viscous disincentive

3. It makes limited partners, investment managers, funds, and other parties that rely on financial statement disclosures of venture-capital investment values skeptical of the amounts reported. If not corrected, this could have a huge impact on future investments into venture capital and therefore a negative impact on innovation and competitiveness in countries that continue to use that definition.

Why Is the Current Definition of Pre-Money Value "Wrong"?

When people refer to the "value" of a venture-backed company, they are usually referring to either pre-money value or a post-money value. This is one of the biggest misunderstandings in all venture-capital valuation terminology and it's a very easy problem to fix. See Exhibit 1.8.

Reason 1 Why Pre-Money Value Is Almost Never Company Value: Shares Purchased in the Latest Round Are Rarely the Same as Shares Purchased in Previous Rounds   Let's do some basic math. The biggest problem with the pre-money/post-money definition and its variations is the assumption that the securities being purchased in B are the same as the securities outstanding in A. In the case of a venture-backed company that is not registered to go public, the securities in B and A are almost never the same. In fact, in most cases, "company value," as defined in A, includes securities that have never been issued or even granted. So based simply on basic math, "company value" before money comes in according to this definition is overstated 100% of the time. See Exhibit 1.9.

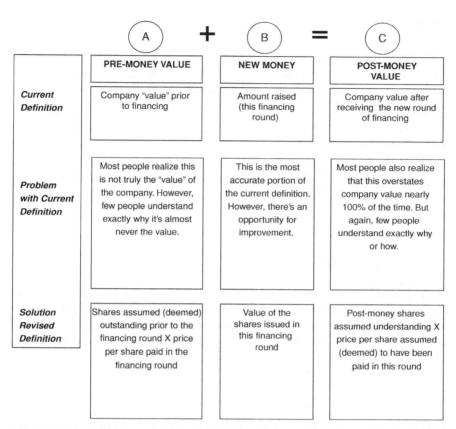

	PRE-MONEY VALUE	NEW MONEY	POST-MONEY VALUE
Current Definition	Company "value" prior to financing	Amount raised (this financing round)	Company value after receiving the new round of financing
Problem with Current Definition	Most people realize this is not truly the "value" of the company. However, few people understand exactly why it's almost never the value.	This is the most accurate portion of the current definition. However, there's an opportunity for improvement.	Most people also realize that this overstates company value nearly 100% of the time. But again, few people understand exactly why or how.
Solution Revised Definition	Shares assumed (deemed) outstanding prior to the financing round X price per share paid in the financing round	Value of the shares issued in this financing round	Post-money shares assumed understanding X price per share assumed (deemed) to have been paid in this round

EXHIBIT 1.8 How Current Definitions of Pre-Money "Value" Are Misleading

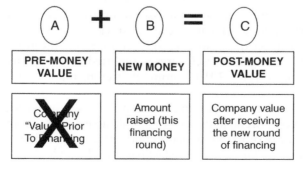

EXHIBIT 1.9 Company Value

EXHIBIT 1.10 2010 IPO Pre-Money Values Using VC Method versus Using Underwriter Method

Q1 2010 IPO Company	Pre-Money IPO Method "Value"	Pre-Money VC Method "Value"	Pre-Money Difference	Post-Money Difference
Meru Networks, Inc. (MERU)	$169,847,775	$312,946,950	84%	39%
MaxLinear, Inc. (MXL)	$353,682,882	$565,435,304	60%	33%
Calix, Inc. (CALX)	$417,701,258	$570,507,756	37%	24%
Financial Engines, Inc. (FNGN)	$346,866,924	$510,732,204	47%	26%

Proof 1—Q1 2010 IPOs To illustrate this, Exhibit 1.10 has four venture-funded companies that went public in Q1 of 2010. The first column shows the pre-money as calculated using market "capitalization" disclosures in the companies' SEC filings. The second column shows how that same company's pre-money value would be interpreted and cited by a VC-funded company using the current definition. The final two columns show the resulting overstatement of company "value" as a result of substantially higher capitalization share counting conventions for private companies versus those used for public companies.

Reason 2 Why Pre-Money Value Is Almost Never Company Value: Last Money in Has Generally Purchased a Class of Security That Has Higher Value Than Prior Rounds Let's take a look at the basic cash flow. Beyond the issue of basic math, overcounting shares that don't exist as well as rights that haven't been granted, there's an issue of investment cash flow potential differences based on when a given class of stock was issued. This is a more difficult problem to explain simply, so we'll use examples from Facebook's valuation-related litigation disclosures as reported by journalists along with disclosures from certain 2010 venture IPO companies disclosed in their SEC filings.

In a very general sense, timing is critical for every investment decision, but perhaps even more so in the case of illiquid assets such as venture capital. This is one of the reasons that so many contractual provisions exist to protect the last party to the table. Also, the last party to the table should, in theory, have a shorter distance between its cash return (cash in) and its investment (cash out). Finally, the price per share paid by those last-round investors is the most objective measurement of the "value" of that specific class of security on that specific day to a buyer similar to the purchasers that bought that same class of preferred stock. The standard for that value, however, is probably not Fair Market Value as defined for 409A.

The Facebook and IPO examples we presented should allow you to get a better feel for this piece of the equation. We will take another look at the Facebook waterfalls as of the Series D, the approximate per share value that was used by ConnectU as a basis for its original settlement negotiations with Facebook.

Proof 2a—Facebook Series D "Value" Versus Litigation "Value" In each of these examples, as well as in cases of all venture-backed companies, understanding rights to investment cash flows is needed to understand the value of every security other than the most recently purchased round of financing. One way to do this is to put yourself in the shoes of each type of investor holding the same exact number of shares but in different types of stock issued by the company. The output in Exhibit 1.11 shows how cash flow to one angel and two VCs that invested in 100,000 shares of Facebook Series A, 100,000 Series B, and 100,000 Series C respectively all get lower investment cash flows than the last money in, the Series D, if the company is sold for anything under $3 billion.

If you could purchase 100,000 shares of **any** of the securities outstanding at that time for $1.00 per share, the Series A, Series B, Series C, Series D, or common stock, which would you purchase for your $100,000? Here's a reminder hint, the 100,000 series D shares give you 6,016 times more cash (that's 601,660% more cash) back than the common stock at even the worse of scenarios. See Exhibit 1.12.

Also, if you buy 100,000 shares of series D with your $100,000, if the company sells for three times as much as the value of the largest venture-backed IPO of 2010, you will still get 505% more cash return to you than if you invested your $100,000 into 100,000 shares of any of the other Facebook securities you could have chosen at $1.00 per share.

So which one would do you chose? You buy the one with the greatest potential.

Since at the same price you are more willing to buy the Series D than the Series A, Series B, Series C, and Common Stock, then we don't really have to go much further in the analysis to prove that the Series D is more valuable than the other classes of stock issued by the company as of that

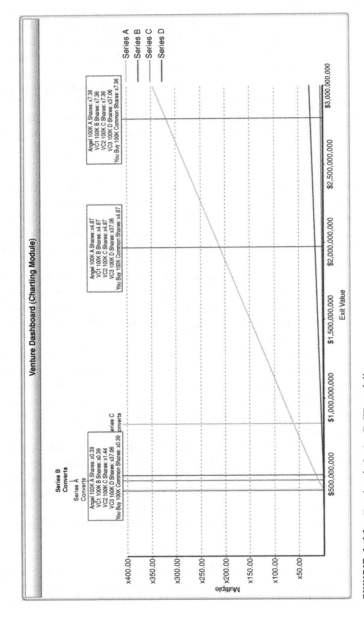

EXHIBIT 1.11 Facebook Series D Waterfall
Source: Liquid Scenarios, Inc.

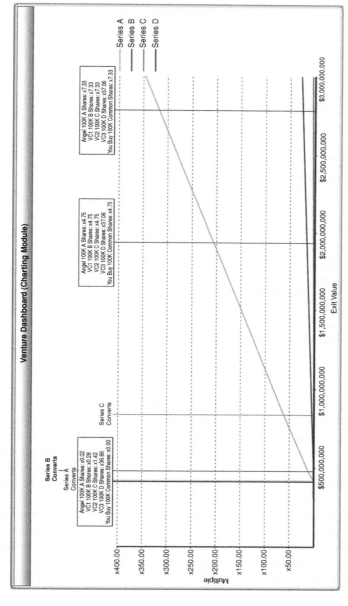

EXHIBIT 1.12 Facebook Series D Waterfall with Carver Deal Term Test

Source: Liquid Scenarios, Inc.

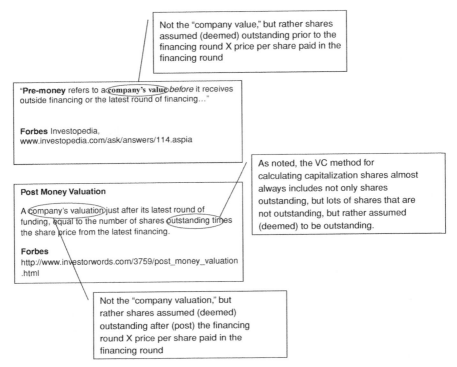

EXHIBIT 1.13   Pre-Money Value Definitions versus "Value of Company" before Financing

date. If that's true, and the Series D shareholders all paid $37.06 per share for the Series D, for instance, then any of the other securities are worth less than $37.06 per share. So multiplying that share price, $37.06 per share, by the shares assumed to be outstanding would overstate the value of the company even if we used the more conservative IPO method of calculating market capitalization. Using the VC method, we would overstate the value even further. See Exhibit 1.13.

Every party involved with the valuation of venture-funded companies is currently applying basic math in a slightly different way (illustrated in Exhibit 1.14). Those differences have profound impacts on the conclusions of value reached. The significance of those differences depends on the stage of a company, its industry, and the objectives of the party seeking to determine value.

EXHIBIT 1.14   VC Valuation Indications and Conclusions Arrived at by Various Parties

Source of "Value" Quote	Typically Refers to	Relative to Company Value
Investing partner at VC fund, company founder, management, and press relying on quotes	Pre- or post-money value, not company fair market value	Overstates company fair market value (FMV) by 50% to 200% Closer to enterprise value later in a company's life The larger (dollar amount) the preferred financing round is, the closer to FMV a VC's pre/post money value will be.
Limited partner financial statements	Carrying value of an LP interest in a VC fund	Overstates or understates FMV by ± 25% to 33%, depending on the auditors, partners finance teams, and liquidity environment
Company 409A (tax) valuation specialist/expert reports	Technically the best assessment of fair market value of common prior to an IPO	Common stock fair market value is typically overstated by 15% to 35% but indicated enterprise values are routinely understated by as much as 100%
Ad hoc enterprise value estimates (times users, revenue, visits, length of stay, clinical trial phase, etc.)	Enterprise value without considering risk, lack of marketability, or uncertainty	All over the map, but still an important exercise to discovering different indications of value
Secondary market transactions (primarily common stock) extrapolated to indicate company value	Price bid (or paid) for common shares times estimated number of fully diluted shares deemed outstanding	Overstates fair market value as a private company by 50% to 200%, but properly values the common shares sold in a given transaction most of the time. The fact that liquidity comes to an asset that was otherwise assumed to be illiquid automatically increases the value of the asset

SUMMARY

The case approach used in this book attempts to allow all parties to quickly find techniques, guides, and samples of how to apply the proper collection of techniques to their real-world situation at the right time to make a better decision. With a relevant case, you should be able to put the facts unique to your situation into a context that will stop you from giving up rights to cash flow or giving advice that will result in your clients giving up those rights unwittingly.

CHAPTER 2

Should Venture-Backed Companies Even Consider a DCF Model?

Introducing the Life Science Valuation Case: Zogenix

I t might seem like almost every company we will use as a case in this book is going to be an Internet-related company. Although not completely true, the reality is that Internet-related VC investments account for 40% of all venture investments today, as illustrated in Exhibit 2.1.

Perhaps more important than the previous statistic is that these investments account for far more than their fair share of VC returns, both in terms of exits and unrealized gains. That being said, it's critical to examine how conventional practices in venture-capital valuation span all industry categories. For that reason, we start our first in-depth case in this book outside of the Internet space, using a life science company, Zogenix.

In this case we will briefly review the major theoretical and practical valuation methods Zogenix used prior to, and after, filing its registration statements with the SEC. As you can imagine, we will likely come up with results that are different than what the investors, founders, auditors, underwriters, and accountants came up with along the way. That's perfectly OK, assuming you (the reader) can distinguish if our differences were due to variations in data quality, differences in assumptions, or differences in the application of business logic. I will try to highlight those differences when available so that you can readily tell when the results were due to a difference in business logic, since the quality of data and the assumptions are of course subject to privacy and price constraints, whereas the search for better business logic is one of the reasons to use a book like this. The goal

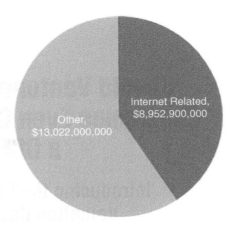

EXHIBIT 2.1   Internet-Related VC
Investments in 2010 versus All Other
Data source: NVCA 2010 Year Book

here is not to revalue the company, but rather to examine the approaches and methods Zogenix used so you can consider how they apply to your company, your portfolio, or your client's company.

This case is referred to, in varying degrees, throughout Chapters 3 and 4. If you are familiar with discounted cash flow concepts, you may find it convenient to skip Chapter 3, which provides a refresher on present/future value concepts and other popular valuation concepts.

ZOGENIX: COMPANY BACKGROUND SUMMARY AND HIGHLIGHTS

From an idea in the early 1990s to a quarter-billion-pound valuation at the turn of the century and a second attempt at going public this decade, Zogenix core technology is anything but an overnight success story. Terry Weston invented the technology in the early 1990s and got a seed round from 3i Ventures in Europe to fund Weston Medical in the UK. Additional investors, including a VC arm of Japan's Normura, participated in subsequent rounds leading up to Weston Medical's listing on the London Stock Exchange during one of the worse market pullbacks in recent history (2000).

However, unlike an Internet company, bugs in production for life science companies can kill a venture's value overnight, due to the risk that its products could kill a patient. That's pretty much what happened to Weston Medical, and it cut the company's 250 million British pounds

Different Kinds of Value at Different Times

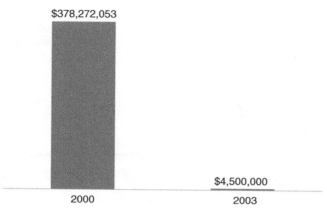

$378,272,053

$4,500,000

2000   2003

EXHIBIT 2.2   Core Technology Once Valued at $350 Million
Then Just $4.5 Million
Data source: Liquid Scenarios, Inc.

(around $350 million) market cap to less than $4.5 million in liquidation
value, which is where the founders and management team from Zogenix
come in. See Exhibit 2.2.

Aradigm Acquires Weston Intraject Assets for Pennies on the Dollar

Following the crash of Weston Medical's stock, and the inability to raise
financing from other sources, Hayward, California-based Aradigm acquired
the Intraject technology out of bankruptcy for around $3 million, including
transaction and transfer costs (see Exhibit 2.3). At the time of the acquisition
Aradigm's stock was bouncing above and below the threshold for NASDAQ
National Market listing requirements (see Exhibit 2.4). Today the company's
stock is on the OTCBB and was trading at under $0.20 when Zogenix filed
for its IPO.

Zogenix Gets Funded—Big Time

At least two of the founders of Zogenix met while working on the Intraject
technology at Aradigm. They arranged to acquire certain rights to the technology in exchange for $4 million up front to Aradigm, provided they could
secure $15 million in VC financing. The founders exceeded that hurdle by
100% to 300%, depending on how you value the deal. Zogenix closed a

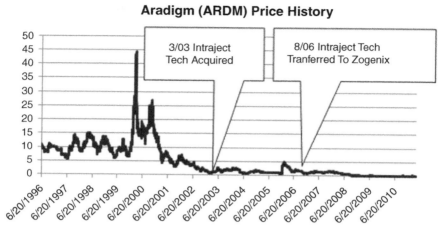

EXHIBIT 2.3   Aradigm Price When Intraject Technology Acquired and When Sold
Source: Liquid Scenarios, Inc. with data from Finance.Yahoo.com.

Series A-1 for approximately $30MM, including the conversion of a $500,000 bridge loan, in August 2006. As part of the deal, Series A-1 holders were issued a "Right" to purchase an equivalent number of shares for the same price, under various conditions. One way to look at this right is as 100% warrant coverage on the Series A-1, with the strike price equal to the Series A-1 issue price. Since warrants issued as part of a round are generally added to the post-money value, as opposed to the pre-money value, one

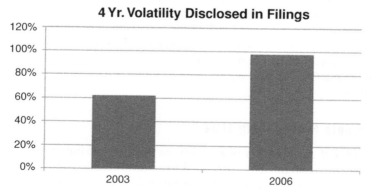

EXHIBIT 2.4   Change in Aradigm Volatility Disclosed in SEC Filings
Source: Liquid Scenarios, Inc. with data from SEC files.

EXHIBIT 2.5 Hypothetical Post-Money Capitalization (Shares) without Rights/Warrants

Security/Class	Shares Issued	Shares Issuable	Fully Diluted Shares
Pre-Money Shares			
Common	11,385,000		11,385,000
Options Pool Increase		20,340,000	20,340,000
Pre-Money Totals	11,385,000	20,340,000	31,725,000
Series A-1	30,775,000		30,775,000
Post Money Capitalization	42,160,000	20,340,000	62,500,000

Source: Liquid Scenarios, Inc. with data from SEC files.

way to view the capitalization of the company after this round might be as shown in Exhibit 2.5.

The first column in Exhibit 2.5 shows the security name, along with subtotals. The next column, Shares Issued, is a number that should match the company's stock ledger, either maintained by a law firm or a transfer agent in some cases. I include a third column, Shares Issuable, to specifically identify shares that are assumed or deemed to be outstanding for purposes of pricing the current round of financing. This column should include the following items:

- Options granted, which can be further broken down into two more categories.
  - Vested Options (those that the holder/grantee has fully earned)
    - If the company sold the day after the round closes, the holder would get proceeds based on his or her adjusted pro-rata ownership. It's important to note that under an M&A (merger or acquisition) scenario, this amount would be higher than his or her pro-rata ownership on a "fully diluted basis" in most cases.
  - Unvested Options (those that the holder/grantee has not earned)
    - So if the company sold the day after the round closes, and there were no "accelerated vesting provisions," the holder would get $0 proceeds as a result of his or her unvested options. It's worth noting that the unvested options would still represent a liability for the acquiring firm and, as a result, theoretically be a portion of the acquisition cost/price

Traditionally, VCs didn't really keep an eye on which options were vested and unvested. In fact, many firms didn't even keep a close eye on the ratio of grants, but instead would focus attention in general to the total size of the option pool as a percentage of "fully diluted shares" outstanding. That practice has started to change as parties have become more focused on specific cash flow potential from period to period, particularly at well-capitalized funds.

Since this is the first round of financing, it's not uncommon to have a completely unissued option pool, so 100% of the pool is simply "reserved" for future issuance. Other items that might populate this column, of "issuable" shares needed to determine fully diluted shares outstanding, would include warrants issued prior to the close of the transaction, or pre-money and any reserved shares issuable to series of preferred stock as a result of conversion price adjustments that cause their conversion ratio to be something other than 1:1. So, for example, if a prior series was issued for $1, but had the conversion price adjusted to $0.50, due to anti-dilution provisions for instance, the original conversion ratio would change from 1:1 to 2:1 and the additional shares "reserved" to satisfy this adjusted price would be included in the issuable column.

It's worth mentioning briefly that the assumed, or "deemed," shares outstanding are defined differently depending on what the calculation is being used for. In this example we are talking about pricing a new round that is not price dilutive, or not a down round, since no prior financing rounds existed. In cases of a dilutive financing, or down round, the number of shares deemed outstanding is generally something less than the fully diluted shares deemed outstanding for purposes of calculating the pre-money value.

Rights and Warrants

There are two key elements still missing from the summary capitalization in Exhibit 2.5. One of the items you don't see in the post-capitalization exhibit presented thus far is the rights or warrants we mentioned earlier. These rights give the investors the option to buy in at the same price, $1.00 per share, at a future date. This raises a number of valuation issues that will impact every holder, whether things go well or not so well in the months following the financing round.

a. Do we simply add the warrants to the post-money value to obtain the post-money "capitalization" of the company?

b. Is the right to an additional superior (preferred) share for each share I currently hold, at a predetermined price, worth more or less than the common stock? Is it worth more or less than the underlying preferred stock?

c. If you were given the choice, which security would you prefer to have, the Series A-1 or the Series A-1 right/warrant?

We'll start with the answer to question a: "Do we add these warrants to get the post-money value?" In general, warrants offered to sweeten a new round of financing are typically included post-money impacting the pricing of the next round of financing. With 100% warrant coverage, or 50% warrant coverage depending on how you calculate it, it's obvious that simply multiplying the post-money fully diluted shares by $1, including the warrants, will describe a value that makes little sense to anyone. In fact, you could easily argue that the warrants actually decrease the value of the company on a fully diluted pro-rata basis, since if the company appreciates rapidly as expected, that growth will go only to the shareholders that hold the warrants.

The next question is how the value of the warrants on the Series A-1 preferred stock compares to the value of the common and the value of the Series A-1 preferred stock. In most cases, the Series A-1 shares, assuming they are the first round of financing, will of course be of greater value than the common stock. Most people would also assume that if the close date for the underlying Series A-1 is the same as the issue date for the warrants then the Series A-1 shares are worth more than the Series A-1 warrants and comparable in value to the common stock. However, there's no way to know the true answer to these questions concerning relative value from one security to another without accurately calculating a payout model first.

The other missing element from Exhibit 2.5 is the presence of two initial tranches for the Series A-1, in the amounts of approximately $15.4 million each; with a future commitment for an equal amount including the warrant exercises, so a total of $60.8 million. Tranches always have pricing and valuation implications. However, those implications are not represented in the form of a changing price per share, since typically the original issue price per share stays the same for each tranche. In this case, the tranches were issued from August 2006 through September/December 2007, so over a year. One year is not a long time for many companies, but for high-growth companies receiving such a large amount of capital at the early stage, you would hope that the value would grow significantly over that period of time. Unfortunately, the reality is that the value could also decrease over that period of time. These changes in the value of the firm, including debt plus equity, or changes in the value of the company's total equity excluding debt, represent volatility, which is a key input to future expectations for venture-backed companies.

Varying Probabilities

One of the unique features of many life-science companies, as opposed to other venture-backed companies, is a sequence of regulatory hurdles that are perceived to represent probabilities of success. There's very reliable data with respect to expected costs for each phase and usable data with respect to how the probability of ultimately being approved for marketing improves as firms move through one stage, or phase in the case of pharmaceuticals, to another stage. Each of these changes can be a clue as to expected volatility, although both are generally used by valuation professionals and analysts to adjust discrete future cash flows and bring them to a present value, which we will discuss further in Chapters 3 and 4.

So why are these varying probabilities so important in the cases of large tranches spread over the course of a year? Because it means that capital appreciation is being earned at a higher rate by those purchasers of these tranches, the VC investors, than it is by the founders and debt holders, under a good scenario. Under a bad scenario, it means that value is being lost at a lower rate for the VCs and a higher rate for founders and employees. As a result, the reliability of recent primary transactions in the company's stock as a market input to find a clue, or indication, of the total equity value of the company diminishes.

Exhibit 2.6 illustrates this by allocating the pre-money and post-money value to each shareholder using the traditional VC convention, which as we've stated is primarily a means of explaining how the new round of financing is explained on a price per share basis, as opposed to truly explaining the value of the company before or after a new round of financing. This is easily proven by simply assuming the company sold for its post-money value, which we do later in this case. Exhibit 2.6 could be effective any time between the initial close of the Series A-1 and the Series A-2, and the implied company value using the traditional VC convention would be the same, even though the amount of cash actually invested, the options granted, and a number of other variables would be different.

We will revisit the implications of this traditional perspective later in this section, but for now you can ask yourself, if the company reached each of its regulatory milestones, would the first tranche issued at $1.00 per share in August 2006 have the same value as the fourth tranche issued in September/December 2007?

LEAPING FORWARD JUST 20 MONTHS, THE COMPANY FILES FOR AN IPO

Less than two years after the first tranche of financing, the new company, Zogenix, was ready to go public. Unfortunately, when it filed its registration statement in March 2008, no one knew it would turn out to be the worst year on record for venture-backed IPOs and one of the worse for securities of any kind. As a result, the company had to raise another round of funding to

EXHIBIT 2.6 Pre-Series B Capitalization Allocated Using Traditional VC Convention

Shareholder	Pre-Money			Invested	FDS %	Avg. Cost
	Invested	Value	FDS %			
Domain Associates, L.L.C.	$75	$75,000	0.39%	$21,100,075	24.08%	$1.00
Stephen J. Farr, Ph.D.	$3,000	$3,000,000	15.68%	$3,000	3.41%	$0.00
Roger Hawley	$2,100	$2,100,000	10.98%	$102,100	2.50%	$0.05
Gamer Investments, LLC	$1,850	$1,850,000	9.67%	$101,850	2.22%	$0.05
Hale Biopharma Ventures LLC	$100	$100,000	0.52%	$100,100	0.23%	$0.50
Windamere LLC III				$100,000	0.11%	$1.00
Clarus Ventures				$21,000,000	23.88%	$1.00
Scale Ventures				$14,000,000	15.92%	$1.00
Thomas McNerney				$12,000,000	13.65%	$1.00
Scott N. Wolfe				$4,167	0.00%	$1.00
Faye Hunter Russell Trust				$4,166	0.00%	$1.00
Cheston Larson				$4,167	0.00%	$1.00
VP Company Investments				$12,500	0.01%	$1.00
Life Science Angels				$235,000	0.27%	$1.00
WSGR/Other				$40,000	0.05%	$1.00
Founder	$6,342	$6,342,188	33.16%	$6,342	7.21%	$0.00
Total Existing	$13,467	$13,467,188	70.41%	$68,813,467	93.56%	$0.84
New Investors	$19,113,721	$5,660,000	29.59%	$19,113,721	6.44%	$3.38
Series A-1 Totals	$19,127,188	$19,127,188	100.00%	$87,927,188	100.00%	$1.00

Source: Liquid Scenarios, Inc. with data from SEC files.

bridge the gap between a withdrawn IPO and continued needs as its offering was commercialized.

VCs Double-Down on Zogenix Convertible Debt

2008, and much of 2009, was probably a record year for convertible debt financings of venture-backed companies for obvious reasons. However, most of those deals converted at discounts to the next round of financing or with multiple liquidation preferences. Those discounts yielded substantial returns for their investors (see the Tesla case in this book). The VCs that invested in Zogenix's latest venture round, along with certain PE investors, did so without any explicit discounts and without any special liquidation preferences (other than those implicit in the Series B financing).

The original issue prices for these convertible debt rounds were only at a slight increase, or step up, in value over the Series A-1 financing. This relatively flat per share pricing is common in private equity, or "PE," deals but not so popular with venture investors outside of certain life science funds. It's important because, as in the case of the large tranches, the reliability of the original issue price per share as an input to the total equity value of the company is decreased. One might argue that the importance of who was participating in those convertible debt rounds, which is always important, was even a more important consideration from a valuation perspective as a result of the relatively flat round to round pricing. See Exhibit 2.7.

VCs Even Offer to Purchase a Portion of the Offering

Similarly, an increasing number of venture-backed IPOs have the VCs as selling shareholders, which is reasonable if there's sufficient market demand

EXHIBIT 2.7   Convertible Debt Purchasers

Investor	2010 Convertible Debt Purchased	Convertible Debt Discount%
Domain Associates	$3,440,206	0%
Clarus Lifesciences	$3,423,902	0%
Chicago Growth Partner	$2,299,963	0%
Scale Venture Partners	$2,282,541	0%
Thomas, McNerney Partners	$2,057,675	0%
Abingworth Bioventures	$1,495,713	0%

Source: Liquid Scenarios, Inc. with data from SEC files.

since these parties took the early risk with the promise of a liquidity event. However, this deal was also unique in that the VCs behind it even offered to purchase a portion (up to $15 million) of the IPO shares being issued.

Some people were skeptical of this willingness to pile cash into a deal at what appears to be essentially the same pricing. And, indeed, in the case of private transactions, such a move can have a profound impact on the perceived value of the enterprise, which we will get into later. On the other hand, others would take these actions to indicate the longer-term value these existing investors see in Zogenix. At the conclusion of this case, you will have the capacity to decide for yourself at every stage of the company's development if you would risk resources as the founder, as an angel, as one of the venture capitalists, or as an investment bank based on changes in the company's value.

ORDER OF VALUATIONS PRESENTED IN THIS CASE

As noted, we are going to examine some of the major theoretical and practical valuation methods Zogenix applied. We will do this across the evolution of the company, including the founding date of the company, the first round of venture-capital financing, subsequent rounds of venture capital financing, convertible debt and venture debt warrant issuances, issuances of employee options, and ultimately the company's IPO.

We could simply start at the beginning, when Zogenix was founded, or start at the end, the date of the public offering. However, I decided to start with the Zogenix IPO disclosures as they are introduced by the company in its SEC filing. For each concept introduced, we will give a background, apply it to the company and security values for Zogenix at different stages, and suggest shortcut ways for trying to do the calculations yourself. Along the way we will identify common pitfalls of both valuation professionals and non-finance professionals in trying to apply these concepts, and how to avoid making those mistakes.

* * *

In Chapter 3 we look at the three approaches to valuation, the asset approach, the income approach, and the market approach, disclosed in the registration statements of most venture-funded companies using Zogenix as an example. We also look at how these indications of value are intertwined with the value allocation methods used by virtually all venture-backed companies in the United States.

Valuation Methods versus Allocation Methods Regarding Zogenix

"The valuation was prepared using the guidance in the American Institute of Certified Public Accounting's Technical Practice Aid, Valuation of Privately-Held Company Equity Securities Issued as Compensation. This process valued our total equity and then allocated it between our common stock and our preferred stock."
—Zogenix 2008 SEC Filing

The epigraph at the start of this chapter, from the Zogenix registration statement filed with the SEC, has three critical pieces of information that impact every investor, founder, and employee of a venture-funded company today:

1. A professional valuation was done, and its preparers relied on guidance from the AICPA's "Technical Practice Aid, Valuation of Privately-Held Company Equity Securities Issued as Compensation."
2. Total equity was valued first.
3. Then the total equity value conclusion was allocated between the other securities.

SEPARATING ENTERPRISE VALUE FROM THE ALLOCATION OF THAT VALUE

The AICPA's Practice Aid in this area lists a handful of methods that can be used to value Total Equity Value as well as a number of methods for allocating that value among different classes of preferred stock, options, warrants, and common stock. Although it's tempting to think that valuing a company in its entirety versus allocating that value to specific securities are distinct processes, unless the tasks are undertaken independently, it becomes an iterative process, where the value allocated to a given security will make a professional reconsider the value of an enterprise, and vice versa.

In the simplest sense, though, you can think of the total company equity value as being the value of the whole pie of equity and the allocation being how much your piece of the pie might be worth. But if you think of this for a moment, it's actually in reverse order of how markets generally work, which is one of many reasons people who don't value these types of securities sometimes have issues with the resulting outcomes.

For instance, if I tell you that there are 10 million shares of stock outstanding and they are being purchased for $5 each, most people will conclude that the company has a value of $50 million. This value is sometimes referred to as a "market cap" or market capitalization. Indeed, each of Zogenix preferred financing rounds, beginning with the Series A-1, was essentially "valued" in this manner, which we referred to as the traditional VC convention previously. See Exhibit 3.1.

Unfortunately, this same methodology was prevalent in how both founders and VCs perceived their respective ownership stakes in private venture-backed companies, until recently. The obvious flaw is that the VCs get a security with superior rights, including characteristics similar to both debt and equity, whereas founders in a company generally get a callable, forfeitable junior security with no debt-like features. That is just one of the obvious reasons why simply taking the value per share for the superior security, the preferred stock purchased by the VC, and multiplying securities outstanding, derivatives outstanding, and derivatives approved for issuance in the future is not a sound valuation method. We covered this topic briefly in Chapter 1 in a section called "The Pre-Money Myth."

Common Stock Outstanding	13,467,188	$1.00	Common @ Series A-1 Price = $13,467,188	"Pre-Money Value"
Unissued Option Pool Deemed Outstanding	5,660,000	$1.00	Unissued Options@ Series A-1 Price = $13,467,188	
Series A-1 Stock Issued in New VC Round	68,800,000	$1.00	$68,800,000 Consideration Received	
Total Post-money FDS "Capitalization"	82,267,188	$1.00	$87,927,188 Post-money Value	"Post-Money Value"

EXHIBIT 3.1   Pre-Series B Capitalization Allocated Using Traditional VC Convention
Source: Liquid Scenarios, Inc.

Another reason it becomes hard for valuation professionals to objectively separate their conclusion of the enterprise value from their allocation of that value to different classes of securities is that a number of methods in the AICPA's practice guide do in fact contemplate solving for enterprise value and security value in a single step. Moreover, many approaches to getting an idea, or "indication," of enterprise value overlap and rely on allocating portions of the value indicated to market data that applies to both debt, common equity, derivatives, and preferred equity, with each of those securities being rewarded according to different rules and rates. We will discuss some of those methods as we move further along in our review of the Zogenix valuation disclosures. We can quickly illustrate some of these features without the use of software by doing a simple calculation of maximum payout per share for preferred versus common, simply taking the liquidation preference of the Series A-1 on the date it was issued, which is:

Preferred

$30.5MM Liquidation Preference Series A-1, with 2.5X Participation Cap—30.5MM Shares

Common

11.39MM Common Shares That "Reverse Vest"—Assume 25% Vest Immediately—3MM Shares

If the company sells at pre-money value the next day, preferred stock gets $30.55MM, with the balance shared between 30.5MM preferred shares and 3MM common shares, so around $0.60 per share. Suggesting value of preferred would be 25% greater than $1.00 per share if sold, and the value of 11.39MM shares of common would be around 90% less.

If, instead of an estimate with respect to the reverse vesting provisions, we used the actual terms, copied below from Zogenix filings, the value of the common stock (using a back of the napkin calculation) would be even lower than 90% of what the pre-money value implies. As stated in Zogenix's S-1 Registration Statement,

> *In May and August 2006, in conjunction with the founding of the Company, 11,385,000 shares of common stock were issued to the founders (Founder's Stock) at a price of $0.001 per share for total proceeds of $11,000. Of the total Founder's Stock issued, 11,200,000 shares vest over periods between two and four years and the Company has the option to repurchase any unvested shares at the original purchase price upon any voluntary or involuntary termination.*

This difference in values, between the common and the Series A-1 preferred, is reflected in the option grant price of $0.05 per share that Zogenix used in February 2007, which is 5% of the price paid in its most recent round of preferred stock. Even if we multiply 100% of the founders' stock by the $0.05 per share common stock value implied by the option grant price, we'll end up with a substantially lower "value of the company prior to receiving a round of financing" than would be suggested by the traditional definition of pre-money value.

It's important to keep in mind that in February 2007, not all venture-funded companies had started using third-party valuation professionals because the effective dates for 409A were still in question. As we have started to discuss, and will continue to discuss at length, had a 409A valuation been done for Zogenix at the end of 2006, gains upon Zogenix's IPO realized by employees receiving those options would have been materially lower. The same can be said for employees of many venture-backed companies, who may be losing up to $1 billion per month due to options that were overpriced as a result of the interactions between auditors and valuation professionals as it relates to 409A.

VALUING TOTAL EQUITY

As noted in the Zogenix disclosure, its valuation professionals "valued our total equity." How they did that is largely what this book is about; fortunately, they go on to tell us the methods they used as of their 2008 and 2010 IPO filings. The 2008 IPO Zogenix filing states, "To arrive at total equity value, the cost approach, the market approach, and the income approach were evaluated." And the 2010 IPO Zogenix Filing states,

> *During 2009 and 2010, the valuation methodologies employed by us in the contemporaneous determination of fair value of our common stock were based on three primary factors: (i) market approach using comparable publicly traded companies, (ii) income approach using discounted cash flow analysis, and (iii) cost approach.*

Although Zogenix states it differently year to year, the same three general valuation approaches were used. Those three approaches to valuation are, more or less, the same ones described in the AICPA practice guide. I say more or less because the AICPA is more specific with respect to what an "asset"-based approach is versus what a "cost" approach is. So before getting into how the company describes its application of these methods, now is a good time to introduce the definitions for each of these approaches for readers who are not valuation professionals. We will use the definitions published by the AICPA on the left hand of Exhibit 3.2 and some practical ways to think of these concepts on the right hand of Exhibit 3.2.

EXHIBIT 3.2   AICPA Practice Aid Definitions of Value Approaches in Plain English

Market Approach – Think "How Much Did My Neighbor's House Sell for?"

FASB/AICPA Definition	Real-World Comparison
"A valuation technique that uses prices and other relevant information generated by market transactions involving identical or comparable assets or liabilities (including a business)..."	In the real estate world you will hear the term "comps," and you will hear the same word used in many cases when people discuss private company "comparables." While technically using "comps" is just one "method" within the market approach, the idea is easy to relate to for most people

Income Approach – Think "How Much Is My House Worth if I Get $X Per Year in Rent Forever?"

FASB/AICPA Definition	Real-World Comparison
"The income approach uses valuation techniques to convert future amounts (for example, cash flows or earnings) to a single present amount (discounted)."	You buy a $1,000 Series EE savings bond today for $500 for your 1-year-old daughter. When she graduates from high school, she redeems it for $1,000. Bonds are the perfect example of where using an income approach to valuation can produce a result you can literally take to the bank.

Asset Approach – Think "How Much Would It Cost to Replace My House?"

FASB/AICPA Definition	Real World Comparison
"A general way of determining a value indication of a business, business ownership interest, or security using one or more methods based on the value of the assets net of liabilities."	Your home is destroyed by a tornado and the insurer has to pay to have each material purchased and for the labor to combine those materials to replace your home. However, you also have a mortgage equal to 60% of the replacement costs. The value to you might be the difference between the replacement costs and the payoff amount of your mortgage.

Source: AICPA and Liquid Scenarios, Inc.

The Income Approach

AICPA's *Technical Practice Aid, Valuation of Privately-Held Company Equity Securities Issued as Compensation* states, "The income approach seeks to convert future economic benefits into a present value for the enterprise." There are two primary methods within the income approach literally used millions of times every day throughout the world. The first is the capitalization of earnings method and the second is the discounted cash flow method, which in many cases also relies on the capitalization of earnings method as we'll describe later. In almost every case, a valuation professional will use some derivative of a discounted cash flow model (or DCF) as at least one of the methods employed to value a venture-capital-financed company. Here's how Zogenix described its application of this particular income approach to valuation in its 2010 S1 filing:

> *The income approach using a discounted cash flow analysis is based on the residual value and debt-free cash flow from our multi-year forecast discounted to present value based on our calculated weighted average cost of capital, or WACC.*

As short and sweet as that explanation sounds, it's critical that every reader fully understand it. As discussed in Exhibit 3.2 with respect to the income approach, the AICPA describes the income approach as "valuation techniques to convert future amounts (for example, cash flows or earnings) to a single present amount (discounted)." That means there are at least two steps:

1. Estimating the future amounts (cash flows, earnings, or other benefits) and
2. Discounting those amounts.

One of the critical concepts embedded there is the process of discounting the future benefits using a formula. This formula is what I call the hammer of finance:

$$(1 + r)^\wedge - t$$

where $r =$ the required rate of return (or interest rate, in which case sometimes the variable I is used)

$t =$ time or term, which can be expressed in any measurement of time (days, months, quarters, or years)

As you can tell from this formula, valuation math is, generally speaking, incredibly simple. However, it's also "deceptively" simple, because how you apply the basic math to a problem at every step can have profound ramifications into what conclusions you draw about the value of a business or a security.

Every valuation-related issue ultimately will be solved for, tested, compared to, questioned, or otherwise considered in the context of this simple formula one way or another. The use of this simple formula applies to almost all other valuation and allocation methods that are not explicitly considered income approaches.

In this case, as with the others, we will try not to gloss over the details of the basic math for two reasons. One reason is that in my experience when this same basic math is applied to venture-capital valuations, failure to properly model the business logic of these transactions results in erroneous conclusions in 80% to 90% of the cases. This conclusion is consistent with results from research from each of the major accounting and consulting firms, which have long asserted that 80% to 90% of Excel spreadsheets contain material errors. Also, although the math is simple, when you apply it across large numbers of rules and multiple scenarios, both precision and accuracy decrease.

Another issue we see in applying these methods simply involves terminology. The word "discount" is used a lot in finance, sometimes as a noun, sometimes as a verb, and sometimes with up to four meanings. For scientists and engineers, it's usually more meaningful to replace the word "discount" in the context of valuation with the phrase "growth/decay formula," since that's all it really is.

Part of the confusion around the use of the term "discount" as it relates to valuations is due to the many definitions for discount that can apply to finance in different circumstances. The definition of discount from Wiktionary here reinforces this reality. As a verb:

to discount (third-person singular simple present *discounts,* present participle *discounting,* simple past and past participle *discounted*)

1. *To deduct from an account, debt, charge, and the like; to make an abatement of; as, merchants sometimes discount five or six per cent for prompt payment of bills.*
2. *To lend money upon, deducting the discount or allowance for interest; as, the banks discount notes and bills of exchange.*
3. *To take into consideration beforehand; to anticipate and form conclusions concerning (an event).*

4. *To leave out of account; to take no notice of.*
5. *To lend, or make a practice of lending, money, abating the discount; as, the discount for sixty or ninety days.*

And as a noun:

discount (plural *discounts*)

1. *A reduction in price.*
2. *A deduction made for interest, in advancing money upon, or purchasing, a bill or note not due; payment in advance of interest upon money.*
3. *The rate of interest charged in discounting.*

So when a valuation professional says he or she is going to "discount" cash flow, take a discount for a lack of marketability, discount management's estimates, or apply a discount rate, that person can easily end up using the same word several different ways in the same paragraph. This of course makes things confusing, especially since most people think of a discount as some kind of a reduction off the stated or usual price. Most people also think of that reduction being determined by multiplying the subject of the discount by one minus some percentage to arrive at the discounted price. As a result, when we use the word "discount" outside of tables for the rest of this book, we will try to include a formula or contextual support so everyone knows exactly how we are using the term in a particular instance.

WACC

The other key terminology used in the Zogenix valuation disclosure was "weighted average cost of capital, or WACC." When you see the term "WACC" used to describe a discount rate (required rate of return) applied to a private company, you should be skeptical. When you see it used in the context of a venture-funded company, you should rarely trust the calculation, unless you've seen (a) a detailed buildup of how the discount rate was arrived at and (b) an estimate of the equity value that you don't notice any material flaws in and believe to be accurate as of a specific point in time close to the company going public or being acquired.

Although this may seem like a strong statement against or criticism of the approach, it's not. Instead, it's simply recognition that even with publicly traded companies, the WACC is a moving target. In the case of a private company, you can't arrive at a weighted average cost of capital until you come up with an estimate for the value of the equity. If you are using the

Weighted by Market Value	W	Weighted
Average of Debt and Equity Cost (Interest and Returns)	A	Average
Cost of Equity	C	Cost of
Cost of Debt	C	Capital

EXHIBIT 3.3   Weighted Average Cost of Capital Mnemonic
Source: Liquid Scenarios, Inc.

income approach, you can't come up with a value for the equity until you arrive at an appropriate discount rate. See Exhibit 3.3.

As the diagram and mnemonic in Exhibit 3.3 illustrate, you need to weight debt and equity by their respective market values in order to apply the WACC. Given the fact that many venture-funded companies are perceived to have little debt in their capital structure, weighting the market value of debt is not usually an issue. Our sample case being used here, the life sciences company Zogenix, does in fact have some debt in its capital structure, around $20MM by the time the company went public. If the rates on the debt are verified to be market value given the risks, we can often simply look at the stated rates as of the valuation date to very easily determine the cost of debt.

Finding the market value of equity, on the other hand, is quite difficult for a private company or other firm whose common shares don't trade actively in a liquid market. In the case of a venture-capital round that just closed, it's not unreasonable to assume that the price paid for that particular security, for instance the Series C, is a fair approximation of the market value for that particular security as of that date. But six months later, even that data point may be a questionable reference for the value of the Series C, for the reasons we mentioned previously concerning progress towards the company's goals. Assuming the Series C original issue price is equal to the Series C market value, what does that say about the market value of the Series B, Series A-1, options at various grant prices, and common stock outstanding?

The answer depends on a number of factors, many of which relate to rights and preferences of those particular securities as compared to the rights and preferences of the Series C. However, even after we've allocated the relative values to each of those other securities, using the Series C as a market input for example, we still don't truly know what the cost, or required rates of return expressed as percentages, are for the Series C, Series A, Series B, options, and common stock. Instead, we just know how we might weight their respective required returns, but how do we differentiate the required returns for one series compared to those of another? To put the steps involved into a context, we can quickly look at how you might determine the WACC for a publicly traded company, compared to doing the same for a private company in the same industry. This is an example of a WACC formula for most public companies and the debt and equity inputs required follow.

WACC = Weighted Cost of Debt (%) + Weighted Cost of Equity (%)

Debt inputs required:

- Market Value of Interest-Bearing Debt
- Rates/Yields on Interest-Bearing Debt
- Marginal Tax Rate

Equity inputs required include (with very simplified definitions for now):

- Equity Market Cap (price per share quoted times number of shares outstanding)
- Beta (the volatility of the stock compared to volatility of the market)
- Risk-free Rate (R_{fr}—for now, just consider this the rate on U.S. Government Securities)
- Long-term Market Return (R_m—generally the S&P 500 return over a long period)

For now, we'll focus on how the equity market capitalization, beta, the risk-free rate, and long-term market return are used to arrive at a cost of equity. These variables are most often expressed in the Capital Asset Pricing Model to arrive at a cost of equity for a public company, as follows:

$$K_e = R_{fr} + \beta(R_m - R_{fr})$$

As you can see, we need two elements, one of which we can only gather directly from publicly traded companies that have been trading for a long enough period from which to derive a meaningful correlation between the volatility of the stock compared to the stock volatility of the broader market. Beta is very easy to interpret for a publicly traded company. If Beta is great than 1, we expect more volatility in the stock than in the market; if Beta is less, we expect less volatility in the stock than in the market of reference.

But without enough data, you can't reliably compare the stock's movements to the overall market's movement. With this in mind, using a beta from publicly traded companies in established industries with established product lines and customers as a "proxy" for privately held companies in emerging industries or product segments is, of course, highly questionable. Still, in the case of a traditional privately held company, the beta can be a useful input in determining a floor of reasonable required returns within an industry.

Without going any further, you can easily see how applying WACC determining to most venture-funded companies requires an increasingly large set of assumptions to arrive at an estimated collection of "costs" or returns for the different types of securities. After all of that effort, we may not be comfortable using the weights implied by the respective market values to appropriately discount the cash flows to the company, or cash flows to the firm.

In a world with lots of computers and a virtually unlimited supply of applications to match any situation, complexity alone should not be a barrier to applying any valuation method that gets us a better conclusion. But the quality of logic and accessibility of relevant, observable inputs into assumptions is a barrier to making decisions that will make money versus those that will ultimately generate losses or smaller returns than one might otherwise realize. That being said, the WACC and the CAPM (capital asset pricing model) can help us prove the reasonableness of other value indications we arrive at, even if they are not ideally suited to explicitly solving for equity and capital costs for venture funded companies. With that in mind, we will transition into the actual income approach methods of valuation that require rates of return, or costs of capital, in order to give us clues to possible values.

USING FUTURE VALUE (FV) AND PRESENT VALUE (PV) TO VALUE FUTURE CASH FLOWS TODAY

Let's consider the statement "I bought this house for $300,000 in 1975 and today it's worth a million." If "today" is 2010, then you've essentially lost money on the home. If today is 1976, then you've not only beat record inflation, but you've managed to beat most alternative asset returns. In 1975, we have cash flow of −$300,000. In the exit year, either 2010 or 1976, we have an asset that we can liquidate for $1,000,000. Note that we've assumed that the true market value of the house is in fact $1,000,000 on that terminal date.

If the discounting formula we described earlier is the hammer of finance, $(1 + r)^{\wedge} t$, then projected cash flows are the nails. Exhibit 3.4 shows one view of the cash flows we've described above at a high level: $300,000 cash out in period 0 and $1,000,000 cash in for period n.

EXHIBIT 3.4   Cash-on-Cash Return Multiples, Present Values and Discounted
Cash Flow

Assuming Exit in 2010	Period 0 (1975)	Period 25 (2010)
Cash In	$0	$1,000,000
Cash Out	$300,000	$0
Cash Flow	($300,000)	$1,000,000
Discount Factor @ 7.5%	$(1+0.075)^\wedge-0=1$	$(1+0.075)^\wedge-1=0.16397906$
Present Value	($300,000)	$163,979
$\sum$ Discounted Cash Flows	($136,021)	
Cash-on-Cash Multiple	$1,000,000/$300,000 = 3.33	
Assuming Exit in 1976	**Period 0 (1975)**	**Period 1 (1976)**
Cash In	$0	$1,000,000
Cash Out	$300,000	$0
Cash Flow	($300,000)	$1,000,000
Discount Factor @ 7.5%	$(1+0.075)^\wedge-0=1$	$(1+0.075)^\wedge-1=0.930232558$
Present Value	($300,000)	$930,233
$\sum$ Discounted Cash Flows	$630,233	
Cash-on-Cash Multiple	$1,000,000/$300,000 = 3.33	

By applying our financial hammer, the present value formula, to a simple set of assumptions we were able to improve our understanding of value quickly and easily. At the assumed discount rate, we would lose at least $136,021 immediately on our investment if it took 25 years to get $1,000,000 in net proceeds from our $300,000 purchase price, assuming a required return of 7.5%. This compares to a present value of more than double our investment if our time horizon is one year and we are able to sell the same property for $1,000,000 in net proceeds within 12 months of our purchase.

There are several key things you've probably observed from the previous sample. First, since there's only two time periods (the cash in and cash out periods), we could simply get the present value of the cash in and subtract the amount we invested (purchase price) from the discounted cash flow in the last year to determine the present value. You will sometimes see the formula expressed like that [Purchase Price – Net Sales Proceeds * $(1 + r)^\wedge - t$].

You also probably noticed that we used a discount rate (or required rate of return) of 7.5% but didn't say where that rate came from. Required rate of return is critical to present value calculations. The higher the required rate, r, the lower the present value (all things being equal). You can view the required rate of return as having two key elements:

1. The Risk-Free Rate: This would be the rate of return you would demand if return of your initial investment (principal) were virtually guaranteed. In most cases, this is the yield (or return if purchased today) on a U.S. Treasury
2. The Risk Premium: In the simplest sense, this is the additional rate of return you require because an investment does not guarantee a return of 100% of your principal. The higher the probability of losing your principal, the greater the risk principal and therefore the greater the required rate of return, resulting in a lower present value compared to a less risky investment with comparable cash flows.

We will review ways to determine an appropriate risk premium later in this book. However, since we can all assume that a real estate investment of any kind has greater risk than a U.S. Treasury, it's fair to say that our actual required rate of return in 1975 would have been higher than 7.5%, which was the 10-year Treasury rate at the time.

You probably also observed that for the longer return horizon, 25 years, there were probably a lot of cash flows in between our purchase date and our exit date. Some of those would have been negative, such as maintenance, repairs, insurance, and so forth, and others may have been positive, such as rental income or having a place to live without paying rent for 25 years. As mentioned before, if the present value formula is the hammer of finance, projected cash flows are the nails, and those are details we would need to nail down further if the 25-year time horizon was otherwise attractive to us.

As a result of this simplifying assumption with respect to cash flows, you will notice that the term "Cash-on-Cash" is used and the amount is the same under both scenarios. This is of particular importance, since investing partners at VC firms are generally more interested in cash-on-cash return multiples than they are in IRR. You will notice, later, that IRR is influenced by time, the same way our discounted cash flows are impacted by time. The longer the time period, the lower our IRR and the lower our Net Present Value, or NPV.

To understand NPV, simply consider the EE bond example we gave earlier, where you purchase a $1,000 face bond that matures in 17 years for $500 today. Now, assume that another savings bond is available for the same face amount ($1,000), but only costs you $100. Which would you chose? The answer probably depends on who the issuer is. If it's another U.S. savings bond, you of course accept the $100 dollar savings bond and the NPV for the other savings bond would decrease. If the issuer is the Central Bank of Iceland, then perhaps you are better off paying $500 for the U.S. savings bond.

When gamblers engage a game of chance, like roulette for instance, and the wheel spins, they are hoping for a return on their investment expressed as a multiple of the amount of money they placed as a bet. In most cases, it will be just a matter of minutes before they know whether 100% of that bet will be lost or if they will get double their money, get five times their money back, or even 100 times their money in certain games. In exchange for a lower chance of losing a given bet, they might bet on red or black, which has a 48% of paying them double their money. If the player chooses to bet on a specific number, their odds of losing 100% of their bet increase dramatically, but so does the payoff multiple (cash-on-cash return) if they are successful.

For better or for worse, all good investors have to make a similar decision with respect to what classes of investments they choose to allocate their assets to in an attempt to realize growth. In the case of venture capitalists, the perception is that they are attempting to get the equivalent of a 35-to-1 payback in roulette, while spreading the risks across multiple bets, or portfolio companies. In reality, only the very best firms have the learned to conduct business in this asset class with that risk profile. As a result of demands from limited partners, the learning curve in transitioning from a successful entrepreneur or engineer into a successful investor and the ever-changing payout table that's tied largely to when you get into an investment and what the larger economy is doing when you'd like to be getting out of that investment means that the majority of VCs actually start out playing Red/Black or Odd/Even (2X returns) on most investments.

So who is the house? By extension, I would have to say the house is really the greater economy, which would include the VCs, the entrepreneurs that founded the companies, the limited partners, the employees they hire, and the customers they serve. In aggregate, the house always wins, which in the case of VC investments generally means that society wins.

SUMMARY

$$(1 + r)^{\wedge}t$$

If an investment grows at a given rate per period, how much cash will you accumulate at the end of a given number of periods? Although the variables here are quite simple, this is probably the most important calculation in of all finance, and is used, to one extent or another, in just about every valuation analysis.

In reality, the simple formula just mentioned applies to valuing venture-backed companies in the earliest stages, but it also kind of depends on the industry. For many venture-backed industries, such as Internet, software, or hardware, you will rarely see investors seriously looking at a pure DCF model in the early stages. Instead, what they will look at is the management team first and foremost, then the market opportunity, and finally the potential competitive advantage, the initial business plan, and proposed product contemplated. Each of these variables is reduced to a required rate of return that the investing partners sponsoring the deal express internally as a multiple of the cash they put in.

So for instance, like in our gambling analogy, the actual investing professionals are thinking, "Can I get 10 times my money on this deal when the company gets acquired five years from now?" This is a key distinction from how other types of investing professionals and hypothetical "financial buyers" make decisions. We'll get more into these details as we explore the Zogenix case, and others, further. However, several key points to keep in mind are as follows:

- Venture-capital fund IRR depends on valuation, and it does so now more than ever.
- Most general partners (GPs), especially early-stage ones, look at cash-on-cash multiples primarily.
- Limited partners (LPs) look at IRR.
- Inexperienced founders tend to focus on "pre-/post-valuation"; whereas experienced founders tend to focus on who's putting the money in and what terms are fair in light of who's putting the money in.

* * *

Having introduced some of the considerations for the income approach to valuation and the discounted cash flow (DCF) method in this chapter, we're now ready to go a little further into considering when and if the DCF is applicable to venture-capital and angel-backed companies.

CHAPTER 4

Applying the Typical DCF Model to a Venture-Backed Company Hardly Ever Works

"Compound interest is the eighth wonder of the world. He who understands it, earns it . . . he who doesn't . . . pays it."
—Albert Einstein

As mentioned, the DCF, or discounted cash flow, method is an income approach to valuation, for the most part. I say for the most part because as you will quickly realize, once we get beyond the cash flows we can "see" or "forecast" reasonably, there has to be a means to account for the value that exists beyond the forecast period. This is often called the "terminal value," but is referred to by some as "residual value," "continuing value," or "horizon value." In the case of venture-backed companies, that "terminal value" is in practice the second most important element driving fair market valuation outcomes, with interim venture financing rounds being the first. As a result, we are going to spend a little time reviewing some of the most popular ways of calculating terminal value for all companies before discussing if, and when, these models apply to venture-backed companies.

THE GORDON GROWTH MODEL

One of the most popular methods of estimating residual value beyond the forecast period is the Gordon Growth Model and variations of it. It's popular, in part, because it is relatively easy to implement and because it's easy to prove the math and logic behind it. It's also worth memorizing for anyone outside of the finance profession, since even if it doesn't fit your particular circumstances for needing to value a security, it can give you a quick test of the reasonableness of an offer for potential future cash flows.

Strictly speaking, the model is composed of three elements:

D = Dividends (Or capacity/ability to pay dividends from earnings)

R = Required Return (For our purposes, the "discount" rate – this variable is usually noted as "k" or cost of capital)

G = Growth (Expected growth of "D" per period—my favorite part of the model)

With those three simple inputs we can calculate a value (V), or price (P), for a security today (V_0 or P_0). I first started to apply this formula to actual companies engaged in financing transactions before completing an undergraduate degree in finance. Many sophisticated angel investors, and their advisors, were receptive to it as a way of agreeing on the potential for companies in mature industries. The key qualifying factor is that—mature industries. If you start plugging variables into the model, you can very quickly see the role of growth on value, but you will also notice that when growth is rapid, as it is with venture capital-backed companies, the model breaks down.

Assume that Company A and Company B both have the ability to pay $5 per share in dividends one year from now (see Exhibit 4.1). With zero dividend growth in either company, the only variable we need in order to calculate a value for both stocks is our required return. If our required return is 8%, then both stocks are worth $62.50 per share based on the model. If Company B, however, is expected to be able to grow its dividend consistently at 4% per year, then its stock might be valued at $125 per share, or 2X the

Company A	Company B
$D_1 = \$5, r = 8\%, g = 0\%$	$D_1 = \$5, r = 8\%, g = 4\%$
$P_0 = \$5/(8\%–0\%) =$	$P_0 = \$5/(8\%–4\%) =$
$62.50	$125.00

EXHIBIT 4.1   Growth versus No-Growth Values

value of Company A's stock. Based on this very simple example, the role of growth in value becomes very clear and very hard to ignore. However, like all good things there are very practical constraints on when this model can be applied explicitly.

The best way to appreciate the limitations of this model, and how they relate to venture-backed companies, is to simply expand the simplified version of the equation to expose a critical variable: infinity. When the symbol "∞" is included in a valuation of cash flows, it's very important to consider the implications, since that essentially means "forever."

$$\sum_{t=1}^{\infty} D^*[(1 + g)^\wedge t/(1 + r)^\wedge t]$$

Without a lot of examination or research, almost anyone familiar with venture-funded companies realizes that most of them are not expected to last forever. This reality is reflected in the contractual lives of the venture capital funds that invest in these companies, which typically span 10 years, the total time horizon for realizing returns from invested capital, not including any extensions granted by limited partners. Similarly, if we look at traditional small businesses, it's clear that businesses started in relatively safe, mature industries with known earning parameters very rarely result in an entity capable of paying a dividend in perpetuity.

That being said, variations of this valuation tool are applicable to almost every company when trying to get a handle on the power of growth. But it's important to review the specific constraints inherent in the Gordon Growth Model as it relates to venture-funded companies. I'll start with the first most obvious constraint that users discover in the absence of the infinity symbol: subtracting growth from required returns when growth is really high.

HIGH GROWTH LIMITS THE GORDON GROWTH MODEL

As beautifully simplistic as the Gordon Growth Model is, it doesn't work so well when there's actual growth that falls outside of a few limiting constraints. A simple and popular example is where growth is high, or rapid, and then ultimately levels out or becomes "stable." See Exhibit 4.2 where, in the column at left (t), periods (rows) numbered 1−5 show rapid growth value, and period (row) number 6 shows stable growth value.

In such a case, it's common to see a bifurcated model that calculates early rapid growth from period to period using more of a typical DCF model and

EXHIBIT 4.2 Simplified Two-Step Model, with Different Rates of Growth

t	D	g	r	PV D @ r	PV Factor
1	$ 1.00	15%	8%	$ 0.93	93%
2	$ 1.15	15%	8%	$ 0.99	86%
3	$ 1.32	15%	8%	$ 1.05	79%
4	$ 1.52	15%	8%	$ 1.12	74%
5	$ 1.75	15%	8%	$ 1.19	68%
			Sum PVs	$ 5.27	
				D/(r-g)	
6	$ 1.84	5%	8%	$ 61.22	63%
			PV of D/(r-g)	$ 38.58	

then stable growth using the Gordon Growth Model. In other cases, you can see models and formulas that break down growth expectations into three or more stages or phases. If this seems like the basic concept we initially introduced, where we specifically forecast as many cash flows as we can reasonably estimate and then capitalize the last period to get a terminal value, that's because it is pretty much the same process. The only variation is the number of growth stages we are addressing.

But what if growth is 30% per period and our required return is just 14% as in the following formula? Some would say that since we end up with a negative outcome, the Gordon Growth Model breaks.

$$D/(14\% - 30\%)$$

This is why one of the recommendations for using the Gordon Growth Model is that your expected growth rate be within a reasonable range of nominal GDP growth. When most people think of nominal GDP growth in the United States today, a figure in the range of 2% to 4% generally comes to mind, often 3% for much of the past two decades. In reality, nominal GDP growth has at times been in double digits, so this is a good general guideline. Exhibit 4.3 shows select nominal GDP rates.

As illustrated in Exhibits 4.4 and 4.5 in the summary rates of targeted and actual VC rates of return, the target return rates for venture-funded companies are substantially higher than nominal GDP growth in most periods.

Some observers might suggest that the more obvious constraint of the Gordon Growth Model as it relates to venture-capital valuation is not growth, but the lack of existence of dividends from a venture-funded company, which even after an IPO is unlikely to pay dividends any time soon,

| American Research and Development Corporation (ARDC) invests $70,000 In Digital Equipment Corp (DEC) | | | | (DEC) IPO 375,000 Shares @ $22 (ultimately a 500X ARDC return) | | | American Research and Development Corporation (ARDC) invests $70,000 In Digital Equipment Corp (DEC) | |

Date	1/1/1957	4/1/1957	7/1/1957	10/1/1957	1/1/1958	4/1/1958	7/1/1958	10/1/1958
GDP Growth Rate - Nominal	8.12%	1.75%	6.27%	-4.20%	-6.50%	3.61%	11.88%	11.28%
Date	1/1/1960	4/1/1960	7/1/1960	10/1/1960	1/1/1961	4/1/1961	7/1/1961	10/1/1961
GDP Growth Rate - Nominal	10.68%	-0.61%	2.13%	-4.01%	3.28%	8.41%	7.72%	9.54%
Date	1/1/1963	4/1/1963	7/1/1963	10/1/1963	1/1/1964	4/1/1964	7/1/1964	10/1/1964
GDP Growth Rate - Nominal	6.14%	5.84%	8.31%	6.15%	10.17%	5.67%	7.10%	3.04%
Date	1/1/1966	4/1/1966	7/1/1966	10/1/1966	1/1/1967	4/1/1967	7/1/1967	10/1/1967
GDP Growth Rate - Nominal	12.47%	4.72%	6.92%	6.91%	5.35%	2.25%	7.10%	7.50%
Date	1/1/1969	4/1/1969	7/1/1969	10/1/1969	1/1/1970	4/1/1970	7/1/1970	10/1/1970
GDP Growth Rate - Nominal	10.55%	6.37%	8.28%	3.25%	5.06%	6.25%	6.78%	0.84%
Date	1/1/1972	4/1/1972	7/1/1972	10/1/1972	1/1/1973	4/1/1973	7/1/1973	10/1/1973
GDP Growth Rate - Nominal	13.51%	11.86%	7.77%	11.94%	15.07%	10.90%	5.63%	11.82%
Date	1/1/1975	4/1/1975	7/1/1975	10/1/1975	1/1/1976	4/1/1976	7/1/1976	10/1/1976
GDP Growth Rate - Nominal	4.27%	9.07%	14.32%	12.39%	13.53%	7.29%	7.40%	10.23%
Date	1/1/1978	4/1/1978	7/1/1978	10/1/1978	1/1/1979	4/1/1979	7/1/1979	10/1/1979
GDP Growth Rate - Nominal	7.27%	23.37%	10.65%	13.83%	7.84%	10.26%	11.57%	9.20%
Date	1/1/1981	4/1/1981	7/1/1981	10/1/1981	1/1/1982	4/1/1982	7/1/1982	10/1/1982
GDP Growth Rate - Nominal	18.62%	4.35%	12.03%	2.23%	-1.20%	7.02%	4.13%	4.66%
Date	1/1/1985	4/1/1985	7/1/1985	10/1/1985	1/1/1986	4/1/1986	7/1/1986	10/1/1986
GDP Growth Rate - Nominal	8.25%	5.72%	7.94%	5.68%	5.90%	3.66%	6.16%	4.65%

| Technology Venture Investors (TVI) invest $1MM In Microsoft's preferred stock | Microsoft IPO 2,795,000 shares @$21 (ultimately 100X return for TVI) | Bill Gates and Paul Allen bootstrap Microsoft partnership |

EXHIBIT 4.3   Select U.S. Nominal GDP Growth versus Venture Financing Events
Source: Liquid Scenarios, Inc. with data from U.S. Dept of Commerce: BEA.

EXHIBIT 4.4   Implied Target Rates of Return as Discussed in AICPA Practice Guide

Stage of development	Plummer	Scherlis and Sahlman	Sahlman, Stevenson, and Bhide
Startup	50% to 70%	50% to 70%	50% to 100%
First stage or "early development"	40% to 60%	40% to 60%	40% to 60%
Second stage or "expansion"	35% to 50%	30% to 50%	30% to 40%
Bridge/IPO	25% to 35%	20% to 35%	20% to 30%

Source: AICPA Practice Aid.

EXHIBIT 4.5   Implied Actual VC Rates of Return as Discussed in AICPA Practice
Guide

Type of Fund	5-Year Return		10-Year Return		20-Year Return	
	2002	2008	2002	2008	2002	2008
Seed/Early Stage	51.40%	3	34.90	25.50	20.40	22.10
Balanced	20.90	7.50	20.90	12	14.30	14.60
Later Stage	10.60	8.10	21.60	7.30	15.30	14.70
All Venture	28.30	8.70	26.30	13.40	16.60	17.20

Source: AICPA Practice Aid.

EXHIBIT 4.6   Dividend History of Leading Venture-Backed Companies

Issuer Offer Year	Dividend Yield
1 Microsoft 1986	16 Years After IPO, 0% Dividend
2 Dell Computer 1988	14 Years After IPO, 0% Dividend
3 Oracle 1986	16 Years After IPO, 0% Dividend
4 Cisco 1990	12 Years After IPO, 0% Dividend

Source: Liquid Scenarios, Inc.

as illustrated in Exhibit 4.6. However, a common explanation of why a
dividend discount model can apply to companies that don't pay dividends is
the "dividend irrelevance theory," which we will simply mention briefly as
we start to transition into other methods of calculating the terminal value
for venture-funded companies.

DIVIDEND IRRELEVANCE AND CAPITAL
STRUCTURE IRRELEVANCE

The phrases "dividend irrelevance" and "capital structure irrelevance" can
be easily misinterpreted in the context venture-funded companies. Miller-
Modigliani's dividend irrelevance theory does in fact relate to venture-capital
valuations in some ways. Coincidently, it's also used outside of venture
capital to explain why adjustments to EBIT (earnings before interest and
taxes) can be used to generate comparable valuations for firms that have the
capacity to pay out dividends but do not declare dividends.

You could argue that Microsoft's stock splits effectively acted as dividends since the stock kept appreciating, which meant that shareholders

could in fact sell shares instead of taking dividends, much in the way Miller-Modigliani theorized a shareholder could do instead of taking retained earnings away from a company that could otherwise use the funds to grow its business. On the other hand, since the practice of splitting shares and thereby keeping the stock approachable by a broader range of individual investors is believed to have impacted liquidity and price appreciation, you might argue that the same item that tends to support their theory with respect to Microsoft's dividends challenges it with respect to Microsoft's capital structure.

The Capital Irrelevance theory also doesn't fit particularly well in the context of venture-funded companies. As you have seen already, and will see at increasing detail throughout this book, the most tangible, objective, and reliable input to the value of most venture-funded companies is in fact their capital structure. Also, the fact that the primary instrument used in venture financings typically has attributes of both debt and equity further complicates strictly applying this model to any element of venture-capital finance.

USING COMPARABLES (GENERALLY MARKET MULTIPLES) TO GENERATE A TERMINAL VALUE

To properly interpret and apply comparables, it's helpful to have a handle on some fundamental elements of the income approaches to valuation. For those who are not valuation specialists, some of the important relationships to remember follow. Keep in mind that these relationships are generalizations that are applicable to many moderate-growth companies, but often not applicable to venture-funded companies. However, they are useful for putting a context to required rates of return that are sometimes used to explain venture-capital valuations.

Capitalization Rate + Growth = Discount Rate (Required Rate of Return)
Discount Rate (Required Rate of Return) − Growth = Capitalization Rate
Discount Rate (Required Rate of Return) − Capitalization Rate = Growth

You should recall from earlier examples that business valuation professionals often will use a "capitalization of earnings" approach to determine the terminal value for traditional businesses that are expected to experience linear, stable growth beyond the forecast period if that growth is comparable to nominal GDP growth. Note that different valuation professionals have varying standards they apply as to what to compare reasonable growth in the Gordon Growth Model to, as opposed to suggesting nominal

GDP growth, as I do here. I've seen some of the best valuation professionals I know use inflation, real GDP growth, and even the risk-free rate as a benchmark for constant, stable growth in perpetuity to be used for a terminal value. I'm emphasizing this again because in order to properly interpret and apply comparables, it's helpful to have a handle on the income approach to valuation. The Gordon Growth Model we presented earlier is an excellent way to appreciate the connection between comparables, discounting, and capitalization, as illustrated in the preceding table.

When people mention the VC Method of valuation, you will often see some reference to an expected price earnings (or PE) ratio. Price earnings ratios, like many multiples, are attractive to many because they appear to be simple to apply and get a quick indication of relative value and, therefore, implied potential value. Despite the difficulties in getting consistent earnings information, there are other limitations to using PE ratios, even when comparing publicly traded companies. Despite these limitations, we will quickly connect the market approach of using a PE ratio to the income approach of using a capitalization of earnings method for those who may not be intimately familiar with the relationship. See Exhibit 4.7.

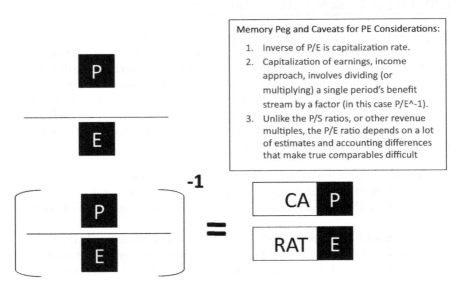

Memory Peg and Caveats for PE Considerations:

1. Inverse of P/E is capitalization rate.
2. Capitalization of earnings, income approach, involves dividing (or multiplying) a single period's benefit stream by a factor (in this case P/E^-1).
3. Unlike the P/S ratios, or other revenue multiples, the P/E ratio depends on a lot of estimates and accounting differences that make true comparables difficult

EXHIBIT 4.7 Price Earnings Multiples Considerations Mnemonic
Source: Liquid Scenarios, Inc.

Ironically, while the limitations of multiples for publicly traded company analysis are critical to value conclusions, for most venture-funded companies, those limitations don't impact conclusions materially. This is because the vast majority of venture-funded companies at any time are so far away from generating meaningful earnings that by the time PE ratios are material, expected returns for the broader market and the industry will have likely changed. As a result, the difficulty with venture-funded companies is projecting the future financial parameter against which to apply the multiple. In general, the further away the estimate is from the bottom line, or earnings, the more likely it will serve as a reliable basis for estimating a potential terminal value. Exhibit 4.8 illustrates this concept.

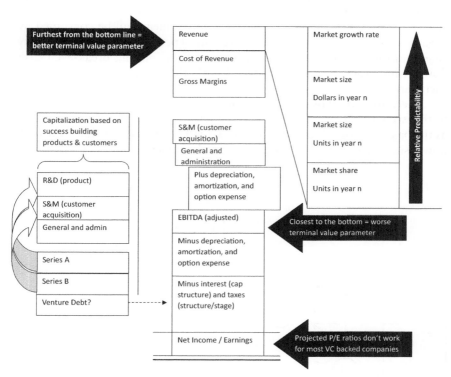

EXHIBIT 4.8   Hierarchy of VC-Backed Company Multiples Far Away from Earnings
Source: Liquid Scenarios, Inc.

Who's Valuing What?

As we've mentioned, different types of investors value high-growth venture-backed companies differently. This is completely rational, since there's often a lack of visibility into entity earnings and operating cash flow when angels and venture capitalists invest, as opposed to when private equity and underwriters are looking at a high-growth company. Referring back to our investment return perspective diagram, reproduced below, you can see that if an early-stage venture investor really had to look explicitly at an investee's free cash flow potential in order to make an investment, very few venture financings would take place.

So, for instance, assume that in period 0, today (P0), an angel investor puts $500,000 into a company knowing that 100% of that investment will be consumed by negative operating cash flow. The angel is counting on, or hoping, that VCs will come in with an investment of $6MM within one year or so (P1), knowing that their entire investment will be consumed by negative cash flow. This pattern continues until period 5, when the company generates only $1,000,000 in negative cash flow, putting break-even cash flow within reach of the company. What's the value of the company in each period?

There are several obvious constraints to applying a discounted cash flow to this scenario. If you use the expected return rate for a venture capitalist as the basis for your discount rate, you actually end up overvaluing the cash flows, since the higher the discount rate, the lower the present value, and

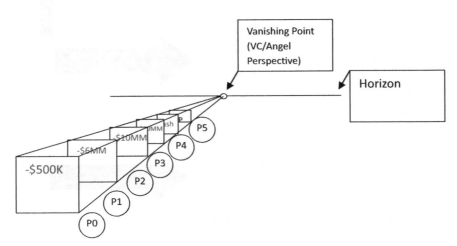

EXHIBIT 4.9   Foreseeable Horizon and Discrete Discounted Cash Flows
Source: Liquid Scenarios, Inc.

the overwhelming majority of free cash flow here is negative. Exhibit 4.10 illustrates this by applying several discount rates to the cash flows described for the hypothetical venture-backed company.

Without intensive examination, it's clear that simply applying our required rate of return to the free cash flows (FCF), we can reasonably generate incorrect conclusions as to the relative acceptability of the investment. That being said, any discount rate we apply results in a negative present value of our investment. Of course, discounting the projected cash flows would only be part of our DCF analysis. The other part would be to estimate a terminal value, or value beyond the point we can reasonably project cash flows. Remember, we assumed that the company could potentially breakeven in period 6, and you can't apply a growth rate to zero. Naturally, there are modifications valuation professionals take into account to address this, but the point is clear. Even if we were to assume a positive free cash flow of $500,000 per year in perpetuity from that point forward, we still end up with a negative present value, as illustrated in Exhibit 4.11.

Obviously, VCs and angels are smart people, so if they were valuing cash flows this way, they wouldn't be making investments in early-stage companies. Also, the method we used, capitalizing earnings to get to terminal value, is not appropriate for these types of companies because they are expected to generate incredible earnings growth ultimately, as opposed to stable growth comparable to the overall economy. With that in mind, let's try to use a more appropriate means of estimating terminal value for these types of companies, such as a multiple of revenue, a market approach to valuation, but, as we discussed earlier, a great way to get a terminal value for a high-growth company.

Market Approaches for Estimating Terminal Value

Within the market approach to valuation, there are a number of methods that use capitalization rates/ratios and/or multiples that are convenient to use to quickly get an indication of a company's value. The three most popular market approaches you will see with respect to a venture-backed company are:

1. Looking at public companies that are "comparable" and comparing their multiples/ratios to the company being valued.
   a. When most people think about valuation, this is the first thing that comes to mind, because it's the most intuitive way to get an idea, or indication, of value.
   b. Getting comps from publicly traded company valuation metrics is often referred to as the "Guideline Company Method."

Discount Rate		Period					
		0	1	2	3	4	5
Projected FCF		$(500,000.00)	$(6,000,000.00)	$(10,000,000.00)	$(8,000,000.00)	$(2,000,000.00)	$(500,000.00)
	Sum of PVs						
3%	$(25,280,613.57)	$(500,000.00)	$(5,825,242.72)	$(9,425,959.09)	$(7,321,133.27)	$(1,776,974.10)	$(431,304.39)
10%	$(21,906,014.24)	$(500,000.00)	$(5,454,545.45)	$(8,264,462.81)	$(6,010,518.41)	$(1,366,026.91)	$(310,460.66)
12%	$(21,078,073.20)	$(500,000.00)	$(5,357,142.86)	$(7,971,938.78)	$(5,694,241.98)	$(1,271,036.16)	$(283,713.43)
15%	$(19,931,052.70)	$(500,000.00)	$(5,217,391.30)	$(7,561,436.67)	$(5,260,129.86)	$(1,143,506.49)	$(248,588.37)
20%	$(18,239,519.03)	$(500,000.00)	$(5,000,000.00)	$(6,944,444.44)	$(4,629,629.63)	$(964,506.17)	$(200,938.79)
25%	$(16,779,040.00)	$(500,000.00)	$(4,800,000.00)	$(6,400,000.00)	$(4,096,000.00)	$(819,200.00)	$(163,840.00)
30%	$(15,508,793.59)	$(500,000.00)	$(4,615,384.62)	$(5,917,159.76)	$(3,641,329.09)	$(700,255.59)	$(134,664.54)
40%	$(13,416,790.62)	$(500,000.00)	$(4,285,714.29)	$(5,102,040.82)	$(2,915,451.90)	$(520,616.41)	$(92,967.22)
50%	$(11,775,720.16)	$(500,000.00)	$(4,000,000.00)	$(4,444,444.44)	$(2,370,370.37)	$(395,061.73)	$(65,843.62)
60%	$(10,462,234.50)	$(500,000.00)	$(3,750,000.00)	$(3,906,250.00)	$(1,953,125.00)	$(305,175.78)	$(47,683.72)
70%	$(9,392,627.92)	$(500,000.00)	$(3,529,411.76)	$(3,460,207.61)	$(1,628,332.99)	$(239,460.73)	$(35,214.81)
80%	$(8,508,476.01)	$(500,000.00)	$(3,333,333.33)	$(3,086,419.75)	$(1,371,742.11)	$(190,519.74)	$(26,461.07)

EXHIBIT 4.10 Impact of Discounting a Series of Negative Cash Flows

Discount Rate	PV + TV	Sum of PVs	PV of Terminal Value	Projected FCF Period 6
				500000
				Terminal Value
3%	$(11,322,542.63)	$(25,280,613.57)	$13,958,070.94	$16,666,666.67
10%	$(19,083,644.59)	$(21,906,014.24)	$2,822,369.65	$5,000,000.00
12%	$(18,967,110.19)	$(21,078,073.20)	$2,110,963.00	$4,166,666.67
15%	$(18,489,960.71)	$(19,931,052.70)	$1,441,091.99	$3,333,333.33
20%	$(17,402,274.09)	$(18,239,519.03)	$837,244.94	$2,500,000.00
25%	$(16,254,752.00)	$(16,779,040.00)	$524,288.00	$2,000,000.00
30%	$(15,163,499.91)	$(15,508,793.59)	$345,293.69	$1,666,666.67
40%	$(13,250,777.74)	$(13,416,790.62)	$166,012.89	$1,250,000.00
50%	$(11,687,928.67)	$(11,775,720.16)	$87,791.50	$1,000,000.00
60%	$(10,412,563.96)	$(10,462,234.50)	$49,670.54	$833,333.33
70%	$(9,363,035.64)	$(9,392,627.92)	$29,592.28	$714,285.71
80%	$(8,490,100.27)	$(8,508,476.01)	$18,375.75	$625,000.00

EXHIBIT 4.11   Too Little Operating Cash Flow Too Late and DCF Still Breaks

2. Looking at sales of similar private companies that have been acquired and comparing some metric of those transactions to the company being valued.

   a. For traditional private companies, the metrics are generally things such as revenue multiples, discretionary earnings multiples, PE multiples, or other financial ratios. Getting comps from actual sales of private companies is often referred to as the "Guideline Transactions Method." The AICPA's Practice Aid describes the "Backsolve Method" as a "version of the Guideline Transactions Method." I don't believe that's an accurate description, since guideline transactions always involve someone else's shares versus sales of the subject company's own shares, which are used for the Backsolve method.

   b. For many Internet-related companies, revenue and earnings multiples are not available for recent private transactions, so other metrics are used. For instance, if one company has recently sold at "$60 per user," multiplying the subject company's users by the same number gives an indication of the range management might have in mind with respect to current valuation.

   c. Alternatively, in the life science space, recent licensing deals are of importance, in addition to recent acquisitions, as licensing deals are often publicized, are accessible, and also give an indication of value for the firm in conjunction with a "sum of the parts" approach.

3. Looking at recent sales of the subject company's stock, including both primary and secondary sales.
   a. This remains the most common method used in practice by venture capitalists, angel investors, and founders of venture-backed companies, largely because it tends to be the most frequent indication of value for these companies.
   b. The vast majority of 409A valuations either rely directly or indirectly on reverse solving, or backsolving, for total equity values that generate preferred values per share that agree with the most recent round of venture financing. This is another example of considering recent sales (primary or secondary) of the company's securities as a market approach input.

In mature industries where there are many comparables, or "comps," to choose from, valuation professionals will narrow their selection based on selection criteria such as the company size, the age of the transaction if applicable, the product focus, and a host of other parameters needed to group only the best match of candidates. Regression analysis and other statistical tests are then run on the list to make sure that potential parameters, such as price to sales, or price to earnings for instance, are correlated to transaction values across the companies selected. This includes, in part, a basic technique very similar to what is used to calculate a Beta. If the covariance is being thrown off by a given company, that candidate will be removed from the list of comparables, or at least removed with respect to the offending metric.

If venture-funded companies had a comparably large group of comps to choose from, that might make market approaches to valuations for those companies easier, but it would also mean that the market was saturated with publicly traded competitors, which of course could lead to very bad consequences for leading-edge companies. As you might expect, the list of true comparables for the most promising venture-backed companies tends to be quite small in most cases, and as a result, compromises have to be made with respect to both quantity of data and the statistical rigor it's subjected to. Despite these limitations, a very often mentioned valuation method associated with venture-capital investors is the so-called "venture capital" or "Chicago" method, which does in theory look to price earnings ratios to determine present and future values of a prospective venture investment.

Do VCs Actually Use the "VC Method" of Valuation?

The so-called "VC method" or "Chicago" method of valuation, as described by academics, is rarely used formally by investing partners at early-stage venture-capital firms. In fact, from what I've observed, it's rarely even used by the analysts at those firms if at all. However, for later-stage venture-capital funds, such an analysis, along with many of the other valuation methods we've discussed, could yield meaningful results. Also, if an early-stage investor happens along the rare high-growth company that's (a) already profitable or about to become profitable and (b) hasn't received any venture financing to date, that's also a great time to apply the VC method and the other valuation methods discussed, such as a DCF model.

With "No Free Cash Flow to Discount," What Are VCs Valuing?

Other than looking at the people involved in the ventures (the founders) and the size of the market opportunity, the next thing on the horizon is the prospects for getting other investors to participate in subsequent rounds of financing. It's those subsequent rounds of financing that will have the biggest impact on how company progress, and therefore valuation, is measured objectively by the market participants (primarily other VCs).

Since late 2006 I tried to convince valuation professionals that their models were more sensitive to future financing rounds for venture-backed companies then those models were to volatility rates, discount rates, or even the anticipated time until a liquidity event. In early 2007 some of those valuation professionals agreed and started including future financing rounds in their calculations. Some even wrote about it and set firm policy around the practice of doing so.

Unfortunately, some of those same professionals ended up paying the price for doing so, since the auditors of the venture-backed companies were relying on authoritative literature that didn't take into account future financing rounds. This meant that valuators had to eat the cost of explaining what they did to auditors and couldn't bill their clients for it.

Many of the valuation teams at audit firms were comfortable with income- and market-based approaches to valuation that emphasized future entity earnings or operating cash flows as a required input. Everyone knows that these methods involve a lot of assumptions for even the most established corporations. However, most venture-backed companies are extremely speculative, since few paying customers exist in many cases, business models change quickly in others, and the competitive realities of approaching a new market with a new product or service result in too many variables to get accurate inputs for in a timely manner.

On the other hand, everyone that's involved in founding or investing in a venture-backed company has some idea of what the financing prospects for that company are from period to period and some idea of what the cash requirements will be from period to period. These two factors, the most reliable and attainable, are also the most reliable inputs into any model for most venture-capital investments. Since the valuation teams at audit firms have become a little more familiar with this reality, and collectively more experienced with these engagements, modeling future rounds of financing has become increasingly accepted in the space.

ACTUAL DIFFERENCES BETWEEN ANGELS AND VCs VERSUS PERCEIVED DIFFERENCES

Angels have long been accused of overvaluing companies. Similarly, VCs have long been accused of, for lack of a better word, "screwing" angel investors. In reality, there are clearly enough cases of both things occurring to justify the existence of these stereotypes. However, there's far more evidence that these parties depend on one another for success in most cases. As a result, it's very important to understand differences in how these parties approach valuing their investments, valuing the companies they invest in, and how their formal and informal rewards systems work. The following attempts to highlight some of the important differences that I've observed as impacting the perspective of most VCs and versus the valuation perspective of most angels.

Let's say an active angel investor with 30 portfolio companies says, "My investment is worth nothing until it sells." The next question might be, then, what happens if the next round is at a very high valuation? The investor says, "It's still worth nothing, but maybe a little more than nothing."

When a VC looks at a deal, the firm, and the individual looking at the deal are being compensated no matter what the outcome. How? Well, the firm is of course charging a management fee to the limited partners (LPs) every year based on the committed capital. If the firm has $500MM under management, than there's typically $10MM per year in fees to divide across partner compensation (salaries) and other administrative expenses of the fund annually. Even if every partner is taking a close look at 100 prospective deals a year, that's $X per deal just for looking. Naturally, these partners want to find the best deals available. But regardless of whether that happens, they will receive actual cash compensation for every deal they take a look at in a given year.

This is in stark contrast to an angel investor that is not associated with a professional fund and hasn't organized his or her fund as such. When an angel looks at a deal, not only does he or she not receive cash compensation, he or she also incurs very real cash expenses: travel, meals, time away from family without cash compensation to make up for it, early due diligence costs, and so forth. So the personal IRR and cash-on-cash for an investing partner at a VC fund is positive when he or she looks at a deal; whereas the personal IRR and cash-on-cash return for an angel is immediately negative. Ironically, this is one of the undocumented areas where the so called "J-curve" really does apply on a cash basis.

Is this alone enough to make a difference in the perceived value of an opportunity? Absolutely. Does that mean that that perception of value ends up finding its way into deal terms, and therefore how securities are priced? Sometimes it does, of course. When you are playing with your own money, your own time, and your family's time (without compensation) at the earliest stages of a venture, most people tend to make decisions differently. One analog might be the differences between entrepreneurs that bootstrapped through the seed and early stages, getting financing only after they achieve meaningful sales traction or technical feasibility, and those that get F&F financing from inception, angel financing at the seed stage, and VC funding for the B and C rounds. The latter model is more likely to efficiently weed out ventures that shouldn't make it to the next stage. However, the former model may ensure that the lessons learned evolve into something that's of greater value to society. The prevalence of Internet-related investments, which tend to be more scalable in both directions than life science and green technology investments, tends to make 100% bootstrapping, 100% angel investors, 100% venture-capital financing, and mixes of each realistic financing alternatives. But with the longer cycles for regulatory approval and testing in life sciences, sometimes bootstrapping is not an option.

These financing realities are reflected in most of the discounted cash flow models you will see in 409A valuation reports, which tend to go out three to five years for venture-backed companies. However, in the case of life science companies, which have to first overcome regulated technical hurdles that generally take much longer than three to five years, a 20-year cash flow model composed of various phases would not be unreasonable. But considering that most venture-capital funds have lives of 10 years, a 20-year cash flow model can quickly become impractical. For these reasons, and many others, the typical DCF model simply doesn't work well with most venture-funded companies until they are about to transition to public companies, be acquired by a public company, or otherwise start generating meaningful operating cash flows. That being said, there are still benefit streams that have to be discounted, or brought to a present value. To do so, an understanding of the relationships between valuation methods and allocation methods is helpful at every stage of a venture-backed or angel-backed company's evolution.

APPLYING VALUATION METHODS AND ALLOCATION
METHODS AT INCEPTION

"The value of an idea lies in the using of it."
—Thomas A. Edison

When you first start a promising company and issue stock, what's it worth? In most cases, the answer, according to accounting records, is the par value of the stock. This practice is largely driven by tax rules and conventions followed by attorneys and accountants familiar with the potentially negative tax consequences to founders that don't follow popular methods for assigning a nominal value to their shares early in the company's life. While there is of course lots of theoretical support for this practice, it's also good for founders and others to understand different ways at looking at the value that's created early in a startup's life.

In almost every case in this book you will see the same pattern:

1. One or two founders start the company and divide the shares (percentage ownership) between one another.
   a. Either additional team members come on prior to funding (and get some restricted stock) or
   b. The company obtains either seed money or a Series A round
2. The founders' shares, common stock, issued in 1 are issued at a par value (often $0.001 per share).
3. The Series A, or some seed round, is issued for 100 times to 1,000 times the nominal (par) value assigned to the founders' shares.

   So, for instance, in the Zogenix case, the Series A shares were sold for $1.00 per share to the outside investors. The common stock was issued to the founders for $0.001 per share, or $1/1,000^{th}$ of what the outside investors paid.
4. When the first outside money comes in, or in some cases prior to the first round, the founders execute a restricted stock purchase agreement that provides for reverse vesting (repurchase) of the shares they were issued.
   a. This has the advantage of keeping a founder who quits early in the process from reaping the rewards for doing no work in the future.
   b. It also has the advantage of giving outside investors and board members a means of invoking management levers that aren't always available when founders control the company.
5. As a result of the lower value, and by filing an 83(b) election within 30 days of getting their stock, the founders in the Zogenix case might pay $30K in taxes today versus a virtually unlimited amount in the future as the shares reverse vest at increasing values.

So, for example, if the fair value of the shares was determined to be $1.00 in a year later when one-third vested, the founders could suddenly have a tax bill of around $1.2 million, for instance. If the company goes out of business the following year, the founders will have lost $1.2 million to the government for no reason, in addition to losing their dream for a successful venture.

With this convention being so practical and prominent, efforts to value the shares at this early stage are rarely done formally. Instead, founders often think, "If the company gets a pre-money value of $10MM and I own 30%, I just made $3MM." Indeed, there's a famous quote from a *Business Week* article on DIGG that makes use of this approach, which is surprisingly accurate in certain cases. In the end, you can't know the value until you apply a reasonable method or until someone buys the stock (or the company) from you.

As a result, we're going to apply some of the valuation methods and allocation techniques introduced thus far to earlier stages of the company's life. We'll be using the same methods Zogenix used as it got closer to an IPO, but doing so long before the management or the investors in the company would have been applying these techniques.

Valuation in the Beginning

In this example, the basic idea of the opportunity is threefold:

- Acquire world's first needle-free injection system for pennies on the dollar.
- Combine it with an existing pain drug that has FDA approval and a huge installed base of prescribing physicians to get to market faster than a traditional drug.
- Raise $60 million in capital over four years to bring the first drug to a market that currently spends $12 billion per year on just one indication addressed by the technology.

Next, we think about the value of each of these parts of the basic idea:

- Zero, it's just an idea and ideas aren't worth anything until you execute on them.
- Apply the "financial hammer" $(1 + r)^{-t}$ to the net cash flows to equity investors projected (C), where r represents a required rate of return and t represents the number of periods (years) required to realize that return and C equals the net cash flow you will realize in t years.
- There's not enough information to answer this question.

EXHIBIT 4.12 Zogenix Founder Common Stock
Startup Allocations

Name	Shares	%
Stephen J. Farr	3,000,000	28%
Jonathan M. Rigby	1,500,000	14%
John J. Turanin	1,500,000	14%
Roger Hawley	2,100,000	20%
Cam L. Garner	1,850,000	17%
Bret Megargel	800,000	7%
Total Founders	10,750,000	100%

So, what is the answer? The answer is always $C*(1+r)^-t$, even if you believe that ideas aren't worth anything until you execute on them (answer A) or if you feel there's not enough information to answer the question (answer C). Here's why (or, the method behind the answer)...

Everyone has to make assumptions with any early-stage deal. Usually the first thing you hear about is in fact the idea, even if the trigger for making a decision to invest time or money into a company is "who are the founders?" (See Exhibit 4.12.) That being said, there's an implicit value to every idea. It may be less than zero and it may be greater than zero, but it is almost never worth exactly $0.

Similarly, although we might like to have more information to make a decision, there's enough information here to easily place a potential value on the idea alone. If we feel there's that more information is needed, we can make r, the required rate of return, higher to reflect the uncertainty. Once we get the facts, we can lower r, assuming the additional information supports the facts as described by the founders.

In this particular case, the fact that the founders are going after a huge market, in a highly regulated industry, with existing products actually makes it easy to test their assumptions regarding the cost, market opportunity, and timing of cash flows being realized. If those assumptions prove true, the idea alone is worth something greater than $0 in this case, even if we assume this is not the best team to execute on that idea.

SUMMARY

In this chapter we've touched upon why traditional discounted cash flow models that would be perfectly suited for private companies in mature industries are rarely appropriate for early-stage venture-backed companies.

Widely used tools, such as the Gordon Growth Model, while not well suited to explicit use for venture-backed company discounted cash flow models, were shown to be useful ways of quickly depicting and grasping the impact of growth on value. We also started to explore the interrelated roles that allocations of rights, values, and proceeds play on value indications and conclusions.

Chapter 5 dives deeper into the current practices concerning enterprise values and allocations of venture capital-backed company values to different classes of securities. It goes on to show how these current practices may be destroying value for some of the most important contributors to venture capital returns.

"Enterprise Value" + "Allocation Methods" = Value Destruction

Undervaluing Companies and Overvaluing Employee Options

T his is perhaps the most important chapter in this book because it gives any reader an opportunity to make money using the information that's about to be presented. How?

In the early chapters of this book, I made the following assertion: The terms "value" and "valuation" are used a lot for high-growth private companies and that's a bad thing. It's bad because when founders, VCs, angels, attorneys, CFOs, CEOs, and employees use these words and don't truly understand what they mean, those same people end up losing lots of money as a result.

If that assertion is true, which every case we've presented thus far supports, then there's an opportunity to realize a profit simply by recognizing verifiable errors in investment cash flow potential embedded in mechanically high- or low-value conclusions related to venture-funded companies.

MOST 409A VALUATIONS UNDERVALUE THE COMPANY AND SIMULTANEOUSLY OVERVALUE EMPLOYEE STOCK OPTIONS

Although we begin the discussion here with respect to employee options, all equity securities in venture-backed companies are essentially call options on an exit opportunity, as opposed to simply rights to future earnings per share. In the case of preferred stock, there are additional options embedded, including calls to roll over the position and related puts to protect prior purchases, through anti-dilution protection. If you can definitively identify logical valuation errors for each of these securities' rights, including each round of preferred stock, common stock, warrants, and options, which we will do in the pages that follow, increased realized and unrealized gains can be achieved. As we look at the real-world cases of VC-funded companies, we are going to identify how different parties in these companies, and outside of these companies, pay the price or realize additional profits because of someone's lack of understanding concerning valuing venture backed company securities.

To that end, here's another assertion we will attempt to prove in this chapter with the cases that follow: "Most 409A valuations undervalue the venture-backed company and simultaneously overvalue the employee stock options." That may seem counterintuitive to many people and almost impossible to others. Many would say that, "if a VC funded company value represents a pie, and the employee stock options represent a piece of that pie, than the difference in value should be proportional." If that's true, than yes, it would appear that my assertion that most 409A valuations undervalue the venture-backed company and simultaneously overvalue the employee options would indeed seem at least not internally consistent. See Exhibit 5.1.

Many venture-capital investing partners would say that it's obvious that 409A valuations understate a company's true value. Some would say the 409A valuation really doesn't matter and, therefore, the prices at which the company is issuing its options don't really matter either, within reason. However, few would note that these differences have an impact on every investing partner's cash-on-cash return and, therefore, impact everyone in a transaction beyond the relatively small expenditure incurred to generate

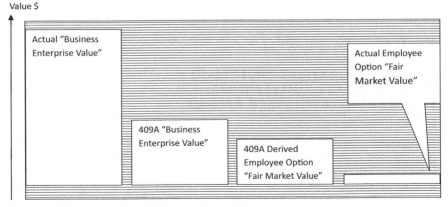

EXHIBIT 5.1   409A Valuations Overvalue Options and Undervalue Companies
Source: Liquid Scenarios, Inc.

these reports and their conclusions. But that is the case. Every investing partner's cash-on-cash return is impacted by how fairly employee options are priced.

So before we get into the details of exactly how 409A valuations typically undervalue companies and simultaneously overvalue employee stock options, please take a moment to assume the assertion is correct. If it is correct, who is making money as a result of overvalued employee stock options and who is losing money as a result? Well, in this case the biggest losers, in fact, would be key employees that have their options granted at a higher strike price than is truly fair as a result of a 409A valuation. As of the writing of this book, most employees can't determine if the strike price for their options are fair, but that's not a condition that's expected to exist in perpetuity, for reasons we'll discuss later.

Who's the second biggest loser of money, from a cash flow perspective, as a result of overpriced employee stock options? Ironically, it's the same organization that set the rules for 409A, the U.S. Department of Treasury. If options are being granted at a higher price than what is "fair," then when a company does realize a successful exit, all things being equal, the gain realized by employees on those options will be lower than it would have otherwise been if a fair price had been used. As a result, the U.S. Treasury actually ends up getting lower receipts due to how the venture-capital industry is attempting to comply with the provisions of 409A.

If you're wondering how that happened, it may be due in part to the fact that few if any of the parties that are most responsible for shaping how venture-backed common stock fair market value calculations are performed for tax purposes are tax professionals. Indeed, they aren't even the investing partners that comprise the primary market participants putting real cash on the line in transactions that drive changes in common stock value fair market value for VC-funded companies. VCs may decide, or more accurately "recommend," who performs the 409A valuations for the companies that they lead investments on, but they certainly don't do this with any objective other than helping their investees, partners on boards, employees, and prospective future acquirers avoid the substantial penalties that accompany being "grossly negligent" in performing those valuations. Instead, the parties that have had the most influence on the common stock value conclusions, from more than a review perspective, are the financial statement auditors.

DID AUDITORS DRIVE VALUATORS TO OVERVALUE EMPLOYEE STOCK OPTIONS?

The accounting rules for employee options, or stock-based compensation, require a value standard that you can't really get to without either

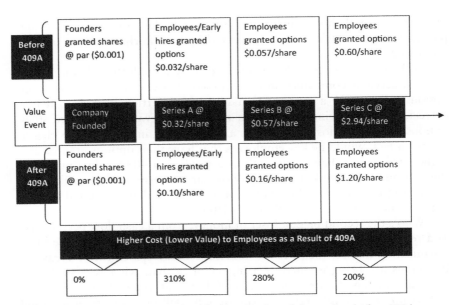

EXHIBIT 5.2   Options Undervalued before 409A and Overvalued after 409A
Source: Liquid Scenarios, Inc.

(a) observing a true market transaction or (b) coming up with an estimate of the market value and then applying some adjustments. Unfortunately for employees of the venture-backed companies, the parties that have paid most heavily for this reality are illustrated in Exhibit 5.2.

A highly successful entrepreneur and angel investor I know, who prefers to remain anonymous, told me, "I don't see why we can't just use 10% of the preferred price like we used to do. No one believes the 409A reports, almost no one even reads them and hardly anyone understands them." The term "fair value" has sometimes been defined, in part, as an unbiased and rational estimate of the potential market price. This definition supports the use of the "10% rule" employed by most venture-backed company boards when pricing employees' options at the early stages for many years before auditors and valuation professionals were heavily involved as a result of 409A. If a preferred financing event had occurred within a reasonable period of time, the boards would simply multiply that round's deemed issue price by 10%, or some comparable fraction (5%, 20%, etc.). The resulting product would be the price at which options were granted, and this was the estimated fair market value of the common stock.

This method, of course, is how we derived the "pre-409A" option grant values in the previous illustration, using 10% until the Series C, for which we used 20%. It's important to note that this practice of simply applying a percentage to the preferred price could be considered a "bottom-up" approach to getting an idea of a security's value. This makes it consistent with how most VCs approach pricing preferred stock, indirectly, when making the investments that trigger nearly 80% to 90% of the changes in value any reporting investee or limited partner will record in a given year.

While on its surface this approach may seem questionable for 409A compliance and Topic 718 (FAS123R) financial reporting, it does in fact meet the test of being both rational and unbiased, especially in the cases of companies that have only issued one round of preferred financing (Series A for instance) within a reasonable window of time around which the options have been granted. Moreover, you could potentially argue that for those same companies, Series A rounds, seed deals, and so forth, it would also meet both the tax and auditing guidelines. We will explore this point at length a little later. The primary point for now is that while the more rigid analysis taking place for early-stage companies in response to 409A may also be generating "rational and unbiased" conclusions, those conclusions may not be fair to employees, who should be considered to one extent or another some of the "willing" buyers or "willing" sellers in these transactions.

Unfortunately, those same buyers and sellers, employees in the case of stock options, clearly don't have reasonable access to one of the requirements for "fair value" used in the definition that applies to venture fund transactions: "having a reasonable understanding about the asset or liability and the transaction based on all available information, including information that might be obtained through due diligence efforts."

If a venture investor told an LP its fund was paying 300% more for every investment in every portfolio company, across the board, in response to a tax regulation and auditor recommendations, what do you think the LPs of that venture fund would do? Their dissatisfaction with that strategy would probably be reflected in immediate attempts to sell their LP interests at a heavy discount to avoid future obligations (capital calls) to fund that investment approach.

One of the reasons you don't see venture-funded company hires, or their spouses, objecting to paying 300% more across the board for rights to purchase the same amount of shares is because of a lack of understanding concerning what they are receiving and how its "valuation" takes away from their earning potential. With the probability of a "grand-slam" rather small, few employees are going to bicker, assuming their cash compensation is comparable to their peers at other VC-backed, and non-venture-backed, companies. So, in some ways the differences between one exercise price and another may not appear meaningful to employees in general.

An analogy might be to the perceived difference between paying $150 in a "Mega Millions" lottery if someone picks 3 out of 5 numbers versus paying $50. Changing the payout from $150 to $50, without changing the probability of winning for getting 3 out of 5 numbers, is unlikely to impact lottery receipts materially. The name of the game is "Mega Millions" not "Mega Hundreds" and it's the prospect of "millions" that drives purchases of a lottery ticket.

MATCH 4 OUT OF 5 WHITE NUMBERS BUT NOT MATCH THE MEGA NUMBER (PAYOUT = $150)

The number of ways 4 of the 5 first numbers on your lottery ticket can match the 5 White numbers is COMBIN(5,4) = 5.

The number of ways your fifth initial number can match any of the 51 losing White numbers is COMBIN(51,1) = 51.

The number of ways your final number can match any of the 45 losing Mega numbers is: COMBIN(45,1) = 45.

The product of these is the number of ways you can win this configuration: COMBIN(5,4) × COMBIN(51,1) × COMBIN(45,1) = 11,475. The probability of success is thus: 11,475/175,711,536 = 0.0000653059000065 or "One chance in 15,312.55."

Source: Bill Butler's Durango Bill Website at www.durangobill.com.

However, hires for venture-funded companies, at all stages, tend to be extremely smart and driven. If the perception became that the options issued by venture-fund startups had a negative present value or negative expected value, while lottery tickets of course have both, stock options might cease to be an effective incentive for new hires. Similarly, VCs, unlike state lotteries, know experientially that it takes a highly motivated and smart management team to achieve a successful exit. As a result, the lack of understanding today (2009, 2010, 2011) regarding artificially higher option grant prices across the board is unlikely to persist indefinitely.

Much of the current lack of understanding is perpetuated by financial industry jargon and accounting pronouncements that are difficult for the auditors themselves to recite accurately without a copy of the rules close by. In this regard, being generally confused by the redundant and inconsistent use of the word "value," the employees are not alone. Venture-fund GPs, investing professionals, limited partner investment managers, and even the accounting firms that sign off on reports used by beneficiaries of these sophisticated parties share that confusion, as we explain in detail later in this chapter. One key cause of this confusion is the use of the terms "market value," "current value," and "enterprise value" interchangeably. Similarly, the use of less-volatile securities, such as publicly traded technology stocks, as the primary source to estimate price and return dispersion for a class of investments that typically has substantially greater volatility is another cause of confusion.

MOST 409A ENTERPRISE VALUE CALCULATIONS IGNORE THE "TAKEOVER" VALUE OF PREFERRED

What's enterprise value? For a public company it's a rather easy calculation, since its equity (usually common stock) is quoted, its debt is on the balance sheet (or trades with a market value), and its cash position is also on the balance sheet and reported quarterly to an exchange as well as regulators, such as the SEC in the United States. So that's one way to explain how to calculate the enterprise value of a company. But it still doesn't speak to the insight a user is supposed to glean from the resulting output of an "enterprise value." One popular alternative description of "enterprise value" is "takeover value."

Takeover value, as the name more clearly suggests, is the estimated cost to buy (take over) a company. A very short version of this relationship is illustrated by the following equation:

Equity Market Value + Debt Market Value − Cash = Enterprise Value
    (Takeover Value?)

It's worth quickly noting that this formula does not fit easily with most venture-backed companies. In the case of venture-financed companies, cash in the enterprise as of a valuation date is like a stack of chips in poker tournament. The bigger the stack, the more chances a company hits the jackpot for investors. But for publicly traded companies, and also for many private companies, you can in fact have too much cash, as in more cash than you need to carry on the operations of a company. Also, for many companies outside of venture capital, the cash on hand is assumed to be an asset that would, or at least could, be distributed to equity holders prior to an acquisition or used to pay down liabilities, for instance. For these reasons, and others, Wall Street analysts and Main Street valuation professionals have a variety of ways of adjusting enterprise values to reflect these realities. Those enterprise values, market values of equity, and market value of debt net of cash represent the cost of taking the company over.

In a publicly traded company, the true takeover value is a moving target. When the stock price changes so does the value of equity. As the value of equity changes, the implied amount required to gain control of the company (the control premium) changes. If an actual offer or rumor of an offer emerges, that control premium will begin to be reflected in the price of the stock. We touched upon this concept briefly in Chapter 1 when discussing control premiums derived from Mergerstat, for instance. You may recall from that chapter that the formula to translate a control premium into a minority discount was:

$$\text{Minority Discount} = 1 - [1/(1 + \text{Mean Premium Paid})]$$

It was also mentioned in Chapter 1 that this premium, which can sometimes be in excess of 50%, is not totally associated with control. In many cases, the premium would also reflect the strategic value of the acquisition. In the case of venture-backed companies that are acquired prior to achieving a clear path to recurring future earnings, or large and growing revenues, you might argue that the vast majority of those acquisitions are in fact strategic in nature. That's important in the context of a venture-backed company because it's that premium, indirectly, that alternative asset investors backing venture fund management teams expect to be pursued if a company does not go public. These same parties realize that not only will most of the companies invested in fail to even return 100% of their capital, but they also know that most of the funds they invest in won't invest 100% of their capital. But one Google, Zynga, LinkedIn, Microsoft, Yahoo!, or Genentech can make up for a world of Webvans. You can't shoot for these kinds of results without an expectation that every transaction invested in has the potential to generate a huge premium above the capital that's been put to work. You might consider that premium part of the "takeover" value of a venture-backed company.

If you search a 409A report, or an MD&A (Management's Discussion and Analysis) section of a registration statement, for the phrase "enterprise value," you will definitely find it in reference to how options were priced. Similarly, if you search the AICPA Practice Aid, you will find enterprise value used in a variety of ways. But if you search for the phrase "takeover value" in this context for any of the venture-funded companies that went public in 2010, or probably any other year, you won't see a reference to it. Why is that important? Because you can't take over a company without paying down or otherwise assuming its interest-bearing debt. This makes sense to most people. So long as the company is judged by its debt holders or the market to have the ability to service its debt, the enterprise value (takeover value) includes payoff costs to those holders.

EXHIBIT 5.3   Netflix Round-to-Round Pricing versus Volatility Used

Date	Series/Round	Shares	Price/Share	Amount Raised
Oct-97	Series A	3,990,000	$0.50	$1,995,000
Mar-98	Series A	454,545	$0.55	$249,999
Jun-98	Series B	5,684,024	$1.08	$6,138,745
Feb-99	Series C	4,650,269	$3.27	$15,206,379
Jun-99	Series D	4,649,927	$6.52	$30,317,524

Source: SEC Filings Imported by Liquid Scenarios, Inc.

How many 409A valuation reports have you seen that state an enterprise value that's close to what VCs in the deal would require to sell their interest? This speaks both to the required return for these investors and the required volatility needed to induce them to invest the first dollar into an enterprise. Looking at the round-to-round price distributions for successful venture-backed companies illustrates true volatility of values within companies that perform as investors expect when placing their bets. Exhibit 5.3 is a summary of preferred stock financing rounds for Netflix, one of the most successful venture-backed companies.

Exhibits 5.4, 5.5, 5.6, and 5.7 summarize the preferred financing rounds of some of the other standout venture-capital returns, including Excite, Yahoo, Google, and LinkedIn.

We can start our discussion with the "takeover" values, or the amounts VCs in each of these deals would require before approving a sale of their portfolio companies. It's obvious by some of the dates listed in the tables above that in a return-rich environment like the late 1990s, few VCs are investing with an eye toward 5X to 10X multiples in 10 years. Notwithstanding that, let's use today's standards, reflecting the required rates you often see cited by investing professionals, venture-capital associations, 409A valuation reports, the AICPA, limited partner associations, and most parties

EXHIBIT 5.4   Excite Round-to-Round Pricing versus Volatility Used

Date	Series/Round	Shares	Price/Share	Amount Raised
Jul-95	Series A	2,250,000	$0.67	$1,500,000
Nov-95	Series B	1,220,000	$1.23	$1,500,000
Dec-95	Series C	309,278	$2.91	$900,000
Mar-96	Series D	1,367,312	$8.00	$10,938,496

Source: SEC Filings Imported by Liquid Scenarios, Inc.

EXHIBIT 5.5   Yahoo Round-to-Round Pricing versus Volatility Used

Date	Series/Round	Shares	Price/Share	Amount Raised
Apr-95	Series A	5,200,000	$0.20	$1,040,000
Nov-95	Series B	2,538,072	$1.97	$5,000,002
Mar-96	Series C	5,200,000	$12.50	$63,750,000

Source: SEC Filings Imported by Liquid Scenarios, Inc.

that have a need to know returns for venture as an alternative investment category.

Exhibit 5.8 is adapted from an interactive form I wrote in the business valuation software I released in 1999, so around three years after Yahoo! and Excite went public, four years before Google went, about the time Netflix started trading, and over a decade before LinkedIn filed for its IPO. Long before then, this approach, reducing a periodic rate of return to a schedule of related payback multiples, was used by valuation professionals, VCs, and other financial professionals to put target returns into perspective. My only contribution at the time was that my software-based form enabled users to simply click on one of the variables, desired multiple, or rate of return and generate an indication of value through the discounted cash flow and capitalization of earnings methods we discussed earlier.

Two things you will notice when looking at the version of the form reproduced here is that to get a required rate of return of 40% in two years, an investment only has to double in value during that time. I say "only" not because a 40% return isn't exceptionally attractive in any market, but partially because in that short period of time few, if any, early-stage VCs are going to exit a transaction. You often hear a 10X multiple cited as a target return by investing partners of early-stage funds. For that reason, I've added emphasis below to amounts closest to a 10X return multiple at the respective exit dates (time horizon row labels, in years found in the left column) and required percentage return rates in the table below. If you look closely for

EXHIBIT 5.6   Google Round-to-Round Pricing versus Volatility Used

Series/Round	Shares	Price/Share	Amount Raised
Series A	15,360,000	$0.06	$960,000
Series B	49,823,000	$0.50	$24,677,332
Series C	6,479,000	$2.34	$15,177,058

Source: SEC Filings Imported by Liquid Scenarios, Inc.

EXHIBIT 5.7   LinkedIn Round-to-Round Pricing versus Volatility Used

Date	Series/Round	Shares	Price/Share	Amount Raised
Nov-03	Series A	3,990,000	$0.32	$4,700,000
Oct-04	Series B	454,545	$0.55	$10,000,000
Jan-07	Series C	5,684,024	$1.08	$12,800,000
Jun-08	Series D	4,650,269	$3.27	$53,000,000
Nov-08	Series D	6,599,987	$11.47	$75,701,851

Source: SEC Filings Imported by Liquid Scenarios, Inc.

a moment, you will find that something very important is missing in years one and two in the chart below.

In Exhibit 5.8, you will notice there are no 10X returns in years one and two (rows one and two) even at an annual return of 110%. So if VCs are really looking for a 10X return at that stage, which there's tons of evidence to support that they are, then in order to take the company over you are going

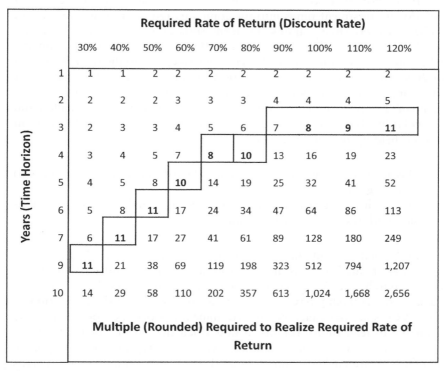

	Required Rate of Return (Discount Rate)									
	30%	40%	50%	60%	70%	80%	90%	100%	110%	120%
1	1	1	2	2	2	2	2	2	2	2
2	2	2	2	3	3	3	4	4	4	5
3	2	3	3	4	5	6	7	8	9	11
4	3	4	5	7	8	10	13	16	19	23
5	4	5	8	10	14	19	25	32	41	52
6	5	8	11	17	24	34	47	64	86	113
7	6	11	17	27	41	61	89	128	180	249
9	11	21	38	69	119	198	323	512	794	1,207
10	14	29	58	110	202	357	613	1,024	1,668	2,656

(Years (Time Horizon))

Multiple (Rounded) Required to Realize Required Rate of Return

EXHIBIT 5.8   Required Rates of Returns to Realize Cash-on-Cash Multiples

to have to give the VCs a return of more than 120% per year in the first two years. To get 10X in two years implies a required rate of return of around 220% per year. This table should remind us of two critical elements that are generally lacking in both the valuations done for venture-fund reporting to LPs in accordance with GAAP as well as virtually every 409A valuation that's used to avoid tax penalties on employees and as a basis for stock-based compensation accounting and disclosures in financial statements. The two missing elements are:

1. An appropriate volatility estimate, and
2. A related acknowledgment of the true takeover values of these companies at different points in time.

In the absence of these elements, a series of questions emerges that most Topic 812, Topic 718, and 409A related valuation conclusions have difficulty answering. For instance:

If investors that "control" a series of preferred and control the flow of additional investment funds into the company, require returns in excess of "120%" over the first year or so of an enterprise, how appropriate is it to use a 60% to 80% volatility estimate retrieved from a publicly traded company where investors consider a "10 bagger" the exception to the rule? If a return of 20X, 10X, or more is required, and there are no financial fundamentals that support those types of returns, is the pool of potential buyers for a company larger or smaller? If the pool of prospective buyers is smaller, and the volatility is greater, what does that say about the marketability of an interest held by an employee who:

- Has no control rights to change any board decisions with respect to financing and exits, and
- Doesn't have access to required information to make a reasonable decision with respect to intrinsic value?

Both volatility and takeover value for a given venture-backed company are closely related to who the investors in a deal are and what securities they've purchased. Also related are the types of investors the current VCs backing the company have worked with previously and the reputation of those VCs, since these factors will determine the pool of additional investors available to lead future rounds, if and when they are needed. Chapter 7 presents additional examples of how volatilities typically relied upon in valuing venture-backed companies tend to be substantially below what's generally observed for these companies in the real world. Before getting into that, I'll review how who's making an investment impacts the range of potential returns and, therefore, the volatility.

THE REALISTIC RANGE OF POSSIBILITIES DEPENDS ON WHO THE INVESTORS ARE

As we've discussed previously, the most likely positive event for a venture-backed company in any given year is not an exit event but rather a financing event, which generally means a new series of preferred or the issuance of some convertible debt. As we've also discussed, and will continue to do so, inputs into the size and potential terms of future financing events, prior to a liquidity event, remain a missing element in most valuations for tax, portfolio company financial reporting, and fund financial statements issued to limited partners. When valuation professionals, auditors, and other parties look at the same inputs that will shape decision making by key stakeholders of the company in the coming year, more reliable value indications emerge. Most of these inputs are easy to obtain, as illustrated in the upcoming list, and begin with the same focus on "people" or "who" that is the foundation for most venture-backed company financing decisions.

Readily Observable Inputs to PCo. Values

- Who (existing VCs were, new investors are, IRRs/stages, GPs)
- What (security/rights they purchased, how does that mix impact their target future returns and present returns/residual value?)
- When (timing of prior financing transactions versus expected timing of future transactions, expected burn rate/runway)
- Why (pro-rata with outside lead? secondary sale?)
- How much (size of the rounds, magnitude of the required returns, implications on future volatility)?

Instead of focusing on this more reliable input to value indications, current valuation efforts filtered through auditor scrutiny and direction rely heavily on future financial results projected out three to five years. These inputs, along with financial data from "comps," or the market approach, are often given more weight than future financings that will occur far sooner than when a venture-backed company will be truly "comparable" financially to a publicly traded company. In addition to the obvious weaknesses of this prevailing approach, which includes the cost of quantifying speculative estimates of future earnings to justify a present value of a future potential exit that will occur at an unknown time period, it takes the attention away from the parties most likely to influence value within any 12-month period.

Who Invested Impacts Volatility, Future Financing Rounds, and Today's Value

Taking a quick look at the Series A shareholders in Yahoo and LinkedIn and you will notice the two share a common investor. If you go a step further and analyze the investors of LinkedIn, Excite, Netscape, and Google, it's clear that a small, small community of investors is generating worlds of opportunities. The power of their networks amplify the range of possible exit multiples as previous endeavors succeed financially, giving founders and funds greater margin to bank critical errors in between. However, take a closer look and you realize that each of the Series A investors are a little different.

Although Netscape, Yahoo, and Excite each relied on professional venture capitalists for their Series A rounds, Google's Series A round was composed of angel investors. Why does this make a difference? Because those investors, in some cases, approach realizing returns and interacting with management teams a little differently than an organized fund does. This means that if we are viewing their investments in preferred stock as debt securities with high, double-digit interest rates (the takeover costs), then they may not have the mandate to swing for the bleachers the same way VCs do. If this assumption is true, then you would expect the volatility of angel-funded deals to be lower than those funded entirely by VCs. Data from the Angel Capital Association suggests that may in fact be the case.

In the case of Netflix, the Series A investor was also the co-founder of the company and ultimately took the reins as CEO. So why does that make a difference? Well, an individual investor/co-founder who's recently come off an extraordinary win, with a personal stake that easily rivals that of many small venture funds at the time, may have a different threshold of financial success for an investment than a venture fund, with multiple portfolio companies will. Again, this can, potentially, impact volatility, assuming professional VCs never come into the deal. But as we've mentioned, volatility is good for options, and each of these Series A investments, whether made by an angel or a founder, are in fact options on future gains in company equity. See Exhibit 5.9. Fortunately, in both cases, VCs came in with valuations

| Enterprise Value / Takeover Value (S) (volatility embedded In required return) | N(d1) (driven by volatility) | Exercise Prices (K) (call options from the waterfall – allocated by volatility) | N(d2) (driven by volatility) |

EXHIBIT 5.9   Volatility (sigma) Is Impacted by Who the Investors Are and as a Result So Is Value
Source: SEC Filings Imported by Liquid Scenarios, Inc.

EXHIBIT 5.10 Netflix Founder Stock Pricing and Ownership Allocation

Netflix Series A – Led by Founders – No Professional VCs

Founder	Founder Shares	Pro-Rata	Per Agreement	Implied Consideration	Per Books (par)
Marc B. Randolph	2,700,000	84%	$0.05	$135,000	$2,700
Reed Hastings	500,000	16%	$0.05	$25,000	$500
Total	3,200,000	100%		$160,000	$3,200

Source: SEC Filings Imported by Liquid Scenarios, Inc.
From internal agreements, it's clear that the founders intended to record their shares at 10% of the preferred price. However, since it's a related party transaction, and also due to potentially negative tax consequences, they ended up recording their common stock at par, which, of course, is the standard.

that represented unrealized appreciation for the founder of Netflix. In the case of Google, the angel investors were of such notoriety that professional VCs were fortunate to get in on the deal. See Exhibits 5.10, 5.11, and 5.12.

In a lot of cases where the founders participate in their own Series A, much less lead the Series A, they don't maintain their pro-rata ownership on subsequent rounds. Some early-stage VCs and angels have an investing discipline that they will only participate on the Series A or first round and not participate in any future rounds. If you are viewing each round of financing as having both a call and put feature embedded in it, then to a certain extent that option is being sacrificed, which means that some value has left the investor. Ideally, that party would have the opportunity to transfer that right to another investor for a fee, but that might not be practical with a small and close-knit industry.

One example of this from earlier would be the case of Twitter we mentioned in Chapter 1. One of the prominent investors in Twitter who had the

EXHIBIT 5.11 Netflix Series A Round Led by Co-Founder versus VC

Netflix Series A – Led by Founders – No Professional VCs

		Series A	Price	Amount	Pro-Rata
17-Oct-97	Reed Hastings	3,800,000	$0.50	$1,900,000	95%
17-Oct-97	Muriel Randolph	50,000	$0.50	$25,000	1%
17-Oct-97	Other Series A Investors	140,000	$0.50	$70,000	4%
Total		3,990,000		$1,995,000	100%

Source: SEC Filings Imported by Liquid Scenarios, Inc.

EXHIBIT 5.12 Netflix Series B VC Increase in Value over Series A

Netflix Series B Investors – "Just" 2.16X the Series A Price

Institutional Venture Partners	3,703,703	$3,999,999	$1.08	68.23%
Reed Hastings	1,655,092	$1,674,999	$1.01	30.49%
Joan Hastings	46,296	$50,000.00	$1.08	0.85%
Muriel Randolph	23,148	$25,000.00	$1.08	0.43%
Total	$5,428,239	$5,749,998		100.00%

Source: SEC Filings Imported by Liquid Scenarios, Inc.

option, or preemptive right, to participate in subsequent preferred rounds chose not to. The value of this option would, as a result, effectively be transferred to other existing investors based on most shareholder rights agreements. Although these rights are not officially accounted for or recorded, they will ultimately show up in fund returns, which was the case with the Twitter investor who chose not to participate on the subsequent financing round. Fortunately, in the case of Netflix, the founder had the inclination and capacity to execute that option and realized a substantial reward as a result of doing so.

At this point, in the Series B round shown in Exhibit 5.12, there's a professional VC in the deal, Institutional Venture Partners, and that VC owes a duty to its LPs to aim for the returns we displayed in the matrix earlier. So what has to happen to Netflix for IVP to either exit or write up its investment by 10X? If the enterprise value of Netflix increases tenfold, will that do it? Not unless that increase is accompanied by another round of venture financing led by an outside investor. Even then, the rights to cash flow for IVP may be slightly less than those of the lead investors, which would mean that even if the round is priced at 10X what IVP paid for the Series B, the full increase might not be reflected in the residual, or unrealized portfolio value, of IVP's fund.

Without looking back at the prior round-to-round increases in the companies we've looked at thus far in Exhibits 5.3, 5.4, 5.5, 5.6, and 5.7, would you guess that the volatility observed in the preferred stock is greater than or less than 100%? Now, considering that most of these companies had IPOs that were offered at prices far below the first-day closes, would you imagine that the volatility of the preferred stock would be below 150%? Below 80%? Interestingly enough, if you look at the registration statements for any of these companies, you will find that only one, Google, has a single period (2001) during which it used a volatility estimate of 100% for the optionality of the derivatives. In each of those cases, except the case of LinkedIn, that approach makes sense because it was simply being used purely to comply with accounting rules and didn't have an adverse impact on the largest group of direct stakeholders in those companies when they were private (employees).

In the case of Yahoo, Excite, and Netflix, the volatility figure they used wasn't actually used to estimate the value of the company's common stock, or to "allocate" an "enterprise value" to the common stock. Instead, those companies were using the volatility input to measure the potential earnings impact of options overhangs and communicate that to public investors in a manner that accounted for the both time value of a range of possible prices for their liquid, marketable, common stock.

If the early-stage venture funds that have invested require a return of at least 220% in the first two years, what does that say about the volatility of the common stock? If the volatility of the common stock is higher, does that make the options on the common stock worth more money or less money? Neither of those are trick questions. However, with even a little bit of experience with traded options you know that higher volatility generally makes options worth more money, not less money. So how could using a lower volatility estimate result in overpricing employee stock options?

Part of the answer lies in the obvious differences between private company options and publicly traded options. Traded options are generally on underlying securities that trade frequently with sufficient liquidity, quoted bids, asks, and volume. In the absence of those characteristics, which we will include in the general category of "marketability" for purposes of this book, one has to reduce the value of the underlying security to account for the inability to realize proceeds until an uncertain future date, at an uncertain future price. As a result, the larger the size of the volatility estimate, the larger the reduction (unfortunately also referred to as a "discount" by valuation professionals) that will be applied against the employee options in general.

This is illustrated in greater detail in the cases at the end of this chapter. In the Yahoo case, for instance, we applied 100% volatility, with two years assumed before a liquidity event, and the same risk-free rate we used for each of the other Yahoo examples for consistency; this resulted in a discount for lack of marketability of around 49%. Applying this DLOM to the $0.13 per common stock value that was produced by backsolving for the Series A price at 100% volatility, we end up with a net value per share of common stock of around $0.06 per share, or 30% of the Series A original issue price of $0.20 per share. This value indication, net of the DLOM, was substantially less than value indicated when we used the 53% volatility disclosed in Yahoo's filings or the 65% benchmark you find in many 2010/2008 filings. Despite a substantially higher enterprise value conclusion generated using our hypothetical estimate of 100% volatility, this same higher volatility generated a lower indicated value per share of common stock due to its impact on the DLOM calculation. The true volatility for these companies, based on observed changes in their preferred share pricing, is certainly higher than 100%.

You could easily use any of the volatility-related functions in Excel, such as STDEV/STDEVP, VAR/VARP/VARA, for instance, to get a good estimate of variability and therefore volatility and applying those measurements to the natural logs of the price chances determined using the NL (natural logarithm) function. For those who don't use Excel a lot, the STDEV function returns an estimate of the standard deviation of a "sample" population, whereas the STDEVP function returns the standard deviation for the population, which is what the P on the end of the function name standards for. Since standard deviation is the square root of the variance, a choice needs to be made as to which estimate of variance to use. One of those choices involves either adjusting the estimated population of values, n, for the reality that we are dealing with a sample by using "n-1" in the denominator of the variance formula instead of using "n."

Without using Excel or even pulling out your calculator, you could simply observe that a private company that's seen its preferred stock go from $0.50 to $6.52 in less than five years is probably more volatile than its publicly traded "peers." In this case, the price appreciation happened in less than 20 months. However, if a third-party 409A valuation was done of that company in the three to four years since the rule became law for these types of companies, you could bet money that the volatility estimated for purposes of estimating stock option value would have been substantially lower than the observed volatility in the company's own stock. In fact, if you thumb through the other cases in this book you will find that most venture-backed companies disclosed public "peer"-based volatility estimates in the range of 60% to 70% in most cases.

The argument for using public comps for volatility estimates is a reasonable one, often emphasizing a lack of quantitative data from a large enough sample size to justify alternative volatility inputs. But in reality, there have been a fair number of studies done of round-to-round volatilities and, perhaps more applicably, venture financing return variability. Each of these studies concludes volatilities in the area of 100% or a little more for VC returns. This raises the question, is the company's preferred stock more volatile or less volatile than its common stock?

The assumption would be that the common stock is more volatile, since its rights to cash flow are derived, netted, from the preferred stock's rights for these companies. Similarly, since most preferred stock has some form of anti-dilution protection, the absolute range of potential downward price adjustments is not as steep as is the case for common stock that does not have this protection. Although the revised AICPA Practice Aid does not acknowledge this, revisions of the AICPA's Practice Aid do acknowledge higher volatility of the common stock in VC-backed companies by including methods used by some practitioners, in theory, to "lever" volatilities. The most recent version of the Practice Aid specifically acknowledges that "[i]n cases where the preferred stock is entitled to a liquidation preference before the common stock begins participating, the common stock is more leveraged and hence has higher volatility than the overall equity volatility."

Since this is almost always the case with a venture-backed company, it's fair to say that most parties agree that common stock in these companies is more volatile than preferred stock. The remaining issue today concerns where the input for volatility comes from and how its magnitude compares to the true dispersion of prices and returns typically experienced by these types of companies. This can be addressed, as we've noted, by focusing on the dispersion of expected prices for the next round of venture financing, as opposed to focusing almost exclusively on anticipated sale scenarios, which tend to be more speculative and further into the future.

Simply observing the values recorded for common stock are not always a good measure of volatility, though. For instance, if you look at any venture-funded company, the founders of the company have the most volatile original issuance of shares in almost every case based on the issue price, as opposed to the intrinsic value. On a practical basis, the deemed issue price for the first common stock issued to founders is typically par value ($0.001 in many cases). Experienced founders recognize that there is in fact substantially more value, but that it requires capital, a first round of financing, and time, which involves subsequent rounds of financing leading to a liquidity event. Valuations, of any kind, for venture-funded companies that are not faced with an imminent IPO or acquisition need to focus on the next round of financing to generate a meaningful conclusion. That conclusion should reflect, in part, the true volatility that's weighing on pricing for that subsequent round as well as required returns for previous rounds. This applies to both 409A valuations for employee stock options and Topic 820 (FAS 157) valuations for venture funds.

OVERSTATING RETURNS AND UNDERSTATING RETURNS ON THE SAME ASSET (SIMULTANEOUSLY)

Applying the same numbers we used in Exhibit 5.2 to illustrate the devestating impact of "fair value" on employee stock option returns, increasing employee return hurdle rates by 900% in some cases, we can effectively convey how a similar potential for LP and fund losses exists. Consider the shared use of "market value," more or less, by LPs to describe "venture-fund book value" in Exhibits 5.14, 5.15, 5.16, and 5.17 and then look at all the possible ways GPs can, and still do, record the value of the exact same investment using examples shown in Exhibit 5.13.

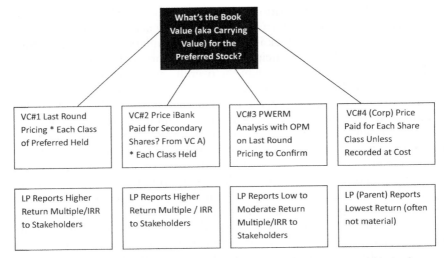

EXHIBIT 5.13   Inconsistent VC Book Value, Fair Value, Reports to Limited Partners

Source: SEC Filings Imported by Liquid Scenarios, Inc.

Note: Each result above is considered "book value" once it passes auditor scrutiny. Each result, however, is materially different. Imagine that LP is a single entity, Limited Partner #1, and each VC in the Exhibit has invested the same amount into the same exact portfolio company's preferred round on the same investment date. LP has committed the same amount of capital to each VC listed on the same date. The LP's "value multiple" reported to stakeholders on VC#1 would be 4.1X, VC#1 would be 3.5X, VC#3 5.0X, and VC#4 (corporate fund) would be 0X, negative IRR%. Each could be in accordance with Generally Accepted Accounting Principles and each would lead a reader of those performance reports to a different conclusion.

Ask a 12-year-old if she wants her money in a fund earning investors 5X or in or a fund earning investors less than 1X their money. Ask a 50-year-old the same question and you will probably get the same investment decision, but perhaps with more qualifiers.

Exhibits 5.14, 5.15, 5.16, and 5.17 illustrate summaries of how certain limited partners report their venture-capital results (returns) to their stakeholders. Note how in this context, higher "market values," or "fair values" both result in higher "return" conclusions. (In these exhibits, please note that boxes in black indicate materially different metrics or definitions for an item.)

As you would expect, and hope, fiduciaries and investment professionals at the limited partners investing in venture-capital funds are considerably

California Public Employees' Retirement System (CalPERS) Format

Cash In (A)	Cash Out (C)	Cash Out & Remaining Value (D) − C = B	Investment Multiple (Not Cash On Cash) A / (C+B)	Net IRR (not cash IRR)

EXHIBIT 5.14   CalPERS Cash-on-Cash versus Residual Return Report Format
Source: Summary of Layout from CalPERS Reports.

University of Texas Investment Management Company (UTIMCO) Format

Capital Invested (A)	Capital Returned to UTIMCO (C)	GP's Assessment of Current Value (B)	Cash-on-Cash Return (Multiple) A/C	IRR (not cash IRR)

EXHIBIT 5.15   UTIMCO Cash-on-Cash versus Residual Return Report Format
Source: Summary of Layout from UTIMCO Reports.

Washington State Investment Board Format

Paid-In-Capital (A)	Capital Distributed (C)	Current Market Value (B)	Total Value Multiple (not cash on cash) A/(C+B)	Net IRR (not cash IRR)

EXHIBIT 5.16   Washington State Cash-on-Cash versus Residual Return Report Format
Source: Summary of Layout from Washington State Investment Board Reports.

Regents of University of California Format

Cash In (A)	Cash Out (C)	Current NAV (B)	Investment Multiple (not cash on cash) A/(C+B)	Net IRR (not cash IRR)

*Boxes in black indicate materially different metrics or definitions for an item.

EXHIBIT 5.17   University of California Cash-on-Cash versus Residual Return Report Format
Source: Summary of Layout from University of California Regents Reports.

more rigorous in how they track the value of portfolios of venture-capital investments than employees are of the options they hold in any particular venture-backed company. That being said, these same institutions have had to struggle with what the true value of their investments are from period to period in addition to the known risk of estimating when any gains will be turned into cash (realized).

With information this specific to an industry and practice area, selecting different data to highlight can sometimes be used to reinforce a biased perspective, including my professional views on valuing these companies for financial reporting purposes. As a result, I've made every attempt to include tables obtained from sources that are generally available on the Web simply by searching for the groups mentioned for those who want to compare my conclusions using the more detailed source documents. Fortunately for our discussion, the four LPs in our example use the terms "Market Value," "Remaining Value," "GP's Assessment of Current Value," and "Current NAV [Net Asset Value]" to describe the same thing, despite using different terminology to do so. This is quite helpful because it speaks to the wide variety of performance conclusions being conveyed from the venture-fund financial statements to the limited partner financial statements and to the stakeholder perceptions of performance for most venture funds. Although the return percentage impact of this confusion is not as significant as it is for employees of venture-backed companies, the magnitude of the cash-on-cash multiple impact is of course substantially greater.

WHAT HAPPENS TO FUND IRRs WHEN YOU ASSUME BOOK VALUE EQUALS MARKET VALUE?

Perhaps the best way for all readers, not just alternative investment professionals, to appreciate this question is to first ask an analogous version of the question at the portfolio company level versus the fund level. See Exhibit 5.18.

With no further information, which company in Exhibit 5.18 looks like it has more traction? Exhibit 5.19 has a little more information about Company A and Company B, showing their relative earnings (EBITDA).

Private equity investors might want to have a closer look at the financial statements for both companies to make a decision. Angels might like to know more about the industry and all investors, especially VCs, will want to know who the existing investors are and who the management team is before saying they would choose Company A over Company B.

Another way to look at the question is to consider a comparison of revenue between two venture-funded companies targeting the same market/customers, with one venture-funded company showing $32 million in revenue for the year ended and the other showing $38 million in revenue for the same period. Both companies represent strong period-to-period momentum, but by and large the company that grew both EDBITDA and "revenue" would get the most attention.

In this particular case, however, both companies have the exact same number of orders/closed deals and the exact same cost structure. One has simply adjusted its contracts so that the accounting rules enable them to

EXHIBIT 5.18 Differences in Revenue Recognition and Perceived Value/Traction

	Portfolio Company A			
	Year 3	Year 5	Growth X	CAGR
Net revenue	1,195,000	32,486,000	27	421%

	Portfolio Company B			
	Year 3	Year 5	Growth X	CAGR
Net revenue	1,195,000	38,209,000	32	465%

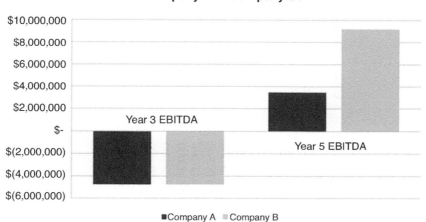

**Which Do You Prefer?
Company A or Company B?**

■Company A ▪Company B

EXHIBIT 5.19 Illustration of EBITDA Reporting Differences and Perceived Value/Traction

record all of the revenue at once. Now, which company do you prefer? Although this may seem like an extreme example, and of course if you dig through the financials you will see that the companies have the exact same free cash flow, perception is obviously very powerful and harder to explain even if you are attempting to be "conservative."

With that in mind, consider the chart we presented in Exhibit 5.13, showing how five different VCs accounted for, reported in their financial statement and, as a result, caused limited partners to report in their financial statements five different performance records for the exact same investment. Now, take a look at the returns displayed in Exhibit 5.20. What does this say about true return volatility versus ongoing improvements in record keeping?

EXHIBIT 5.20 Variation in Fund Returns Reflect Even Higher Volatility in Underlying Assets

Partnership Name	Capital Invested	Capital Returned to UTIMCO	Current Value	Cash-on-Cash Return	IRR
Fisher Lynch Venture Partnership, L.P.	28,640,000	2,040,340	23,164,959	0.07	−5.05%
Foundation Capital IV, L.P.	20,004,870	1,517,513	24,532,058	0.08	5.55%
Foundry Venture Capital 2007, L.P.	24,650,000	4,530,594	57,948,661	0.18	72.44%
Sofinnova Venture Partners VII, L.P.	11,400,000	0	9,914,580	0	−7.62%
Spark Capital II, L.P.	9,918,500	0	13,008,615	0	19.18%
TCV V. L.P.	27,441,000	19,546,425	19,632,527	0.71	9.63%
TCV VI. L.P.	28,861,000	9,644,412	21,188,830	0.33	2.90%
TCV VII. L.P.	11,290,000	0	9,975,374	0	−11.56%
Union Square Ventures 2004, L.P.	22,250,000	14,287,506	55,870,113	0.64	54.71%
Union Square Ventures 2008, L.P.	7,500,000	0	6,894,491	0	−8.99%

Source: UTIMCO Reports.

Let's switch gears briefly back to volatility, which is directly related to required returns. As we transition back to the symbiotic relationship between required returns and volatility, it's a good time to take a look at a shortcut way to appreciate this relationship using a simple formula, the Sharpe Index. Although sometimes criticized for its primary purpose, comparing risks and returns associated with more liquid asset classes than venture, this tool still provides a meaningful way to explain venture dynamics in the context of competing objectives and risk dynamics of stakeholders with different classes of securities.

The beauty of the Sharpe Ratio is that it's easy to calculate and easy to understand. For our purposes here, explaining the role of often inappropriate volatility assumptions on VC security pricing makes the tool perfect. You can read it like you read a grade point average, so a higher number is generally better, compared to someone else's lower number. The three components are described in Exhibit 5.21.

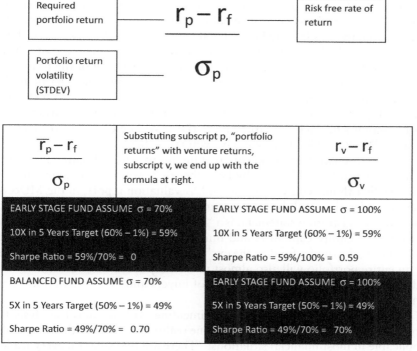

EXHIBIT 5.21 Sensitivity of VC Return Risks to Perceived/Disclosed Volatility
Source: Liquid Scenarios, Inc.

Beyond some legitimate technical issues with using the Sharpe Ratio for this type of an analysis, there are two obvious issues that bring the output into question. First, notice how the early-stage venture fund appears to be a better bet using the hypothetical inputs. That is to say that it receives a better risk adjusted performance grade than the balanced fund under each scenario calculated. On the surface, anyway, we would expect that a fund with a lower target return would have somewhat lower risks. As such, we would expect the variability of the returns to be lower. This may or may not in fact be the case in reality. However, it's highly likely that the volatility of returns for the early-stage fund is going to be different than the volatility of the balanced fund over certain time periods. As a result, the time period for our volatility estimate is an important one, as illustrated in Exhibit 5.21.

THE REAL COST OF FAIR VALUE, FAIR MARKET VALUE, AND ENTERPRISE VALUE

The most evident cost of the terms fair value, fair market value, and enterprise value (or business enterprise value) to the venture-capital community goes beyond the fees incurred for fair value opinions, 409A, Topic 820 (FAS 157), or audit field work for Topic 718. Fortunately, the biggest cost is also the easiest to address. In order to do so, an understanding of the terminology is needed. Fair value has sometimes been defined by others, particularly certain valuation professionals long before 409A and Topic 718 (FAS123R) had an impact on venture funded companies, as follows, "Fair market value with discounts for lack of marketability (DLOM) and discounts for lack of control (DLOC) added back will give you fair value."

This particular definition is of great importance to us because it implies that "fair value" would generally be higher than fair market value. One of the very first things you will see in a 409A valuation report, in the MD&A section under the stock-based compensation portion of a venture-backed company's registration statement, is a "marketability discount" or "liquidity discount." Venture capitalists and limited partners who have experienced the winding down of a fund or the exchange of an LP interest versus the sale of an entire portfolio will also almost universally see in these transactions a "discount" that reflects a limited pool of buyers and other restrictions that impact liquidity.

When I was a young adult experimenting with technical analysis to program option trading strategies, the one reality that stuck with me remains applicable in most financial situations: "There are two sides on every trade, so if one party is making money, they are getting that profit from another party that's losing profit." That sounds like a "zero-sum" game, but doesn't always have to be. For instance, one party gained liquidity and some capital appreciation, and another party gained an opportunity to realize future capital appreciation. When someone takes a small profit, another party may be taking a loss as a result, or simply realizing a smaller profit as a result.

Here's an example that's directly applicable to our discussion regarding enterprise value, liquidity, and control as it relates to allocating value to venture-backed companies. The market rallies by 20% in a period and some of your holdings are up 50% at the close. You immediately put in a sell order, and a fair amount of other investors do the same thing. Assume you realize your 45% of your gain in cash and that by the close of that trading day the market is down. The financial press says the "market was down on profit taking." Naturally, there were parties taking profits, but many parties that sold or held positions took losses on that day and that process happens each and every day. If venture-backed companies in that liquid market are realizing volatilities in excess of 60%, with public investors reasonably seeking appreciation of perhaps 8% to 12% per year, it's obvious that investors seeking higher returns such as those in the tables below are realizing substantially higher volatility. Using this lower volatility rate for venture-backed companies, along with a longer time period that doesn't take into account new financing rounds means that even when "profits are taken" or realized, someone in a deal has lost value along the way. See Exhibit 5.22.

What's an Allocation Method?

As you've come to realize from the previous chapters, there's a lot of terminology that appears redundant in the valuation space. In the beginning of this book, before getting into the income approaches to valuation, we attempted to clarify some of the confusion caused by multiple uses of the word "discount" in the context of valuing a company. As we start to explore what many valuation professionals refer to as "allocation" methods,

EXHIBIT 5.22   Implied Rates of Returns from Studies in AICPA Practice Aid

Implied "Target Rates of Return" as Discussed in AICPA Practice Guide

Stage of Development	Plummer	Scherlis and Sahlman	Sahlman, Stevenson, and Bhide
Startup	50% to 70%	50%–70%	50%–100%
First stage or "early development"	40% to 60%	40% to 60%	40% to 60%
Second stage or "expansion"	35% to 50%	30% to 50%	30% to 40%
Bridge/IPO	25% to 35%	20% to 35%	20% to 30%

Source: AICPA Practice Aid.

it's important to explain why and how the term is being used for valuations of venture-capital-financed companies.

If you look at recent registration statements for venture-funded companies, as we've done throughout this book, you will notice that the MD&A sections (Management's Discussion and Analysis) generally repeat text found within valuation reports that essentially say "first we estimated an enterprise value—then we allocated those values." This is in accordance with AICPA guidelines and also with valuation guidelines for private equity funds. The rationale is that you can't allocate portions of the company equity value to different equity classes until you've first valued the total company value separately using one of the three valuation approaches discussed previously. See Exhibit 5.23.

That logic, of first getting an enterprise value independent of recent market indications the security values before "allocating," seems to make sense if we are talking about valuing a security that:

a) has a liquid market,
b) does have at least some history of meaningful revenue, and/or,
c) does have at least the reasonable prospect of generating growing free operating cash flow within the next 18 to 24 months.

Of the cases we've referenced thus far in this book, only one of the venture-funded companies meet the three criteria noted above. It's for this reason that the first thing a party looking at a venture-funded company is going to look at with respect to valuation is the last-round pricing, and that makes perfect sense. In the context of a valuation, the longstanding approach of examining the last-round price per share paid for a given series of preferred and applying a discount to arrive at the value of common stock, or the value of other junior stock in some cases, is more or less how things still work, assuming the last round has closed within three to six months. The real difference today has a lot more to do with how the discount (reduction in value) is arrived at, quantified, and validated.

STEP 1. Estimate Enterprise Value	**STEP 2.** Allocate Enterprise Value to Securities
(in many venture-backed cases, this is total equity, since there's no significant debt)	(again, this generally involves equity securities or quasi-equity securities for venture-backed companies)

EXHIBIT 5.23   Popular Two-Step, Top-Down 409A VC-Backed Company Valuation Process

So a practical interpretation of disclosures that says "we first estimated an enterprise value and then allocated that value" might be as follows:

> *First we looked at the price per share paid by VCs in the most recent round of financing. Then we looked to see if the company had revenue and if so how much. If the company didn't have significant revenue but did have a recent round of venture financing, we assumed that the common stock value would be worth something greater than 10% of the last round financing price per share and something less than 50% of the last round pricing per share, which we immediately tested for by backsolving for the last round using an option pricing method. This was done if the last round occurred within six months of our valuation. Next, we looked for comparable companies to use in assessing enterprise values using a market approach. In the case of public guideline companies that were comparable we used an average of their, volatilities as an input to the Black-Scholes or binomial models. We also considered the betas of those guideline public companies as an input to betas to apply in the capital asset pricing model used to support the discount rate used in our discount cash flow (DCF) model. Revenue multiplies of the guideline public companies we felt were comparable to the company being valued we used in our terminal values and sanity tests.*

While that type of disclosure might not sound as elegant to auditors or some 409A valuation professions, it's a logical approach to both revealing a "fair market value" in accordance with Revenue Ruling 59-60 and a "fair value" in accordance GAAP. See Exhibit 5.24.

Note that despite the efforts of Topic 820 (FAS 157) to create a unified definition of fair value, it's worth noting that accounting rules that define "Fair Value" for equity-based compensation in financial reporting use a slightly different standard. We aren't going to distract you from the primary focus of this chapter, which has more to do with your actual rights to investment cash flows and how that impacts value. Still, it would be reckless not to include a side-by-side comparison of these separate definitions. The AICPA Practice Aid effectively specifies the fair value to be used in 409A engagements as: "A valuation performed for the purpose of valuing privately held company securities issued as compensation under US GAAP should be based on the definition of fair value used in FASB ASC 718 and 505-50." It should also be noted that this definition of fair value is slightly different from the definition under FASB ASC 820, Fair Value Measurements and Disclosures, in which fair value is defined as: "The price that would be received to sell an asset or paid to transfer a liability in an orderly transaction between

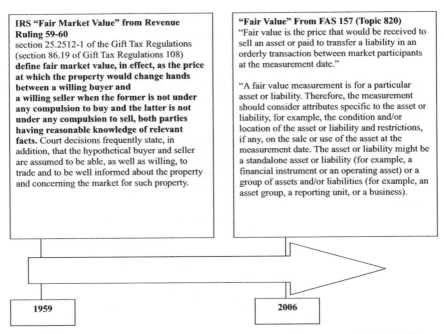

IRS "Fair Market Value" from Revenue Ruling 59-60
section 25.2512-1 of the Gift Tax Regulations (section 86.19 of Gift Tax Regulations 108) **define fair market value, in effect, as the price at which the property would change hands between a willing buyer and a willing seller when the former is not under any compulsion to buy and the latter is not under any compulsion to sell, both parties having reasonable knowledge of relevant facts.** Court decisions frequently state, in addition, that the hypothetical buyer and seller are assumed to be able, as well as willing, to trade and to be well informed about the property and concerning the market for such property.

"Fair Value" From FAS 157 (Topic 820)
"Fair value is the price that would be received to sell an asset or paid to transfer a liability in an orderly transaction between market participants at the measurement date."

"A fair value measurement is for a particular asset or liability. Therefore, the measurement should consider attributes specific to the asset or liability, for example, the condition and/or location of the asset or liability and restrictions, if any, on the sale or use of the asset at the measurement date. The asset or liability might be a standalone asset or liability (for example, a financial instrument or an operating asset) or a group of assets and/or liabilities (for example, an asset group, a reporting unit, or a business).

1959   2006

EXHIBIT 5.24   Revenue Ruling 59-60 Fair Market Value versus FASB Fair Value

market participants at the measurement date." In addition, the definition from Topic 718 (FAS123R) is: "The amount at which an asset (or liability) could be bought (or incurred) or sold (or settled) in a current transaction between willing parties, that is, other than in a forced or liquidation sale."

Who Are the "Market Participants"?

The "market participants" referred to in Topic 820 (FAS 157) are buyers and sellers in the principal (or most advantageous) market for the asset or liability who are:

- Independent (i.e., not related parties);
- Motivated (or, freely willing, not forced) to buy/sell; and
- Have the authority and resources to buy/sell.

When VCs and founders discuss "deal terms" or "valuation," they aren't truly discussing the "enterprise value of the company," the "discounted cash flow value of the enterprise," or even the "VC-method-derived value of the company." As noted previously in Chapter 1, after the investor has validated the people and the opportunity, the question before him or her is "What fully diluted ownership percentage are we getting?" Granted, that fully diluted percentage ownership target does get expressed as a pre-money value and post-money value during negotiations and does hold a psychological significance to more than a few founders and investors. Still, "What percentage of the company will I own?" is really at the heart of the discussion. In the context of a company with no material physical assets and often solely the consensus promise of creating intangible assets that have yet to be completed or yet to be validated as fitting a customer/market opportunity, does that sound more like a "valuation" or more like an "allocation"?

If you're thinking, "It kind of sounds like a little of both," that's because it is in fact a little of both. So if that approach is a good starting point for the primary "market participants," it makes sense that it should be the natural starting point for those attempting to quantify the behaviors, past, present, and future, of market participants. The cases that follow examine each of the "allocation" methods and go on to illustrate how these methods can successfully be used to obtain a superior indication of value than applying traditional valuation techniques to early-stage companies. As you review the case studies and related calculations that follow, you will find that allocation and valuation are in fact integral when it comes to valuing venture-funded companies.

YAHOO! CASE

Application of OPM, Backsolve, Protective Puts, Waterfalls, CVMs, and Various Volatilities to Yahoo's Securities and Major Shareholders

Exhibit 5.25 shows one of the ways the backsolve method was used to reverse into a total equity, or "business enterprise value," for Yahoo. This was done in a manner consistent with how a valuation profession would match the Series A original issue price (split adjusted) to the Black-Scholes values based on the "claims" on Yahoo's equity due to deal terms, most significantly the $1 million liquidation preference of the Series A in this case.

In this first illustration, there were no stock options included in the calculations. While this may seem unusual, Chapter 6 discusses why this is not an unusual thing to see in a valuation analysis when the company doesn't have vested or granted options. Another missing element in this analysis was the discount for lack of marketability, or DLOM. Using a protective put to calculate the DLOM, assuming 65% volatility, a 2% risk-free rate, and an assumed exit time horizon of two years results in an estimated marketability discount of around 33%. This reduces the net value indication for the common stock from $0.11 per share to $0.07. As you will read in a

EXHIBIT 5.25 Yahoo! Backsolved Option Pricing Method Model at 65% Volatility

	Total	Series A Liquidation Preference	Common Participates	Series A Converts
Breakpoints		Breakpoint 1	Breakpoint 2	Breakpoint 3
Strike Price (K)		$0	$1,040,000	$3,040,000
BEV Estimate (S)	$2,125,901	$2,125,901	$2,125,901	$2,125,901
Breakpoint Call Value	$2,125,901	$853,531	$727,307	$545,063
Call Value at Floor		$2,125,901	$1,272,369	$545,063
Term in Years (t)		2.00	2.00	2.00
Risk-Free Rate (r)		2.00%	2.00%	2.00%
Volatility		65.00%	65.00%	65.00%
d1		26.37	1.28	0.11
d2		25.45	0.36	−0.81
N(d1)		1.00	0.90	0.55
N(d2)		1.00	0.64	0.21
S * N(d1)		$2,125,901	$1,913,076	$1,159,467
K * e^-rt		$0	$999,221	$2,920,800
Times N(d2)		$0	$640,707	$614,405
C Value at Ceiling		$1,272,369	$545,063	$0
Common	$1,085,901	$0	$727,307	$358,594
Proceeds Prior Breakpoint		$0	$0	N/A
Proceeds This Breakpoint Ceiling		$0	$2,000,000	N/A
Difference		$0	$2,000,000	N/A
% of Range Proceeds		0.00%	100.00%	65.79%
Pro-Rata Percentage		0.00%	100.00%	65.79%
Option Value to Security	$1,085,901	$0	$727,307	$358,594
Value per Share	$0.11	$0.00	$0.07	$0.04
Series A	$1,040,000	$853,531	$0	$186,469

Source: Liquid Scenarios, Inc. Used under license agreement. Copyright 2003–2011 bpCentral, Inc. Patent pending.

moment, the risk-free rate in 1995 was in fact much higher than the 2% we used in this first illustration. The rate used in the first illustration is closer to the rates you would find disclosed by companies that were actually guided to use this methodology in order to comply with tax and financial reporting requirements. Yahoo! went public over a decade before these rules went into effect, but still provides an excellent example of longstanding weaknesses

EXHIBIT 5.26   Yahoo! Back Volatility and Risk-Free Rate Assumptions in 1995 and 1996

	Expected life	Interest rate	Volatility	Dividend yield
1996	30 months	5.1%–6.5%	53%	0%
1995	30 months	5.3%–6.0%	NA	0%

Source: Yahoo! SEC Filings.

with the volatility inputs used in models for high-growth, venture-backed companies.

Another opportunity to test my assertion that these valuation tools, as they are often applied, result in understating the value of the company while simultaneously overstating the value of the common, is to use the volatility estimate actually disclosed in Yahoo's filing with the SEC, 53%, and compare the resulting backsolved enterprise value, as well as the resulting DLOM adjusted common stock value.

Recall that the prevailing instinct is that as the volatility is increased, the value of the options will increase. So if we are applying a lower volatility estimate to Yahoo using the Black-Scholes option pricing method and backsolving to an enterprise value based on the Series A issue price, we should end up with a lower indicated enterprise value, which we do. See Exhibit 5.27.

Whereas the Exhibit 5.25 used 65% as the volatility estimate, to make the outcome more comparable to what you see used for post-409A companies (based on public peer volatility in 2007, 2008, 2009, and 2010), using the 53% from Yahoo's 1996 financial statements produces a backsolved enterprise value of $2,082,844 as illustrated in Exhibit 5.27. If the process stopped there, we would simply end up with a slightly lower indicated value for the company and a somewhat lower value for the common stock. However, in most cases the volatility will be considered as an input into how the common stock discount for lack of marketability is calculated. As a result, we end up with a lower put value when the volatility input is lower and therefore a lower discount for the common stock. The lower discount results in an estimated value for Yahoo's common stock that's 14% higher than was indicated at the higher volatility, despite an enterprise value that's actually about 2% lower. See Exhibit 5.28.

In the next iteration we'll apply a volatility that's closer to what venture-capital investors tend to experience, 100% volatility, and see how that impacts the values indicated before and after discounting the common stock for a lack of marketability based on Yahoo's Series A price. See Exhibit 5.29.

EXHIBIT 5.27   Yahoo! Backsolved Option Pricing Method Model at 53%
Volatility

	Total	Series A Liq. Pref.	Common Participates	Series A Converts
Breakpoints		Breakpoint 1	Breakpoint 2	Breakpoint 3
Strike Price (K)		$0	$1,040,000	$3,040,000
BEV Estimate (S)	$2,082,844	$2,082,844	$2,082,844	$2,082,844
Breakpoint Call Value	$2,082,844	$909,683	$792,234	$380,928
Call Value at Floor		$2,082,844	$1,173,161	$380,928
Term in Years (t)		2.00	2.00	2.00
Risk-Free Rate (r)		2.00%	2.00%	2.00%
Volatility		53.00%	53.00%	53.00%
d1		32.13	1.35	−0.08
d2		31.38	0.61	−0.83
N(d1)		1.00	0.91	0.47
N(d2)		1.00	0.73	0.20
S * N(d1)		$2,082,844	$1,900,070	$978,046
K * e^-rt		$0	$999,221	$2,920,800
Times N(d2)		$0	$726,909	$597,118
C Value at Ceiling		$1,173,161	$380,928	$0
Common	$1,042,844	$0	$792,234	$250,610
Proceeds Prior Breakpoint		$0	$0	N/A
Proceeds This Breakpoint Ceiling		$0	$2,000,000	N/A
Difference		$0	$2,000,000	N/A
% of Range Proceeds		0.00%	100.00%	65.79%
Pro-Rata Percentage		0.00%	100.00%	65.79%
Option Value to Security	$1,042,844	$0	$792,234	$250,610
Value per Share	$0.10	$0.00	$0.08	$0.03
Series A	$1,040,000	$909,683	$0	$130,317
Proceeds Prior Breakpoint		$0	$1,040,000	N/A
Proceeds This Breakpoint Ceiling		$1,040,000	$1,040,000	N/A
Difference		$1,040,000	$0	N/A
% of Range Proceeds		100.00%	0.00%	34.21%
Pro-Rata Percentage		N/A	N/A	34.21%
Option Value to Security	$1,040,000	$909,683	$0	$130,317
Value per Share	$0.20	$0.17	$0.00	$0.03

Source: Liquid Scenarios, Inc. Used under license agreement. Copyright 2003–2011
bpCentral, Inc. Patent pending.

Last Round Test	⌄
Last Round	Common ▾
Adjusted Issued Price	$0.00
OPM Value Per Share	$0.11
Marketability Discount (DLOM)	32.80%
Control Discount (DLOC)	0.00%
OPM Value Net of Discounts	$0.07
Imlied Enterprise Value	$2,125,901
	Test

Last Round Test	⌄
Last Round	Common ▾
Adjusted Issued Price	$0.00
OPM Value Per Share	$0.10
Marketability Discount (DLOM)	26.72%
Control Discount (DLOC)	0.00%
OPM Value Net of Discounts	$0.08
Imlied Enterprise Value	$2,082,844
	Test

EXHIBIT 5.28   Yahoo! Protective Put at DLOM 65% and 53% Volatility
Source: Liquid Scenarios, Inc.

Applying a more appropriate, higher volatility to the venture-funded company, as we propose, yields a more reasonable estimate of both business enterprise value and common stock value without making any of the further adjustments recommended in this book. At 100% volatility a backsolved enterprise value of $2,297,027 is generated, as illustrated in Exhibit 2.29. This is the highest enterprise value produced thus far, but it generates the lowest common stock value, net of the DLOM, since the higher volatility generates a higher DLOM.

At 100% volatility, with two years assumed before a liquidity event, and the 2% risk-free rate we've used for each of the Yahoo examples thus far for consistency, a discount for lack of marketability of around 49% is calculated. Applying this to the $0.13 per common stock value that was produced by back-solving for the Series A price at 100% volatility, we end up with a net value per share of common stock of around $0.06 per share, or 30% of the Series A original issue price of $0.20 per share. While simply adjusting the volatility input doesn't get us all the way to 10% of the Series A price Yahoo's early hires were fortunate enough to get, it's a whole lot better for modern optionees than the result that would likely be generated by a 409A valuation using the lower volatilities based on public "peers." Equally as important, the logic is more consistent with reality and requires fewer "judgment"-based inputs to explain how the conclusions were reached.

One of the recent additions to the AICPA Practice Aid can offset this problem, in part, by effectively increasing the volatility input used for

EXHIBIT 5.29   Yahoo! Backsolve Value Indication at 100% Volatility

	Total	Series A Liq. Pref.	Common Participates	Series A Converts
Breakpoints		Breakpoint 1	Breakpoint 2	Breakpoint 3
Strike Price (K)		$0	$1,040,000	$3,040,000
BEV Estimate (S)	$2,297,027	$2,297,027	$2,297,027	$2,297,027
Breakpoint Call Value	$2,297,027	$676,528	$558,043	$1,062,455
Call Value at Floor		$2,297,027	$1,620,499	$1,062,455
Term in Years (t)		2.00	2.00	2.00
Risk-Free Rate (r)		2.00%	2.00%	2.00%
Volatility		100.00%	100.00%	100.00%
d1		17.61	1.30	0.54
d2		16.19	−0.12	−0.88
N(d1)		1.00	0.90	0.70
N(d2)		1.00	0.45	0.19
S * N(d1)		$2,297,027	$2,072,976	$1,618,131
K * e^-rt		$0	$999,221	$2,920,800
Times N(d2)		$0	$452,477	$555,676
C Value at Ceiling		$1,620,499	$1,062,455	$0
Common	$1,257,027	$0	$558,043	$698,984
Proceeds Prior Breakpoint		$0	$0	N/A
Proceeds This Breakpoint Ceiling		$0	$2,000,000	N/A
Difference		$0	$2,000,000	N/A
% of Range Proceeds		0.00%	100.00%	65.79%
Pro-Rata Percentage		0.00%	100.00%	65.79%
Option Value to Security	$1,257,027	$0	$558,043	$698,984
Value per Share	$0.13	$0.00	$0.06	$0.07
Series A	$1,040,000	$676,528	$0	$363,471
Proceeds Prior Breakpoint		$0	$1,040,000	N/A
Proceeds This Breakpoint Ceiling		$1,040,000	$1,040,000	N/A
Difference		$1,040,000	$0	N/A
% of Range Proceeds		100.00%	0.00%	34.21%
Pro-Rata Percentage		N/A	N/A	34.21%
Option Value to Security	$1,040,000	$676,528	$0	$363,471
Value per Share	$0.20	$0.13	$0.00	$0.07

Source: Liquid Scenarios, Inc. Used under license agreement. Copyright 2003–2011 bpCentral, Inc. Patent pending.

purposes of calculating the discount. This is accomplished by a rather simple formula (variables from the actual draft revised practice aid):

$$\text{Class Volatility} = \text{Equity Volatility}$$
$$\times (\text{Equity Value} \times \text{Class N(d1)})/\text{Class Value}$$

Although "levering" the volatility does in fact increase the discount for lack of marketability on common stock to a figure that's more appropriate, the fundamental assumption that the volatility of the company's total equity value is comparable to the volatility of a public company still results in lower indications of total company value. Still, it's a step in the right direction to reduce the impact on employees of overvalued stock options. The actual elements that contribute to the appropriate volatility input for a venture-backed company are similar to the elements that impact an appropriate discount rate (or required rate of return) buildup for a privately held company.

Having improved the correlation between Yahoo!'s volatility, the appropriate discounts, and the resulting indicated values, now's a good time to move on to generating an even more accurate, higher, enterprise value estimate while verifying that a fair common stock value estimate and resulting fair option grant price is generated. We can start by reviewing our checklist of readily observable inputs and then placing them into waterfalls, OPM models, PWERMS (covered later), and CWERMS (also covered later) with future rounds taken into account to reach realistic value indications that account for the takeover value of the company and the related volatility of the various target returns by investor type and stage.

Yahoo's Readily Observable Valuation Inputs

Imagine Yahoo was founded by PhD candidates in Mobile, Alabama, had the same amount of traffic when it got venture capital, and was able to recruit a successful, high-growth CEO, albeit one without substantial tech experience. It's possible that the company could have raised a Series A financing that was comparable in size. So if we were to simply backsolve for an indication of the total equity value of the company using standard inputs we would find in a 409A valuation or Topic 820 valuation, we would of course end up with comparable results (the same value indication). Before going any further in this case, you might want to ask yourself, does that seem reasonable? You can also ask some questions while referring to the inputs from the following list.

Readily Observable Inputs Checklist

- Who (existing VCs were, new investors are, IRRs/stages, GPs)
- What (security/rights they purchased, how does that mix impact their target future returns and present returns/residual value?)
- When (timing of prior financing transactions versus expected timing of future transactions, expected burn rate/runway)
- Why (pro-rata with outside lead? secondary sale?)
- How Much (size of the rounds, magnitude of the required returns, implications on future volatility)?

If the entire state of Alabama, where you can certainly find comparably intelligent and motivated innovators, were helping Yahoo become the leader in its space using all their connections, it would be unlikely to rival the connections within one or two degrees of Sequoia and Stanford. What impact do you suppose being based in Alabama would have on Yahoo's Series B financing prospects? How would Yahoo's ability to recruit team members with the strong local professional networks needed to maximize traction and execution when a business model emerged have been different if Yahoo were based in Alabama, versus Silicon Valley?

Approaches to valuation used by professionals to appraise private companies in mature industries would use adjustments to the discount rate, as explained earlier, to adjust the risk and required return for Yahoo! of Mobile, Alabama. But as we've seen, companies like Yahoo don't fit easily within the constraints of a traditional discounted cash flow model. Even if it did, simply increasing the discount rate to reduce the present value to the amount invested would be perceived as what it was, a financial "plug," as we discussed earlier. Still, it's worth quickly reviewing how a valuation professional might adjust the required rate of return and therefore the valuation of Yahoo! assuming it was a private company that was not venture-funded. We then compare this to how a Wall Street analyst or M&A investment bank would make adjustments for enterprise or takeover value and how that relates to the backsolve methods being currently applied to many venture-backed company valuations today.

As discussed in Chapter 3, to apply a discounted cash flow method or capitalization of earnings method, we need our "financial hammer," the discount formula and an appropriate discount rate to use in that formula. We also need a future benefit stream to discount or capitalize (the "nails"). Since Yahoo!'s earnings before interest, taxes, depreciation, and amortization (EBITDA) are projected to be negative for each of the three years ending 1995, 1996, and 1997, the discounted cash flow approach is probably not going to work very well if we use EBITDA as the benefit stream. We could, however, look at a multiple of projected revenue in 1995, 1996, or 1997 to get an indication of value as of any of those periods. If we use only "Lycos" and "Excite" as comparables to get a clue as to Yahoo!'s value as a multiple of projected revenue, we would give up statistical significance but make up for it with a superior indication of equity market demand for a brand new market sector, Internet Information Companies.

As discussed, this method of comparing metrics for comparable companies that trade publicly to the private company we are valuing would be considered by valuation professionals and auditors as a "market" approach to valuation. Since we are using projected revenue for the subject company, Yahoo!, we would still need to discount that future revenue to bring the value back today. That exercise, of discounting the future benefit stream (revenue), would be considered an income approach to valuation and would of course require us to use an appropriate discount rate. The discount rate we use will be composed on three general elements for a privately held company:

1. The risk-free rate (which we've discussed).
2. The required return in excess of the risk-free rate investors demand for bearing the risks of equity securities in general (what we referred to as the equity risk premium earlier).

   In the case of a smaller company like Yahoo!, it could be appropriate to include an additional premium to reflect the increased risks that come with dealing with investing in a smaller company.
3. A company-specific risk premium, which in the case of a privately held company would typically be arrived at based on an analyst's judgment.

You may recall from Chapter 1 that the risk-free rate plus the equity risk premium represent systematic risk that can't be diversified simply by owning equity interests in a variety of companies. Combing these premiums to arrive at an appropriate discount rate is known as a "buildup" approach. Since systematic risk (Risk-Free Rate + Equity Risk Premium + Industry Risk Premium + Size Premium) accounts for a larger portion of the required return in a traditional private company than in a venture-funded company, small differences can have a big impact. Fortunately, these inputs are generally sourced from reliable information providers.

How a Valuation Analyst Would Build Up a Discount Rate for Yahoo!

A valuation analyst builds a discount rate by summing the risk-free rate, the equity risk premium for large publicly traded stock, the industry risk premium for the company's industry, and the size premium. Each of these elements can be obtained from independent sources such as Ibbotson Associates' *Stocks, Bonds, Bills and Inflation Yearbook,* which tracks average total returns (capital appreciation and dividend income) on large corporate equity issues from 1926 and to present. Duff & Phelps Risk Premium Report is another trusted resource for such data, albeit generated with slightly different criteria and methodology than Ibbotson.

The rate of return on a U.S. Government Treasury Bond is easily obtained from many reliable sources, such as Bloomberg, of course. This leaves only the company-specific risk. There are a variety of ways an analyst will support the company-specific risk premium he or she uses. A rough example that might apply to Yahoo! if it were a typical privately held company is as follows:

Company Specific Risk =

Management Team:0%

+ Dependence on Key Personnel: 2%

+ Technology Risk: 1%

+ Competitive Landscape: 1.5%
    = Total Specific Company Risk Premium: 4.5%

In reality, the true company-specific risk for a venture-backed company would have to be a lot closer to the required rates of return capital providers, venture capitalists, and angels demand minus the risk-free rate, equity risk premium, size premium, and industry risk premiums sourced from the information providers previously mentioned. If you wanted to mix the two approaches to arrive at a discount rate, you might build it up as follows (all amounts are hypothetical for illustrative purposes only):

Risk-Free Rate: 6%

+ Equity Risk Premium: 9%
    + Industry Risk Premium: 3%
    + Size Premium: 2%
        = Discount Rate before Adding Company-Specific Risk: 20%

Company-Specific Risk =

+ Management Team: −5%

+ Board of Directors: −5%

+ Capital Structure: 15%

+ Key Management Dependence: 6%

+ Competition: 12%
+ Burn Rate: 5%
+ Technology Risk/IP: 6%
   = Specific Company Risk Premium: 19%
   Discount Rate: 39% (Risk Free Rate + Equity Risk Premium +
   Company Specific Risk Premium)

Note, it's not often that you actually see negative amounts included in a company-specific risk buildup. But given the fact that management teams at venture-backed companies often have qualifications that rank in the top 0.01% of the world, and board members that rank even higher, it's not unreasonable to assume that these elements would counterbalance other specific risk. However, those same advantages would be offset by the dependence on key personnel, which generally increases risk and the return requirements embedded in the instruments used in the company's capital structure (preferred stock with sophisticated terms designed with a liquidity event in mind for instance).

Now that we have a hypothetical input, the discount rate, for our financial hammer, we can use it to get the present value of the benefit stream (projected revenue times the comparable multiple). Assume the comparable multiple was around 18 times revenue based on the guideline public companies and Yahoo! projected revenue of $22 million in 1996, you would simply multiply the 1996 revenue projection by 18 to arrive at a terminal value indication of $396 million. Since Yahoo!'s current revenue may be $0 or approaching $1 million depending on the date, we have to use our discount rate and time to bring the $396 million to a present value. If an analyst ends up with a number that seems high, naturally the company-specific risk will be increased. Alternatively, if an analyst ends up with a number that seems low, the company-specific risk can be decreased. But with this rather subjective input accounting for such a large amount of any value conclusions, prior to discounts for lack of control, you can easily see how the result can be perceived as a "plug." This is one of the reasons using an option-pricing methodology has become so popular, because it allows a more objective answer to be generated quickly and within the confines of the complex capital structures of venture-backed companies, as illustrated in Exhibits 5.30, 5.31, 5.32, 5.33, 5.34, and 5.35.

To successfully illustrate an accurate backsolve model requires an accurate capitalization table from which to derive pre- and most money "values." I will quickly review some of the sources of information that were used to generate the preceding models so that you can adjust the numbers yourself if appropriate and see how your conclusions differ due to better information concerning the pre-IPO capital structure and deal terms.

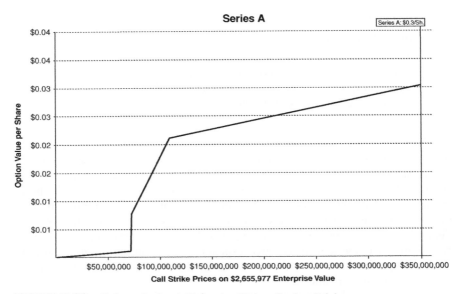

EXHIBIT 5.30 Yahoo! Series A Valuation Using Option Pricing
Source: Liquid Scenarios, Inc.

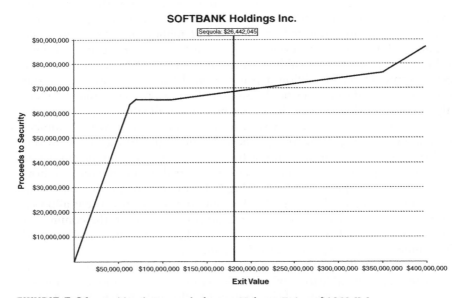

EXHIBIT 5.31 Softbank Proceeds from a Yahoo! Exit at $180MM
Source: Liquid Scenarios, Inc.

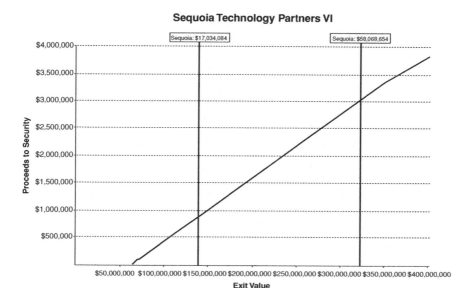

EXHIBIT 5.32   Sequoia Proceeds from a Yahoo! Exit at Various Values
Source: Liquid Scenarios, Inc.

I've seen, and heard, a number of resources suggesting that the initial Sequoia investment in Yahoo! was "$2 million." Since the only public record of the exact amount is available indirectly through the SEC filings, this is another reason for illustrating the methodology behind how we arrived at the figures. What's the difference between the $1 million we've noted below and the $2 million you see referenced elsewhere when a company skyrockets to over $100 billion in market cap (equity value)? Well, for purposes of the valuation techniques being illustrated here the difference is significant. Also, assuming it was $2 million instead of $1 million, the difference to investors that would have held those shares from original issue to the peak market cap would have been $10 billion.

One easy way to either source or confirm capital structure is financial statements if you don't have access to an actual cap table. In Yahoo!'s case, the financial statements filed with the SEC, particularly the statement of shareholders equity, suggest the amount was actually around $1 million. The relevant portions are reproduced in Exhibit 5.36 along with the related calculations.

The Statement of Shareholders' Equity doesn't include information about increases in the option pool. As noted earlier in this book, as well

	30%	40%	50%	60%	70%	80%	90%	100%	110%	120%
1	1	1	2	2	2	2	2	2	2	2
2	2	2	2	3	3	3	4	4	4	5
3	2	3	3	4	5	6	7	8	9	11
4	3	4	5	7	8	10	13	16	19	23
5	4	5	8	10	14	19	25	32	41	52
6	5	8	11	17	24	34	47	64	86	113
7	6	11	17	27	41	61	89	128	180	249
9	11	21	38	69	119	198	323	512	794	1,207
10	14	29	58	110	202	357	613	1,024	1,668	2,656

	Common Stock Equivalents	Price per Share	Amount Raised
Sequoia	5,382,614	$0.37	$1,975,000
Sequoia Capital VI	4,898,180	$0.37	$1,797,252
Series A	4,436,250	$0.20	$887,250
Series B	461,930	$1.97	$910,002
Sequoia Technology Partners VI	269,130	$0.37	$98,749
Series A	243,750	$0.20	$48,750
Series B	25,380	$1.97	$49,999
Sequoia XXIV	195,000	$0.20	$39,000
Series A	195,000	$0.20	$39,000
Sequoia 1995	20,304	$1.97	$39,999

EXHIBIT 5.33   Sequoia Series A and Series B Yahoo! Investments by Fund
Source: Liquid Scenarios, Inc.

as in Chapter 6 on option pool calculations, the size of the pool reserve has a material impact on venture fund returns especially when a company realizes an "early" exit. You can occasionally find information about the size of the option pool reserve at different times in a company's history, prior to going public, by simply looking at the options note in the financial

EXHIBIT 5.34 Yahoo! Reverse Solve Exit Value That Yields $19.70 per Share

Net Exit Value by Security: as of 12/31/1996

	$447,440,018	%	$/Sh.	×	$44,976,144	%	$/Sh.	×
Series A	$102,440,000	22.89%	$19.70	×98.50	$10,400,000	23.12%	$2.00	×10.00
Conversion	$102,440,000	22.89%	$19.70	N/A	$10,400,000	23.12%	$2.00	N/A
Liquidation Preference	$1,040,000	0.23%	$0.20	N/A	$1,040,000	2.31%	$0.20	N/A
Series B	$50,000,018	11.17%	$19.70	×10.00	$5,076,144	11.29%	$2.00	×1.02
Conversion	$50,000,018	11.17%	$19.70	N/A	$5,076,144	11.29%	$2.00	N/A
Liquidation Preference.	$5,000,002	1.12%	$1.97	N/A	$5,000,002	11.12%	$1.97	N/A
Warrants	$0	0.00%	$0.00	N/A	$0	0.00%	$0.00	N/A
Common Stock	$197,000,000	43.98%	$19.70	×197.00	$20,000,000	43.98%	$2.00	×20.00
Options - Vested Pro-Rata	$98,500,000	21.99%	$19.70	N/A	$10,000,000	21.99%	$2.00	N/A
Total:	$447,940,018	100.00%	$19.70	N/A	$45,476,144	100.00%	$2.00	N/A

Source: Liquid Scenarios, Inc. Estimates from SEC filings.

Security/Class	Shares Issued	Issuable	Fully Diluted
Pre-Money Shares	10,000,000	0	10,000,000
New Anti-Dilute Shares		0	0
Options Pool Increase		5,000,000	5,000,000
Pre-Money Totals	**10,000,000**	**5,000,000**	**15,000,000**
Proposed Series A	5,200,000		5,200,000
Post-Money Capitalization	15,200,000	5,000,000	20,200,000

Multiplying the pre-money capitalization (15,000,000) by the new round/Series A price per share ($0.20), we end up with $3,000,000

EXHIBIT 5.35   Yahoo! Series A Pre-Money Estimates
Source: Liquid Scenarios, Inc.

statement. These amounts sometimes don't go far back enough for you to get an exact number for the unissued pool, though. This is because if the company is beyond the development stage, it doesn't have to disclose as many prior-period financial details. In the case of Yahoo!, we were able to get the original option pool reserve simply by looking at the notes to its financial statements since the company was so young when it went public.

Exhibit 5.37 is from the Yahoo! 1996 Annual Report to Shareholders (10K) filed with the SEC.

As discussed previously, although the capitalization table, or cap table, is probably the most relevant record of valuation data for the majority of venture-backed companies, it's not an official financial statement. As a result, it's rare, but not impossible, to find a pure capitalization table in SEC filings. You can sometimes find a partial capitalization in the following documents and exhibits to the securities filings:

- Investors Rights Agreements: Look toward the end of the document in the signature area for a "schedule of investors" or "schedule of purchasers," which in some cases includes a detailed cap table. An example follows for Yahoo. Although it doesn't include common stock or options, it does have a breakdown of exactly how many shares (pre-split) are held by each preferred investor in Yahoo. This enabled us to discover more precise estimates of the rights to investment cash flow-specific holders had at different times leading up to Yahoo's IPO.
- Venture Leasing Documents and Related Forms of Warrants: In certain filings, there are warrant agreements filed in connection with a venture lease, or look toward the end of the document in the signature area for a "schedule of investors" or "schedule of purchasers," which in some cases includes a detailed cap table.
- Stock Purchase Agreement: There have been cases where the schedule of purchasers is filed as an exhibit to the stock purchase agreement. In

EXHIBIT 5.36 Yahoo! Shares Outstanding Post Series A

	Convertible Preferred Stock		Common Stock		Additional Paid-In Capital	Accumulated Deficit	Total
	Shares	Amount	Shares	Amount			
Issuance of Common Stock in connection with the formation of the Company	–	$–	10,000,000	$–	$–	$–	$–
Issuance of Series A Convertible Preferred Stock at $0.20 per share	5,200,000	5,000	–	–	1,018,000	–	1,023,000

Source: SEC Filings.

EXHIBIT 5.37 Yahoo! Option Pool Activity 1995 and 1996

	Available for Grant	Options Outstanding		Price per Share
Shares reserved	5,000,000	–		–
Options granted	(3,454,910)	3,454,910	$0.02	$(0.20)
Options exercised	–	(189,400)		$0.02
Balance at December 31, 1995	1,545,090	3,265,510	$0.02	$(0.20)
Additional shares reserved	3,000,000	–		–
Options granted	(3,716,343)	3,716,343	$0.20	$20.88
Options canceled	281,000	(281,000)	$0.02	$18.50
Options exercised	–	(496,377)		$0.02
Balance at December 31, 1996	1,109,747	6,204,476	$0.02	$20.88

Source: Liquid Scenarios, Inc. with data imported from SEC Filings.

certain filings, there are warrant agreements filed in connection with a venture lease, or look toward the end of the document in the signature area for a "schedule of investors" or "schedule of purchasers," which in some cases includes a detailed cap table.

Exhibit 5.38 shows the Yahoo! Series A Investors from Shareholders Rights Agreement Filed with the SEC.

EXHIBIT 5.38   Yahoo! Series A Investors

Series A Investors

Name/Address	No. of Shares
Sequoia Capital VI 3000 Sand Hill Road Building 4, Suite 280 Menlo Park, California 94025	2,218,125
Sequoia Technology Partners VI	121,875
Sequoia XXIV	97,500
Fred Gibbons, Trustee of The Fred Gibbons Separate Property Trust U/T/D 2/26/93 c/o Sequoia Capital	62,500
Timothy Koogle c/o Yahoo!, Inc. 110 Pioneer Way, Suite F Mountain View, CA 94041	50,000
VLG Investments 1995 2800 Sand Hill Road Menlo Park, CA 94025	21,250
Craig W. Johnson 2800 Sand Hill Road Menlo Park, CA 94025	21,250
James L. Brock 2800 Sand Hill Road Menlo Park, CA 94025	3,750
Tae Hea Nahm 2800 Sand Hill Road Menlo Park, CA 94025	3,750
Total:	2,600,000

Source: SEC Filings.

As mentioned, the shareholder rights agreement contains lots of relationships and agreements that should impact risk for different holders and securities. In a DCF analysis, these should be reflected in the discount buildup. If you are building up a volatility input, that's also a place to reflect some of these elements. But the most obvious, and easy, place to reflect them may be in your consideration of a discount for lack of marketability and control, since many of the control rights typically available to equity holders are superseded or enhanced for different parties, based on the shareholder rights agreement.

Secondary Sale of Common and Series A to SOFTBANK

Secondary sales of private company shares have always had an important impact on valuation. Although no formal venues for these transactions existed for VC-backed companies when Yahoo was funded, they still occurred when one party had realized appreciation and needed to "take money off the table" and provide liquidity to investors and the purchasing party was looking to increase its stake in a venture it believed had upside potential with reduced risk. Recent examples of this include transactions completed by DST in its purchases of shares of Zynga stock from Foundry Group, Union Square Ventures, the founder, and Avalon Ventures. That transaction was very similar to the one done between SOFTBANK and Yahoo!'s shareholders. The economic impact of SOFTBANK's purchase of around $12 million each from both founders, $24 million total, less than 24 months after they created their project, certainly changed some lives in a way that's hard to reduce to a valuation analysis. It's fitting that SOFTBANK's founder also obtained his first fortune from an invention he created as a student (at Berkeley, California).

Sequoia, who had also sold around $12 million to SOFTBANK at the Series C price, was able to realize a true cash-on-cash multiple on its investment prior to the IPO and still have substantial shares in the company that would go on to become worth billions.

Our next analysis in this case illustrates what happens to valuation when an anticipatory secondary sale takes place in advance of an IPO. Obviously, there's the risk that the IPO doesn't happen. A venture-funded example of that is the eProcrates case.

In addition, here is an excerpt from Yahoo's 10K filed with the SEC:

In April 1996, SOFTBANK purchased certain shares of the Company's capital stock from shareholders of the Company at a price of $12.50 per share, including shares held by Mr. Filo and an affiliated trust (996,250 shares), Mr. Yang and an affiliated trust

(996,250 shares), and Mr. Koogle (100,000 shares), and entities affiliated with Sequoia Capital (996,250 shares).

During March 1996, the Company issued to SOFTBANK 5,100,000 shares of Mandatorily Redeemable Convertible Series C Preferred Stock at a price of $12.50 per share. All shares of Preferred Stock were converted into shares of the Company's Common Stock at the time of the Company's initial public offering of securities in April 1996. SOFTBANK is entitled to certain registration rights with respect to such Common Stock.

Exhibit 5.39 shows the impact of the secondary sale on potential payouts to various parties after selling, or buying, shares of Yahoo! prior to the public offering becoming effective. In today's world, these transactions would become market inputs used to value grants of options on common stock. Also, you can see from all of the illustrations here that the nature of Black-Scholes to bring the values of different classes of securities closer and closer together as they become comparable in the money due to escalating enterprise values is consistent with the real-world practice in the marketplace.

Also for reference, here are a few prices from the Yahoo! 1996 Annual Report to Shareholders (10K) filed with the SEC. This shows some of the additional appreciation realized by Softbank shortly after its private, secondary purchases of Yahoo's stock.

1996		
	High	Low
-		
Second Quarter	$33.00	$18.25
Third Quarter	$24.00	$15.75
Fourth Quarter	$22.63	$17.00

For most of the other cases, we obtained the deal terms for the preferred stock from the company's certificate of incorporation or certificate of designation for the particular series. In the case of Yahoo!, we used the notes to the financial statements, since that was the most accessible resource. Based on those notes, there was 1X liquidation preferences for each series, and Series C also had cumulative dividends.

Yahoo! Case Conclusions

By applying the basic techniques of looking at (a) who invested, (b) the cash flow potential of their securities, and finally, (c) comparing potential outcomes using various observed and imputed rates of volatility, we were able to value each security as well as get objective indications for the company as a

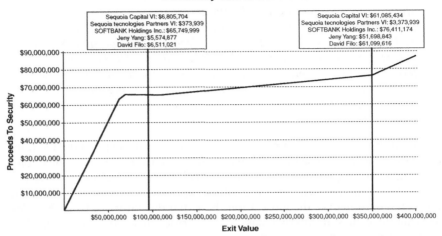

EXHIBIT 5.39   Payout Diagram Impact of Yahoo! Secondary Sales to Softbank
Source: Liquid Scenarios, Inc. with data imported from SEC filings.

Note: As an indication of volatility during first year trading, the original issue price is not reflected in "high/low," just close prices. True volatility impacting the value of the shares issued prior to the IPO, including common stock underlying the options and convertible preferred stock, would include the first-day gains above the original issue price. This can be appreciated somewhat by reviewing the disclosures in Yahoo!'s 10K filed after the company had been trading. Note that the offer price of $13 per share does not show up in the record since it was not a close price.

whole. Unlike traditional backsolve or other 409A-inspired methodologies, which make reconciling indicated values to value indications expressed by actual market participants problematic, the techniques we applied generated fair market values that were internally consistent using a market approach.

*   *   *

Before getting into the next case, Kayak.com, we are going to examine some of the other areas where valuation professionals, auditors, and venture-fund finance teams often struggle to reconcile rights to cash flow as of a given day using popular shortcuts and conventions. Particularly, we look at how the employee option pool is treated when determining payouts. We also touch upon similar conventions concerning cumulative dividends, in the Kayak.com case, as well as warrants in general. I refer to these derivatives as reasons to "D.O.W.T" venture-capital returns, which is an acronym for dividends, options, warrants, and time.

CHAPTER 6

Why You Should D.O.W.T. (Doubt) Venture Capital Returns—Option Pool Reserve

Differences in how venture capitalists, valuation professionals, underwriters, and auditors treat stock options when valuing a company's securities has a huge impact on the differences in conclusions reached by these parties.

In this chapter, we take a look real VC-backed cases to illustrate how the varying perspectives (VC, valuation professional, underwriter, and auditor) result in value conclusions that can be internally inconsistent in many cases or simply wrong in some cases. We take the various assumptions, such as considering that the ungranted (reserved) option pool is totally vested on the valuation date, that the reserved pool is ignored, and other variations, apply those to the cases presented and see how big the differences in value conclusions are in different circumstances. Being aware of these differences should allow you to D.O.W.T. (doubt) venture returns, to carefully consider the impact of assumptions concerning how dividends, options, warrants, and time impact investment cash flow. See Exhibit 6.1.

UNISSUED OPTION POOLS

In the simplest sense, there are three alternatives for how to treat the unissued option pool for purposes of venture-capital valuation:

1. Ignore the unissued pool and don't include it in any of the analysis.
2. Assume that the entire option pool is both granted and vested in its entirety at each step of the analysis.
3. Specifically estimate changes in the unissued option pool to match changes in time incorporated in the analysis.

D	**Dividends** (Cumulative)	Do They Convert (PIK)?
O	**Options**	Actual Payouts on Valuation Date?
W	**Warrants**	Underlying Preferences and Rights?
T	**Time**	As of Exit or as of Valuation Date?

EXHIBIT 6.1   Payout Error Mnemonic D.O.W.T. VC Returns
Source: Liquid Scenarios, Inc.

Why is this so important? We can take another home ownership analogy to get some insights. Imagine you and a partner invest in a home together. A clear opportunity to sell the home for $500,000 to $600,000 within one year seems apparent, so long as you can do $50,000 to $100,000 in improvements. You don't know exactly how long the improvements will take and, as a result, don't know exactly how much they will cost. You do, however, know that the total cost will be at least $50,000 prior to getting a buyer to pay $500,000 to $600,000 for the home.

Your partner agrees to bear the cost of the first $50,000 in improvements for you, and split any amount above that with you based on your pro-rata ownership share. Also, since your partner will be bearing most of the costs, and the first costs of the project, it's safe to assume he or she will get multiple detailed estimates before starting work. This is important, because in some cases an argument for not modeling detailed costs is that meaningful estimates are not easily obtainable or accessible.

Assuming you want to have an idea of the net present value of the improvements to your investment interest, should you ignore the costs of the improvements entirely, since they occur in the future and you know your partner will bear most of the cost (dilution)? Should you assume that the whole $100,000 in improvements takes place immediately and base your NPV calculations on that? Obviously, neither of those are reasonable courses of action if you really want to understand the change in the value of the investment you've already made and very well may have to add more cash to.

It's clear that with a single investment of a few hundred thousand, max, most people would like to have a reasonably arrived at estimate of the potential cost of realizing their investment return. That being the case, should funds with millions in multiple companies want to do the same? Of course, and they all do desire to manage their funds responsibly. However, truths and myths about how to properly model one of the biggest potential costs that will reduce, or enhance, their investment returns (options), are many times treated across the board with simplifying assumptions that result in erroneous conclusions.

VALUE CONCLUSION ELEMENTS IMPACTED BY OPTION POOL RESERVE ASSUMPTIONS

Each of the seven valuation elements in Exhibit 6.2 are clearly impacted by how one decides to treat the option pool reserve of a venture-capital-backed company when reaching a value conclusion. We will briefly cover how each of these areas are impacted using the examples referred to previously starting with some basic sanity tests that should be applied when reaching a value conclusion.

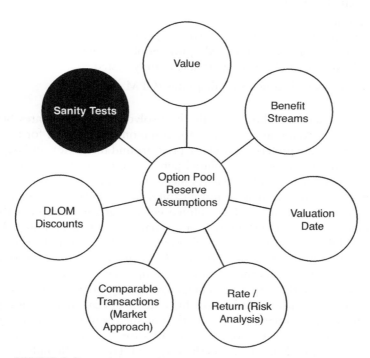

EXHIBIT 6.2   Bad Option Assumptions Cause Sanity Tests to Fail
Source: Liquid Scenarios, Inc.

Sanity Tests

We start our simple sanity tests using the Microsoft case initially, since it is one of the few venture-backed companies, other than Zynga, that has substantial earnings so early in its life. Because of those earnings, we are able to get a better sense of the impact of various option pool reserve assumptions on traditional discounted cash flow analysis as well as the current, OPM, and PWERM models. Also, since the company completed only one venture-capital financing round prior to realizing liquidity, that gives us room to include hypothetical rounds in between that would be more common for venture-backed companies. After the Microsoft case, you can easily perform a similar analysis on Excite and Google, since those companies had a lot more rounds of financing.

The Simple Version

Microsoft Corporation June 30, 1981, Hypothetical Valuation Date

Estimated Waterfall 1

Assumptions:
    Single average grant price ($0.475 per share)
    Assume the entire unissued option pool is vested
    Assume that all existing grants are fully vested

Summary benefit conclusion diagrams (OPM and current)

As illustrated in Exhibit 6.3, the backsolve method generates $0.42/ share before marketability discounts for common, $0.50/share for the preferred (which is the preferred purchase price around that date), and payouts that match the estimated fully diluted percentage ownership of Microsoft Corporation as of June 30, 1981. As mentioned previously, most venture-fund analysts, and also many venture-capital fund CFOs and finance staff, would assume that since the fully diluted percentage ownership equals the percentage payoff chart in the lower-right-hand corner of Exhibit 6.3, the model is valid. But as you learned earlier in this book, the complete opposite of that assumption is true, especially just following a new round of venture financing, as is the case in the Microsoft example here above.

The way that the target percentage ownership of the preferred stock investors matches fully diluted ownership and payout calculations using this simplifying assumption with respect to the unissued option pool may explain why this method has been popular with VCs for so long. However, if we were to assume that Microsoft sold the very next day for $100 million, none of the percentage payouts in our waterfall would be realized. Particularly, the sole venture capitalist in the deal, Technology Venture Investors, or

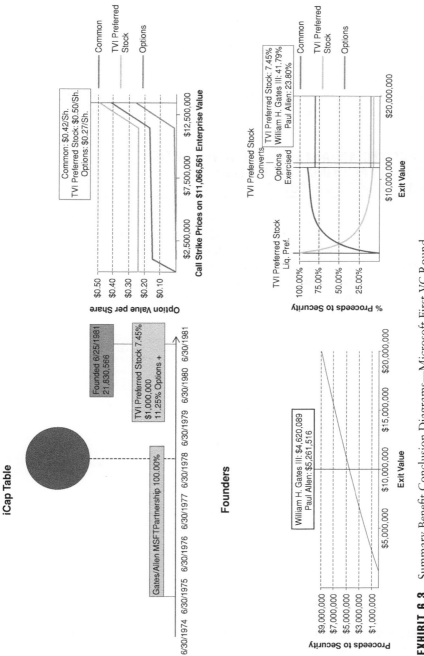

EXHIBIT 6.3 Summary Benefit Conclusion Diagrams—Microsoft First VC Round
Source: Liquid Scenarios, Inc.

TVI, would get something greater than 7.5%, and it's highly unlikely that it would be willing to give some of that excess to future employees of the acquiring company. We can easily illustrate this by changing the date to July 1, 1981, and comparing the proceeds that parties would receive based on the assumption that all options (granted and reserved) were vested (top diagrams) opposed to the actual payouts that would occur based on actual company sale the very next day (the lower charts). See Exhibit 6.4.

PERCEIVED ADVANTAGE—UNISSUED OPTION POOL SIMPLIFYING ASSUMPTION: VERY EASY TO CALCULATE

IF 100% of option pool is assumed granted and vested, AND 100% of granted options are assumed vested, THEN payout percentages in waterfalls and payout diagrams will equal fully diluted ownership percentages for each preferred class and the fully diluted target ownership percentage of the most recent round closed (assuming no warrants and no debt are outstanding as of the valuation date).

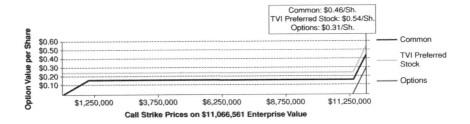

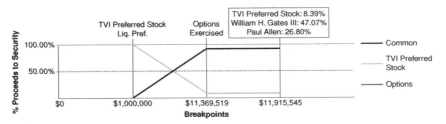

EXHIBIT 6.4   Impact of Common Simplifying Option Assumption on Bill Gates
Source: Liquid Scenarios, Inc.

Different parties explain the rationale behind this assumption, especially with respect to financial reporting of venture-capital funds to the insurance companies, pension funds, and other institutional limited partners that have to rely upon these assumptions, indirectly, for their reporting to plan holders, states, universities, public servant retirement funds, and so forth. These are the most common explanations I've heard. . .

"Assuming that the entire option pool is vested, even if it hasn't been issued yet, is conservative, since it will likely take 100% of the option pool being used in order to get the company to the point where it would be attractive to an acquirer." Obviously there's some merit to this argument. However, as you look at it closer you realize that it fails on several fronts.

First, what is the exercise price that's being assumed for the options that are fully vested? In the previous iteration of our sample case, we used an average exercise price of $0.475 under both scenarios for consistency (the simplifying assumption that the entire unissued pool vested the next day, and the more realistic assumption that only those options that were granted would dilute other holders from proceeds).

The second problem is that if we are assuming that the entire option pool will be needed to get the company to the point of an exit, where's our assumption concerning the additional financing required to get the company to that exit? Is leaving that out also conservative?

Another major problem with this logic is suggesting that it is in fact conservative. In some cases, it results in more value being allocated to common stock, which is unrealistic, and in other cases it results in more of a company's value being allocated to preferred stock or options. There are more variables at play to determine if it's conservative (results in a relatively lower value conclusion for the security you are valuing) or aggressive (results in a relatively higher value conclusion for the security you are valuing).

"That's just the way it's done in the industry. It's been that way since the beginning and it's not going to change." There's no way to prove that this has, in fact, or hasn't been done, since the concept of reserve a pool for employee options doesn't pre-date the modern venture-capital industry. That being said, there's no doubt that it's a popular approach at venture funds. In a world where the methods of reporting IRRs and residual fund values to fund investors simply involve reporting the amount invested (the cost method), not an estimate of the upward change in value, you could also argue that the option pool doesn't matter with respect to what the limited partners are relying on. Again, however, the industry hasn't lived in such an environment for several decades, since many firms routinely wrote up investments based on new up rounds and wrote down investments based on

down rounds or other significant events clearly indicating an impairment of some kind. In both of these cases changes to the option pool are routine and have been for some time. As a result, failure to properly consider such a potentially dilutive, or anti-dilutive, security can come at a very high cost in terms of understanding the value of the security a fund actually holds.

"The option pool isn't significant (material) to the calculations." Ironically, I've heard this from almost every group, to varying degrees. Primarily from VCs investing partners, VC analysts, and, surprisingly, even some valuation professionals. As we've illustrated in the first of many examples, this is simply not true. If a 20% difference in rights to proceeds is not significant, in a business where IRR is a measuring stick for the limited partners making the investments, it's hard to argue that even 5% or 10% is not material when you can account for it simply by making a more realistic assumption.

Most importantly, the significance of the option pool can't be substantively opined upon until one has does at least a few sanity tests similar to the one we did on the previous page.

So, as you can see from the preceding example, assuming that the entire reserve option pool has been vested as of a date when it's definitively known not to be vested can cost millions of dollars in fees due to incorrectly achieved, or not met, hurdle rates. More importantly, the inherent value of an investment and the urgency of a sale offer at a given price are substantially reduced by this popular practice. If that's not enough, the impact on audited fund values, and therefore the information limited parties receive from the fund and rely on to make additional investments in new funds, become distorted due to this process. Next, we'll take a look at the other extreme: ignoring the option pool reserve in its entirety.

Ignoring the Unissued Option Pool

Microsoft Corporation June 30, 1981, Hypothetical Valuation Date

Estimated Waterfall 2

Assumptions:
　　Single average grant price ($0.475 per share)
　　Ignore the entire unissued option pool (remove from model)
　　Assume that all existing grants are fully vested

Summary benefit conclusion diagrams (OPM and current)

In this example, we started by using the same backsolved enterprise equity value, $11,066,561, as illustrated in the prior sample, which assumed 100% of the unissued option pool was issued and vested immediately. As illustrated in Exhibit 6.5, using that same total equity value we end up with a substantially higher value allocated to our common stock, $0.46 per

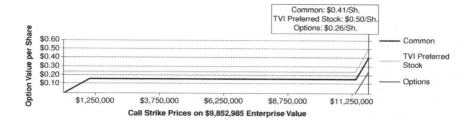

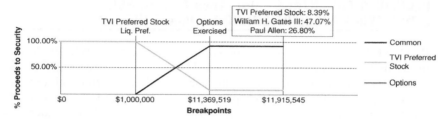

EXHIBIT 6.5 Impact of Ignoring Unissued Option Pool on Bill Gates, Paul Allen, and TVI
Source: Liquid Scenarios, Inc.

share before marketability discounts for common assuming 0% of the unissued pool is outstanding versus $0.42/share assuming that 100% of the unissued pool was vested.

Without further information, it's clear that ignoring the unissued option pool effectively increases the hypothetical proceeds available for common stock. This means that the value of the common stock we conclude, regardless of what valuation methodology or approach we use, will be higher with this assumption than it is if we assume that some of the unissued option pool reducing our return at certain points in time.

If the goal is to minimize the intrinsic value of the common stock for tax purposes, as some valuation professionals believe, then ignoring the unissued option pool might be at odds with that objective. If the goal is to provide a reasonable, conservative, and defensible position of the common stock value, then it appears that assuming 100% of the unissued pool has been issued would work against that goal, since the value conclusion for common stock would be understated on most dates. Using either of these prevalent simplifying assumptions results in conclusions that yield unanticipated variations in value conclusion, depending on the date of the valuation and its proximity to the latest option pool reserve being authorized.

So why are these simplifying assumptions so popular? In both cases valuation practitioners, venture capitalists, and even auditors using these methods argue that they are less subjective than having to estimate changes in the option pool at a more detailed level. The real-world cost of the simplifying assumption can be illustrated by simply applying the backsolve method to determine an enterprise value for Microsoft on June 1, 1981, with the sometimes popular valuation assumption that none of the unissued option pool will impact the benefit flows to common stock, preferred stock, or other issued securities of Microsoft.

PERCEIVED ADVANTAGE—UNISSUED OPTION POOL SIMPLIFYING ASSUMPTION: NO ESTIMATE NEEDED

IF 0% of the option pool is assumed granted and vested, AND 100% of granted options are assumed vested, THEN payout percentages in waterfalls and payout diagrams will be higher than the fully diluted ownership percentages for each preferred class and the fully diluted target ownership percentage of the most recent round closed under every scenario.

As you can see in Exhibit 6.6, ignoring Microsoft's unissued option pool entirely on July 1, 1981, results in a backsolve enterprise value, based on

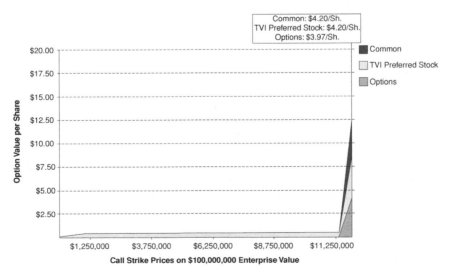

EXHIBIT 6.6   Bad Option Pool Assumptions Cause Backsolve to Fail
Source: Liquid Scenarios, Inc.

the preferred stock market value on June 30, of around $9.9 million. This is a full 10% lower than the approximately $11.1 million backsolved value we generated assuming that 100% of the unissued option pool had actually been issued and vested. See Exhibit 6.7.

Sanity Test—Increasing the Enterprise Value Estimate

Another quick sanity test of these popular assumptions is to have an equally large exit value—perhaps 100X the last-round proceeds—and see what OPM value we end up with for common stock under both assumptions. So, for instance, Exhibit 6.8 ignores the option pool and assumes a company equity value of $100 million on July 1, 1981.

As you can see in Exhibit 6.8, these assumptions result in an estimated OPM value of $4.20 per share for common stock.

In Exhibit 6.9, we kept the assumed company equity value at $100 million and assumed the same date, but assumed that 100% of the unissued option pool was both issued and vested on that date. The result of changing that simple assumption is a value conclusion of just $3.75 per share for the common stock before discounts, or roughly a value of $81 million for Microsoft's outstanding common shares, $7.5 million for outstanding preferred shares, and the remaining $10MM allocated largely to options that were not yet granted. This implies that the ungranted options were worth more than the preferred stock actually outstanding. As you can see, these assumptions result in an estimated OPM value of $4.20 per share for common stock.

Is the difference of more than $10 million in common value material? Exhibit 6.10 assumes 100% of the unissued pool is vested, while Exhibit 6.11 assumes 0% of the unissued pool has a claim on equity.

If for some reason you have to choose between one of these two simplifying assumptions, which method is better? The answer depends on timing. As Exhibit 6.12 illustrations, you can still generate a perfect waterfall and current date OPM without even knowing the size of the unissued option pool. However, if you want to create a lattice, or compound OPM, take into account future financing rounds, model claims on future expected cash flows or terminal values, or otherwise look to the future capital structure of the company, you can't do so accurately without modeling the unissued option pool.

As a result, if you believe that a sale or liquidation of the company is imminent, then ignoring the unissued option pool is the better simplifying assumption of the two. If you don't believe a sale or liquidation of the company is imminent, and the unissued option pool is relatively small as a percentage of fully diluted shares (perhaps 1% to 2%), then assuming that 100% of the unissued pool is actually granted and vested might be a better simplifying assumption in some cases.

EXHIBIT 6.7 Microsoft OPM Backsolve with Typical Option Pool Assumption

	Total	TVI Preferred Stock Liq. Pref.	Common Participates	Options Exercised	TVI Preferred Stock Converts
Breakpoints		Breakpoint 1	Breakpoint 2	Breakpoint 3	Breakpoint 4
Strike Price (K)		$0	$1,000,000	$11,369,519	$11,915,545
BEV Estimate (S)	$9,852,985	$9,852,985	$9,852,985	$9,852,985	$9,852,985
Breakpoint Call Value	$9,852,985	$486,554	$3,139,452	$106,438	$6,120,541
Call Value at Floor		$9,852,985	$9,366,430	$6,226,979	$6,120,541
Term in Years (t)		5.00	5.00	5.00	5.00
Risk-Free Rate (r)		13.95%	13.95%	13.95%	13.95%
Volatility		60.00%	60.00%	60.00%	60.00%
d1		20.06	2.90	1.08	1.05
d2		18.72	1.55	−0.26	−0.29
N(d1)		1.00	1.00	0.86	0.85
N(d2)		1.00	0.94	0.40	0.38
S * N(d1)		$9,852,985	$9,834,359	$8,481,622	$8,403,802
K * e^-rt		$0	$497,828	$5,660,069	$5,931,896
Times N(d2)		$0	$467,929	$2,254,643	$2,283,261
C Value at Ceiling		$9,366,430	$6,226,979	$6,120,541	$0
Common	$8,850,242	$0	$3,139,452	$106,387	$5,604,403
TVI Preferred Stock	$1,000,000	$486,554	$0	$0	$513,446
Options	$2,743	$0	$0	$51	$2,692

Source: Liquid Scenarios, Inc.

Name	Test
Chart	Default Breakpoints
Term	5.00 Years
Risk Free Rate	13.95%
Volatility	60.00%
BEV Estimate	$100,000,000

Back Solve Last Round

Last Round	Common
Adjusted Issued Price	$0.1700000
OPM Value Per Share	$4.1955816
Marketability Discount (DLOM)	16.19%
Control Discount (DLOC)	0.00%
OPM Value Net Of Discounts	$3.5163483
Implied Enterprise Value	

Back Solve

EXHIBIT 6.8   Using Extremely High Exit Value as Sanity Test for OPM
Source: Liquid Scenarios, Inc.

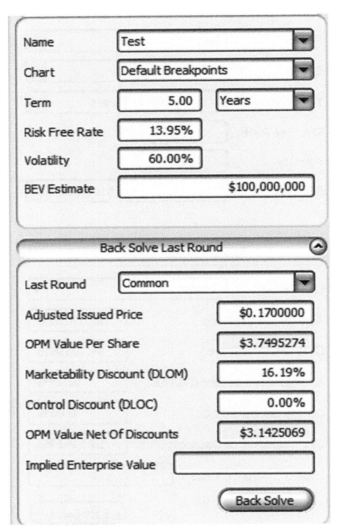

EXHIBIT 6.9 Using Extremely High Exit Value as Sanity Test for OPM
Source: Liquid Scenarios, Inc.

EXHIBIT 6.10 OPM Payouts and Backsolved Microsoft Value

	Total	TVI Preferred Stock Liq. Pref.	Common Participates	Options Exercised	TVI Preferred Stock Converts
Breakpoints		Breakpoint 1	Breakpoint 2	Breakpoint 3	Breakpoint 4
Strike Price (K)		$0	$1,000,000	$11,369,519	$11,990,783
BEV Estimate (S)	$100,000,000	$100,000,000	$100,000,000	$100,000,000	$100,000,000
Breakpoint Call Value	$100,000,000	$497,760	$5,008,137	$286,522	$94,207,581
Common	$81,854,307	$0	$5,008,137	$251,702	$76,594,468
TVI Preferred Stock	$7,514,937	$497,760	$0	$0	$7,017,176
Options	$10,630,756	$0	$0	$34,820	$10,595,936

Source: Liquid Scenarios, Inc.

EXHIBIT 6.11 OPM Payouts and Backsolved Microsoft Value

	Total	TVI Preferred Stock Liq. Pref.	Common Participates	Options Exercised	TVI Preferred Stock Converts
Breakpoints		Breakpoint 1	Breakpoint 2	Breakpoint 3	Breakpoint 4
Strike Price (K)		$0	$1,000,000	$11,369,519	$11,915,290
BEV Estimate (S)	$100,000,000	$100,000,000	$100,000,000	$100,000,000	$100,000,000
Breakpoint Call Value	$100,000,000	$497,760	$5,008,137	$251,796	$94,242,307
Common	$91,591,923	$0	$5,008,137	$251,793	$86,331,993
TVI Preferred Stock	$8,407,037	$497,760	$0	$0	$7,909,277
Options	$1,040	$0	$0	$3	$1,037

Source: Liquid Scenarios, Inc.

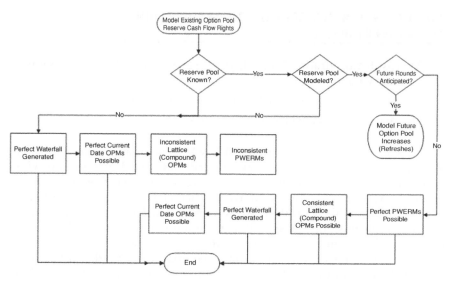

EXHIBIT 6.12   Value Indication Impact Flow Chart for Option Assumptions
Source: Liquid Scenarios, Inc.

Time Invalidates Both Simplifying Assumptions

As we move the date from the day immediately after a financing round to some other future date, the distorting impact of these popular simplifying assumptions regarding the option pool become even more pronounced. As you saw previously, unless a sale and liquidation of the company is imminent, a forward-looking calculation is required to properly arrive at a value conclusion. As you look into the future of a venture-funded company, there are few things you can project with a great deal of accuracy. However, one of the things you can project reasonably and rather simply is granting and vesting of shares that are in the unissued option pool.

In the sanity tests, we were able to demonstrate rather easily that our value conclusions under the simplest conditions were extremely sensitive to the two most popular assumptions concerning the option pool. If we move the date out under both examples by just one year, the results continue to vary significantly for each of the valuation and allocation approaches we've illustrated thus far in the Microsoft case. Before showing the impact of these assumptions on other valuation approaches, we will take a quick look at how these popular shortcuts can cost millions of dollars to limited partners (pension funds and endowments), employees, venture-fund general partners, responsible reporting parties (auditors, tax accountants, company officers), and founders.

IMPACT ON PARTIES RELYING ON ASSUMPTIONS OF VC INVESTMENTS

Microsoft Corporation June 30, 1982, versus June 30, 1981 Hypothetical Valuation Dates

Assuming 100% of unissued pool is granted and vested

Summary benefit conclusion tables (OPM)

As you can see from Exhibit 6.13, when we assume that 100% of the unissued option pool has been granted and vested, we end up with nearly the same value allocation today as we do one year from now. As a result, the value conclusions we draw for each class of stock remain fixed, which is highly unlikely for the reasons we mentioned earlier in this chapter. The impact of this popular simplifying assumption on some of the parties reviewing, distributing, and relying on this information can be substantial. Next, we briefly review the impact on several parties that either develop or rely on these types of simplifying assumptions concerning venture-capital investments.

Venture-Capital General Partners (GPs)

For general partners, assuming 100% of the unissued option pool has a constant claim on equity directly impacts their fund's compensation, its progress toward meeting return hurdles, and, potentially, the ability to distribute gains on winning exits to partners that were responsible for those gains. We will discuss this aspect further as we explore the other valuation approaches impacted by the popular simplifying convention.

Venture-Capital Limited Partners (LPs)

A venture-capital fund that assumes 100% of the unissued employee option pool has vested in the Microsoft case, where only one round of preferred stock has been issued, would understate its returns in 1981, 1982 and 1983, 1984 and 1985. This would cause limited partners to report lower returns from the venture fund invested in Microsoft that followed this methodology and lower IRRs at each period. When management fees were taken into account, and in the absence of an outside round, it's possible that limited partners could in fact be showing a loss on this fund, due to management fees and the failure to receive cash flow.

Obviously, in the case of a fund that had invested in Microsoft this would lead to poor decision making by its LPs concerning future allocations to that

EXHIBIT 6.13 Impact of Differences in Time on Indicated Value

1982 t=4	Total	TVI Preferred Stock Liq. Pref.	Common Participates	Options Exercised	TVI Preferred Stock Converts
Breakpoints		Breakpoint 1	Breakpoint 2	Breakpoint 3	Breakpoint 4
Strike Price (K)		$0	$1,000,000	$11,369,519	$11,990,783
BEV Estimate (S)	$100,000,000	$100,000,000	$100,000,000	$100,000,000	$100,000,000
Breakpoint Call Value	$100,000,000	$572,339	$5,831,422	$338,149	$93,258,091
Common	$81,950,972	$0	$5,831,422	$297,055	$75,822,495
TVI Preferred Stock	$7,518,791	$572,339	$0	$0	$6,946,452
Options	$10,530,237	$0	$0	$41,094	$10,489,143

1981 t=5	Total	TVI Preferred Stock Liq. Pref.	Common Participates	Options Exercised	TVI Preferred Stock Converts
Breakpoints		Breakpoint 1	Breakpoint 2	Breakpoint 3	Breakpoint 4
Strike Price (K)		$0	$1,000,000	$11,369,519	$11,990,783
BEV Estimate (S)	$100,000,000	$100,000,000	$100,000,000	$100,000,000	$100,000,000
Breakpoint Call Value	$100,000,000	$497,760	$5,008,137	$286,522	$94,207,581
Common	$81,854,307	$0	$5,008,137	$251,702	$76,594,468
TVI Preferred Stock	$7,514,937	$497,760	$0	$0	$7,017,176
Options	$10,630,756	$0	$0	$34,820	$10,595,936

Source: Liquid Scenarios, Inc.

particular VC fund and venture-capital investments in general. Similarly, if all VC funds were using a similar assumption in how they accounted for the unissued option pool, pension funds would erroneously be estimating their funded status, expected returns, and related assumptions.

Pension Fund Estimates

Pension fund estimates, especially those of large pension funds covering civil servants, can have a global impact for many reasons. Perhaps the most direct impact of public pension fund estimates is on how state and local governments tax their citizens to meet projected benefit obligations of retirement plans that have been used to retain public servants that might otherwise have to seek more competitive employment opportunities. A less obvious but equally important impact is on the market for all securities globally, across all asset classes. To see how a very small change in pension plan assumptions can have a massive impact on conclusions and investing patterns, look at the following letter from the Center for State and Local Government Excellence.

Why should decision makers care about the debate between actuaries and economists over what the appropriate discount rate should be to value pension liabilities? As Alicia H. Munnell, Richard W. Kopcke, Jean Pierre Aubrey, and Laura Quinby write in this issue brief, the stakes are high. They also argue that the debate over the discount rate should be separated from decisions over how to fund pension liabilities and how to invest pension assets.

What caught my eye was the CalPERS pension history they cite. In 1997, CalPERS reported that assets equaled 111 percent of liabilities using the traditional actuarial model. That upbeat report led the California legislature to enhance the benefits of both current and future employees. The legislature reduced the retirement age, increased benefit accrual rates, and shortened the salary base for benefits to the final year's salary.

If CalPERS liabilities had been valued at the riskless rate in 1997, the plan would have been 76 percent funded. The authors suggest that a riskless rate of valuing liabilities would minimize the temptation for elected officials to become overly generous in good financial times and would better protect funding levels when there is a downturn.

> *The authors acknowledge that reducing the discount rate from about 8 percent today to 5 percent under the riskless rate would raise new policy questions:*
>
> ▪ *Should the amortization period be increased from 30 years to a longer period?*
> ▪ *Are changes needed in retirement ages and other provisions for new employees?*
> ▪ *How would plans pay for increases in their required payment for normal costs?*
>
> *These are important issues to consider as governments grapple with financial pressures and public skepticism.*
> *The Center for State and Local Government Excellence gratefully acknowledges financial support from the ICMA Retirement Corporation to undertake this research project.*
> *Elizabeth K. Kellar*
> *President and CEO*
> *Center for State and Local Government Excellence*

Although the context of that analysis was across a much larger base of assets, and venture-capital investments account for only a portion of public pension funds assets, it's clear that a recursive relationship exists. So when you change one variable slightly, the assumptions, conclusions, and decisions that result can change substantially. You saw earlier in this book that when a high discount rate is applied to a future negative cash flow (such as a liability being settled), the conclusion can be erroneously interpreted as suggesting that a given investment opportunity has a higher present value than is the case. That's similar to the arguments being made in the letter above concerning how pension funds discount their future obligations. Applying too high a discount rate to future obligations can, in some cases, have a bigger impact than applying too high a return estimate to current investments.

Officers and Tax Advisors

For officers of the company, and tax advisors, the risks are that the amounts disclosed to investors, as compensation expense in the case of financial reporting or as fair value in the case of tax calculations, are not properly stated. If it's assumed that 100% of the option pool has been vested and the

Name	Test
Chart	Default Breakpoints
Term	5.00	Years
Risk Free Rate	13.95%
Volatility	60.00%
BEV Estimate	$11,066,561

Last Round Test

Last Round	Common
Adjusted Issued Price	$0.17
OPM Value Per Share	$0.42
Marketability Discount (DLOM)	16.19%
Control Discount (DLOC)	0.00%
OPM Value Net Of Discounts	$0.35
Implied Enterprise Value	

Test

Name	Test
Chart	Default Breakpoints
Term	5.00	Years
Risk Free Rate	13.95%
Volatility	60.00%
BEV Estimate	$9,852,985

Last Round Test

Last Round	Common
Adjusted Issued Price	$0.17
OPM Value Per Share	$0.41
Marketability Discount (DLOM)	16.19%
Control Discount (DLOC)	0.00%
OPM Value Net Of Discounts	$0.34
Implied Enterprise Value	

Test

EXHIBIT 6.14 Volatility and Discount Percentage Remain Constant—but Value Changes
Source: Liquid Scenarios, Inc.

valuation date is close to the date of the option pool creation, then the fair value of the common stock will be understated and compensation expense will be understated also. This means that for 409A tax calculations, the grant prices for options, and their assumed fair values, will be understated, which is not conservative for tax purposes. In the case of tax reporting, this risk is partially offset by the use of rather heavy discounts, such as DLOMs.

In Exhibit 6.14 we calculate a discount for lack of marketability using the protective put methodology discussed previously. As you can see, the discount applied is not sensitive to the changes in the total equity value estimate. As a result, when we generated a backsolve enterprise value of $11.07 million 100% of the reserved (unissued) option pool had vested, we ended up with a DLOM of 16.19%. We got the same discount when we ignored the unissued option pool entirely.

In the prior examples, the discount for lack of marketability (DLOM) was calculated using a protective put. To do this, we set the strike price (K) and underlying OPM value net (S) to the backsolved enterprise values we obtained previously, $11,066,561 for in the case where the unissued option pool was ignored and $9,852,985 in the case where 100% of the unissued option pool was assumed to be vested. So in the former case we set the strike price, K= $11,066,561 and the stock or total company equity value S=$11,066,561. In the latter case, where 100% of the unissued option pool was assumed vested, we set the strike price, K= $9,852,985 and the stock or total company equity value S=$9,852,985. In both cases, volatility, risk-free rate, and expected term were set equal to the active model, 3%, 60%, and 3 respectively.

With these inputs, the final step was simply to reverse, more or less, the default Black-Scholes calculation (which is a call option currently) so it becomes a put option. So we applied a formula with $P = Ke^{-rt} N(-d2) - SN(-d1)$. Dividing the resulting answers by their respective backsolved company equity values, $11,066,561 for the case where the unissued option pool was ignored and $9,852,985 in the case where 100% of the unissued option pool was assumed to be vested, generates the same percentage discount for lack of marketability (DLOM) of approximately 16.19%. Changing the expected exit horizon, variable t, from five years to three years increases the DLOM percentage, from 16.19% to 18.15%, but that percentage stays the same regardless of which of the two simplifying unissued option pool assumptions we use.

*   *   *

We could conclude that neither of these simplifying assumptions has an impact on the discount applied. If that were true, then the impact of these shortcut methods might appear more significant with respect to common stock than with respect to preferred stock being valued. However, as we expand our analysis of option pool reserves to other valuation approaches and techniques, such as the Market Approach and the PWERM, it will become clear that the option pool assumptions we make impact both the gross values and the net values concluded for common stock.

To illustrate this, we look at another case in addition to the Microsoft case using a company that had multiple rounds of funding, and multiple quarters of negative cash flow, prior to its liquidity event.

CHAPTER 7

If Valuation Can't Make You Money, Do You Really Need It?

Learning Practical Applications from Kayak.com

For many people, truly understanding a complex topic is best achieved by experiencing it first-hand. With the previous cases and methods presented thus far, you should be able to do the following:

1. Make more money *as an investor* by recognizing potential valuation conclusions that create opportunities for arbitrage and "abnormal" profits.
2. Make more money *as a practitioner* by better appreciating the perspectives of the market participants, both hypothetical ones and actual ones, and adjusting valuation inputs and methods to enlighten the parties that depend on your insights and expertise.
3. Make more money *as a founder, employee, or executive* by ensuring that you and your team (be it your managers, your family, your advisors, or others who influence your decisions) have several ways of comparing the "fairness" of compensation awards based on the way known risks and expected benefits have been distilled into an exercise price, or value that determines the grant price of your options.

As discussed, the vast majority of VCs, CFOs, founders, attorneys, angels, and other parties that come into contact with a 409A valuation, the most popular form of an independent venture-backed company appraisal, believe they've received a compliance-driven commodity. Most have indicated that they essentially see 409A valuations as a prophylactic against severe tax penalties and, to a lesser degree, against financial statement auditor irritability.

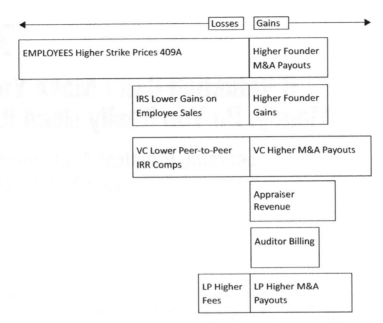

EXHIBIT 7.1   The Economic Impact of 409A Is Not the Valuation
and Audit Fees
Source: Liquid Scenarios, Inc.

Interestingly enough, each of those parties has made and lost at least $10 billion in each of the four years since 409A became effective. During that same period, valuation professionals may have made around $240MM in fees, while auditors may have billed around 50% of that amount ($120MM) to review the 409A work and comply with FAS123R and SAS 101. Even after reading this book, the alphabet soup needed to describe these relationships is hard to digest, so Exhibit 7.1 should be helpful in clarifying the winners and losers of 409A and fair value pronouncements.

As you read the venture-backed IPO cases here and apply the techniques covered, it's important to remember that there's not necessarily a single "right" answer. However, there is always, in every case, an opportunity to optimize your investment outcomes by better understanding the perceptions of reality implied by using the inputs you've come to learn in this book versus those others might apply. If you wield a hammer without any expertise, it's still a hammer and will likely get you further toward your goal of driving a nail into something than using your hand or a rock for the same task. Similarly, if you use the "financial hammer" described in this book, you will find that converting the promise of future rewards into a cash value today will become a lot easier for you than it will be for those who continue to use their hands or rocks for the same task. Before we introduce the next set

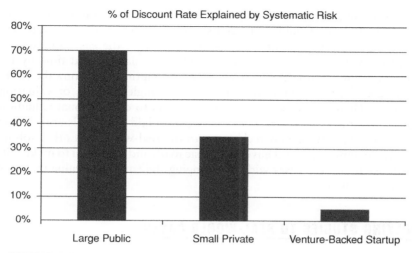

EXHIBIT 7.2   The Equity Risk Premium/Systematic Risk Is Less Important Than Volatility
Source: Liquid Scenarios, Inc.

of cases, you should take a look at the "financial hammer" again in light of what we've discussed concerning two small and simple variables that we've shown to have very large impacts on value indications and conclusions.

You will recall that the two elements of the hammer are r, the required or expected return, and t, time or the term. You may also recall that I said if $1.r\hat{}t$ is the "financial hammer," then the benefit stream, often cash flows, are the nails. We also discussed how valuation professionals will "build up" a discount rate. For most publicly traded companies, the "market rate of return" component is a substantial portion of that discount rate. For most non-venture-backed private companies, the highest single component of risk is still the ERP (equity risk premium), industry risk premium, and size premium, although company-specific risks tend to be much higher than they would be for small publicly traded companies. For venture-backed companies, the highest single component of risk is rarely systematic risk, unless the company is on the eve of an IPO. Looking at the three bars in the chart of Exhibit 7.2, you see the following:

- Public company: Most risk (50%+) is systematic/ERP
- Non VC private company: Substantial risk (35%+) is ERP
- VC backed company: Highest risk is not ERP but driven by volatility and based on t

In order to apply this same methodology to venture-backed companies, using traditional approaches, the company-specific risk component would have to become the largest component of risk. This substantial difference reflects the failure of publicly traded securities to match the volatility and return requirements of venture investments. One of the easy solutions to this problem that I proposed is to "build up" volatility and time by focusing on round-to-round dynamics versus attempting to capture the entire investing cycle, from cradle to grave, with a single formula or valuation approach. Therein lies most of the adjustments to conventional valuation approaches and industry practices that we have laid out in this book. Now it's time to apply these new techniques to the real-world cases that follow and identify how you could have used basic math and valuation to make millions in each of these cases without changing the enterprise value that was ultimately realized.

APPLYING STUDIES TO REAL-WORLD CASES

The following cases include one extended case, Kayak.com, and a number of quick cases that simply include the "rapid models." Cases other than Kayak.com are available at www.wiley.com/go/venturecapitalvaluation for additional review. The Kayak.com case allows you to apply the techniques shared in this book as follows:

1. Kayak.com Eyeball/Napkin Models: Just looking at pricing information draw some conclusions about who lost and made money based on valuation errors.
   a. Here, we simply array price history for each security to the extent it is available.
   b. If you've read more than one of the previous chapters, you should be able to draw meaningful, actionable conclusions without getting a calculator out.
   c. After presenting the raw data, we review how you could have applied the techniques and insights shared in this book in your analysis of the pricing patterns.
2. Kayak.com Rapid Models/Carver Deal Term Test—Certificate Plus Press Releases: For use when you have access/rights to little or no detailed company information.
   a. Using the Certificate of Incorporation and data from press releases, Crunchbase, and secondary marketplaces, such as SecondMarket and Sharespost, we demonstrate how to very quickly generate value indications that will be either equal to or superior to those discussed in the registration statements of Kayak.com and the other case companies in this chapter.

    b. First, we present the unmarked source document (the certificate of incorporation) so you can identify the key characteristics needed to run the Carver Deal Term Test (which we mentioned in Chapter 1 and demonstrated for Facebook) and determine relative value under an M&A scenario.

    c. After that, we review a version of the certificate that I've marked up, which highlights the key attributes you should have captured to create a quick and accurate Deal Term Test.

    d. Finally, we run a full set of venture-capital valuation calculations (OPMs, PWERMS, and CWERMS) to compare the outcomes to those presented in the company's MD&A section.

3. In this case, we generate the same models (OPM, PWERM, CWERM) we used in the rapid models, but using the more detailed (and accurate) information that major investors and valuation professionals generally have access to.

    This involves using the official sources of "who, what, when, why and how much" for Kayak.com as opposed to just the certificate and publicly released or crowd sourced data, including Kayak's...

    i. Shareholder rights agreement
    ii. Audited financial statements (balance sheets, income statements, etc.) and related notes
    iii. Option plans
    iv. Options grants
    v. Employment agreements
    vi. Founder repurchase agreements
    vii. Restricted stock purchase agreements
    viii. Specific secondary sales
    ix. Debt schedules
    x. Other information as needed

The readily observable inputs to Portfolio Company (PCo.) values were given in Chapter 5, but here they are again to refresh your memory as we use them in the following cases:

- Who (existing VCs were, new investors are, IRRs/stages, GPs)
- What (security/rights they purchased, how does that mix impact their target future returns and present returns/residual value?)
- When (timing of prior financing transactions versus expected timing of future transactions, expected burn rate/runway)
- Why (pro-rata with outside lead? secondary sale?)
- How much (size of the rounds, magnitude of the required returns, implications on future volatility)?

EXHIBIT 7.3   Kayak.com per Share Transaction History Implies Its Own Volatility

Date(s)	Common Stock	Options	Preferred
1/14/2004	$0.001		
3/14/2004	N/A	$1.00	$1.00
11/14/2004		$1.40	$2.00
2/14/2005		$1.40	$1.40
4/14/2006		$1.40	$1.40
5/14/2006		$2.98	$2.98
5/14/2007		$5.00–$16.50	$20.73
4/2008	$15.50		

Source: Liquid Scenarios, Inc.

Kayak.com Eyeball/Napkin Model—Price History

Combining some of the techniques discussed previously, and using nothing more than the history of option, common, and preferred stock pricing below, you should be able to rather quickly see how parties may have lost or made millions as a result of not understanding valuation.

Where do you see opportunities to make (or lose) money based on the pricing in Exhibit 7.3?

Two-Minute Analysis   Let's make a quick analysis of the pricing patterns in Exhibit 7.3. Options were grossly overpriced in Q1 2004, by at least 900% based on conventional practices at the time of issuance (which means probably overpriced by 200% to 300% based on prevailing 409A practices today). This is accretive to venture investors and founders, although neither party wants to make money that way, in the vast majority of cases.

Further, the $2.00 per share February 2005 preferred financing round was price dilutive (a down round) to the November 2004 preferred financing round. Whereas the preferred stockholders would have protection against the dilutive issuance, any option grants would have no official price protection. I say no "official" protection for two reasons. One, the simple fact that investors are participating at the lower price (continuing to fund the company) is a great sign with respect to investment prospects.[1] Similarly, in cases where the impact on grantees is substantial, repricing grants is not uncommon.

---

[1]See the article *"Down Rounds + Cramdowns = 2009 Top VC Exits?"* at http://vator.tv/news/2009-08-13-downrounds-cramdowns-2009-s-top-vc-exits.

Ultimately, the options issued in early 2004 were in the money by at least 15X, which makes it easy for a grantee to forget (or not recognize) that they were overpriced to begin with. That being said, had they been priced in a manner consistent with most other venture-backed companies at the time, they would have been in the money by 150X, that's a 15,000% unrealized gain (think Facebook Series A investment returns) versus a 1500% unrealized gain (think Zynga Series A investment returns). See Exhibit 7.4.

In this particular case, simply looking at the price pattern is enough to draw meaningful and actionable valuation-related conclusions, without answering the question of "Who" or drilling down further into the deal terms. In the next analysis, we go further into the deal terms, which, as we have emphasized in the book, are critical.

As previously demonstrated, there are some conclusions/benefits that can be obtained with little more than pricing history, including:

- Identified opportunity for optionees to earn 15,000% versus 1,500%
- Identified multiple instances of options being grossly overvalued
- Noting the potential impact of a dilutive round on optionees, without protection, versus preferred shareholders, with price protection

From a valuation perspective, a key question would remain as to whether the sophisticated, independent, third-party purchaser of 626,664 shares of Kayak's common stock (the $15.50 per share paid on 4/2008, as shown in Exhibit 7.3) made the purchase based on "fair market value" versus "investment value." Although the terminology can be confusing, the semantics can have very real impact on whether that same price should apply to employee stock options or not, as we discussed in Chapters 1 and 5, and discuss further in this chapter.

Kayak.com Rapid Model/Carver Deal Term Test—Certificate Plus Press Releases

The rapid model approach relies on a combination of crowdsourced records of amounts raised (Crunchbase) and certificates of incorporation (via SecondMarket and Sharespost) to apply slightly more refined analysis to the company, such as the Carver Deal Term Test. The Crunchbase data is of course not always accurate. However, it is accessible for free, and if you use its API, you can literally run a year's worth of analysis in several hours.

With that kind of power, you can use its API to build templates and then refine those templates using other data sources, either manually or programmatically depending on what kind of resources are available. For our purpose, this example does it both ways, initially using just the raw

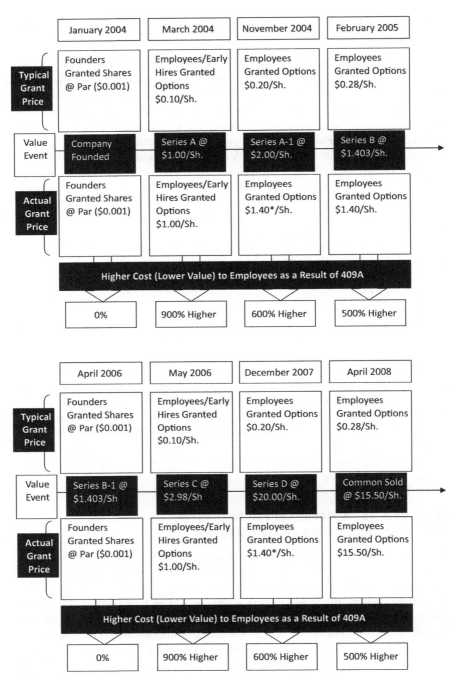

EXHIBIT 7.4 Fairness Grid for Kayak.com Option Grants
Source: Liquid Scenarios, Inc.

Crunchbase data, a certificate, and a handheld calculator. Then we use a program to see what additional insights we might gain, still recognizing the limitations of the data quality.

Manual Analysis Using Crunchbase Data Academics are skeptical of even premium databases, much less free databases and crowdsourced records like Crunchbase. However, you may recall that to apply the Carver Deal Term Test, the most important variable is the amount raised, in most cases. This tends to be the most accessible variable also, since many companies issue press releases after a round has closed.

With Crunchbase, those releases are put into a structured format that allows good use or comparison, listing amounts raised and the estimated dates the rounds closed. While SEC filings of Form Ds are sometimes useful also, simply getting an approximate amount raised is often enough for someone trying to get a quick but meaningful feel for the valuation dynamics of a given venture-backed company. In addition, as we've demonstrated before, Crunchbase is a quick and easy way to get an answers to the critical question of "Who?"—who financed the company, founded it, competes against it, and works for it are obtainable with pretty good reliability. So, here are the amounts raised generated by Crunchbase for Kayak.com (see Exhibit 7.5).

Without further information, we would generally assume that the company has to sell for at least $223 million before the common stockholders and optionees participate, as of the December 2007 round based on the information from Crunchbase. That compares to a hurdle rate of

Kayak.com Amounts Raised per Crunchbase

	Amount Raised
■ Dec-07	$196,000,000
■ May-06	$11,500,000
▨ Dec-04	$7,000,000
■ Jan-04	$8,500,000

EXHIBIT 7.5 Crunchbase Amounts Raised per Crunchbase for Kayak.com Valuation
Source: Liquid Scenarios, Inc. via Crunchbase API.

$27 million prior to the December 2007 round, meaning the company has to sell for at least eight times more than it would have the day before the round in order for common stock to get $0.01. Crunchbase doesn't track liquidation preferences, but we can easily get those for free from the certificate on SecondMarket or Sharespost or, in some cases, for free from other sites.

Included on the companion Web site to this book at www.wiley.com/go/venturecapitalvaluation is Kayak.com's Certificate of Incorporation in PDF format with a few notes from me. When you consider it alongside the following questions, you will see you can find the answers to the questions accurately and quickly in order to complete the Carver Deal Term Test on the data. It shows that the actual liquidation preference is substantially greater than 1X. The key questions to consider alongside the certificate include:

- What date was the company founded?
- What series of preferred stock are outstanding and what's their liquidation preference?
- Do any of the series have dividend rights?
- What's important to know about those rights?
- Are any of the series "Participating Preferred"?
- Which ones?
- What's the original issue price for each series?
- What's the conversion price for each series?

Finding these elements can be difficult, even for experienced finance executives at venture funds who may see more of these than a typical CFO and certainly more than the typical founder. Here are some more tips about how to find these items and where to look, using the actual Kayak.com certificate that's available on the companion Web site just mentioned.

1. Date company was founded: You can generally find this on the first page of the certificate (although not always). It often references "the original certificate" and a filing date. So, for instance, here's an excerpt of the reference from which we derived the date that Kayak.com was founded from page one of the Certificate of Incorporation:

That the name of this corporation is Kayak Software Corporation, and that this corporation was originally incorporated pursuant to the General Corporation Law on January 14, 2004 under the name Travel Search Company, Inc.;

2. Series of Preferred outstanding: This is almost always found on pages one or two right after the certificate notes the "Classes" of stock (preferred and common, in most cases). All you have to look for are key words like "Series" and "Designated" or "Designation" as we did here with Kayak.com's certificate:

> *The Corporation is authorized to have two classes of shares, designated as Common Stock and Preferred Stock. The total number of shares of Common Stock which the Corporation is authorized to issue is 40,000,000 shares, and the par value of each of the shares of Common Stock is one tenth of one cent ($.001) (the "Common Stock"). The total number of shares of Preferred Stock which the Corporation is authorized to issue is 26,876,384 shares, and the par value of each of the shares of Preferred Stock is one tenth of one cent ($.001) (the "Preferred Stock"). A total of 6,600,000 shares of Preferred Stock shall be designated the "Series A Convertible Preferred Stock", a total of 1,176,051 shares of Preferred Stock shall be designated "Series A-1 Convertible Preferred Stock", a total of 4,989,308 shares of Preferred Stock shall be designated "Series B Convertible Preferred Stock", a total of 2,138,275 shares of Preferred Stock shall be designated "Series B-1 Convertible Preferred Stock", a total of 3,897,084 shares of Preferred Stock shall be designated "Series C Convertible Preferred Stock" and a total of 8,075,666 shares of Preferred Stock shall be designated "Series D Convertible Preferred Stock". The Series A Convertible Preferred Stock and the Series A-1 Convertible Preferred Stock are sometimes referred to herein, collectively, as the "Series A Stock", the Series B Convertible Preferred Stock and the Series B-1 Convertible Preferred Stock are sometimes referred to herein, collectively, as the "Series B Stock", the Series A Stock, the Series B Stock, the Series C Convertible Preferred Stock and the Series D Convertible Preferred Stock are sometimes referred to herein, collectively, as the "Convertible Preferred Stock", and the Convertible Preferred Stock and any other series of Preferred Stock hereinafter authorized are sometimes referred to herein, collectively, as the "Preferred Stock".*

3. What's their (preferred series) liquidation preference? This usually comes after the dividends are described in a certificate, but all you have to look or search for are keywords like "liquidation," "liquidation preference," "original issue." The words you want to be on the lookout for are "multiplied by," "plus," and "the remaining." Here's the example from Kayak.com. You'll notice the word "multiplied by" followed by

"1.5," which means that preferred shareholders will get at least 1.5X their money back before common shareholders, including optionees, start to participate. In addition, the preferred shareholders get their cumulative dividends. Fortunately for common holders and optionees, the liquidation preference multiple (1.5) is not applied to the dividends also, which you will sometimes see in certain transactions particularly in some regions and industries. From a preferred investor's valuation standpoint, you can also see that each of these securities rank equally with respect to its liquidation preference based on the proportion of capital (cash) it provided (pari passu). This, of course, is not always the case. From a pure liquidation standpoint, the impact on common stock proceeds in a liquidity event is often the same regardless of where the seniority, or rank, of various classes of preferred. However, from a value perspective there can be differences, since the optionality and breakpoints are different if all preferred series are pari passu with respect to liquidation preference versus if certain series are junior to others in the order of their claims. Here's an excerpt from that portion of the Kayak.com certificate.

Upon any liquidation, dissolution or winding up of the Corpora-tion (a "Liquidation Event"), whether voluntary or involuntary, the holders of the shares of Convertible Preferred Stock shall first be entitled, before any distribution or payment is made upon any stock ranking on liquidation junior to the Convertible Preferred Stock (including, without limitation, the Common Stock), to be paid (a) an amount per share of Series A Convertible Preferred Stock equal to (i) $1.00 per share of Series A Convertible Pre-ferred Stock (as adjusted from time to time to reflect any stock split, stock dividend, reverse stock split or similar event affecting the Series A Convertible Preferred Stock, the "Series A Original Issue Price") multiplied by 1.5, plus (ii) an amount equal to all Series A Accruing Dividends per share unpaid thereon (whether or not declared) and any other dividends per share declared but unpaid thereon (such aggregate amount described in clauses (i) and (ii) payable with respect to one share of Series A Convert-ible Preferred Stock being sometimes referred to as the "Series A Liquidation Preference Payment" and with respect to all shares of Series A Convertible Preferred Stock being sometimes referred to as the "Series A Liquidation Preference Payments"), (b) an amount per share of Series A-1 Convertible Preferred Stock equal to (i) $1.403 per share of Series A-1 Convertible Preferred Stock (as adjusted from time to time to reflect any stock split, stock dividend, reverse *stock split or similar event affecting the Series A-1 Convertible Preferred Stock, the "Series A-1 Original Issue Price") multiplied by 1.5, plus (ii) an amount equal to all Series A-1 Accruing Dividends per share unpaid thereon (whether or not declared) and any other dividends per share declared but unpaid thereon (such aggregate amount described in clauses (i) and (ii) payable with respect to one share of Series A-1 Convertible Preferred Stock being sometimes referred to as the "Series A-1 Liquidation Preference Payment" and with respect to all shares of Series A-1 Convertible Preferred Stock being sometimes referred to as the "Series A-1 Liquidation Preference Payments"), (c) an amount per share of Series B Convertible Preferred Stock equal to (i) $1.403 per share of Series B Convertible Preferred Stock (as adjusted from time to time to reflect any stock split, stock dividend, reverse stock split or similar event affecting the Series B Convertible Preferred Stock, the "Series B Original Issue Price") multiplied by 1.5, plus (ii) an amount equal to all Series B Accruing Dividends per share unpaid thereon (whether or not declared) and any other dividends per share declared but unpaid thereon (such aggregate amount described in clauses (i) and (ii) payable with respect to one share of Series B Convertible Preferred Stock being sometimes referred to as the "Series B Liquidation Preference Payment" and with respect to all shares of Series B Convertible Preferred Stock being sometimes referred to as the "Series B Liquidation Preference Payments"), (d) an amount per share of Series B-1 Convertible Preferred Stock equal to (i) $1.403 per share of Series B-1 Convertible Preferred Stock (as adjusted from time to time to reflect any stock split, stock dividend, reverse stock split or similar event affecting the Series B-1 Convertible Preferred Stock, the "Series B-1 Original Issue Price") multiplied by 1.5, plus (ii) an amount equal to all Series B-1 Accruing Dividends per share unpaid thereon (whether or not declared) and any other dividends per share declared but unpaid thereon (such aggregate amount described in clauses (i) and (ii) payable with respect to one share of Series B-1 Convertible Preferred Stock being sometimes referred to as the "Series B-1 Liquidation Preference Payment" and with respect to all shares of Series B-1 Convertible Preferred Stock being sometimes referred to as the "Series B-1 Liquidation Preference Payments"), (e) an amount per share of Series C Convertible Preferred Stock equal to (i) $2.983 per share of Series C Convertible Preferred Stock (as adjusted from time to time to reflect any stock split, stock dividend, reverse stock split or similar event affecting the Series C Convertible Preferred Stock, the "Series C Original*

Issue Price") multiplied by 1.5, plus (ii) an amount equal to all Series C Accruing Dividends per share unpaid thereon (whether or not declared) and any other dividends per share declared but unpaid thereon (such aggregate amount described in clauses (i) and (ii) payable with respect to one share of Series C Convertible Preferred Stock being sometimes referred to as the "Series C Liquidation Preference Payment" and with respect to all shares of Series C Convertible Preferred Stock being sometimes referred to as the "Series C Liquidation Preference Payments") and (f) an amount per share of Series D Convertible Preferred Stock equal to (i) $20.727 per share of Series D Convertible Preferred Stock (as adjusted from time to time to reflect any stock split, stock dividend, reverse stock split or similar event affecting the Series D Convertible Preferred Stock, the "Series D Original Issue Price") multiplied by 1.5, plus (ii) an amount equal to all Series D Accruing Dividends per share unpaid thereon (whether or not declared) and any other dividends per share declared but unpaid thereon (such aggregate amount described in clauses (i) and (ii) payable with respect to one share of Series D Convertible Preferred Stock being sometimes referred to as the "Series D Liquidation Preference Payment" and with respect to all shares of Series D Convertible Preferred Stock being sometimes referred to as the "Series D Liquidation Preference Payments"). The Series A Liquidation Preference Payments, the Series A-1 Liquidation Preference Payments, the Series B Liquidation Preference Payments, the Series B-1 Liquidation Preference Payments, the Series C.

Liquidation Preference Payments and the Series D Liquidation Preference Payments are sometimes referred to collectively herein as the "Liquidation Preference Payments". If upon such Liquidation Event, whether voluntary or involuntary, the assets to be distributed among the holders of Convertible Preferred Stock shall be insufficient to permit payment in full to the holders of Convertible Preferred Stock of the Liquidation Preference Payments, then the entire assets of the Corporation to be so distributed shall be distributed ratably among the holders of Convertible Preferred Stock in proportion to the portion of the aggregate Liquidation Preference Payments which each such holder would have received on the date of such Liquidation Event had the Liquidation Preference Payments been paid in full.

4. Do any of the series have dividend rights? In many cases, the answer to this is found on the second or third page of the certificate, right after authorized classes of stock and the series designations are noted. In addition to the obvious key word to look for, "dividends," the more

important ones to look for, for all investors, are the words "cumulative," "accrue," "accruing," and "accrued." It's also worth noting if cumulative dividends, when applicable, are to be paid in cash or "in kind." Dividends paid in kind, or "PIK" dividends, can seem rather innocuous in the world of venture finance compared to their impact in the world of private equity finance. However, I've personally seen many cases where parties entitled to PIK dividends were not clear on how those accrued benefits (or claims on equity) were to convert into shares of the company's stock. If a company has had a large run up in value and has an offer on the table, the difference between converting at the Original Issue Price of the underlying security versus converting based on the proceeds per share payable to the underlying security can make a big difference to every investor and employee. A portion of Kayak.com's dividend clause is below.

In addition to the dividends required to be paid to the holders of Convertible Preferred Stock pursuant to subparagraph 2A, (i) from and after the date of the issuance of any shares of Series A Convertible Preferred Stock, the holders of such shares of the Series A Convertible Preferred Stock shall be entitled to receive, out of funds legally available therefore, dividends at the rate per annum equal to 6% of the Series A Original Issue Price (as defined subparagraph 3A) per share (the "Series A Accruing Dividends"), (ii) from and after the date of the issuance of any shares of Series A-1 Convertible Preferred Stock, the holders of such shares of the Series A-1 Convertible Preferred Stock shall be entitled to receive, out of funds legally available therefore, dividends at the rate per annum equal to 6% of the Series A-1 Original Issue Price (as defined subparagraph 3A) per share (the "Series A-1 Accruing Dividends"), (iii) from and after the date of the issuance of any shares of Series B Convertible Preferred Stock, the holders of such shares of the Series B Convertible Preferred Stock shall be entitled to receive, out of funds legally available therefore, dividends at the rate per annum equal to 6% of the Series B Original Issue Price (as defined subparagraph 3A) per share (the "Series B Accruing Dividends"), (iv) from and after the date of the issuance of any shares of Series B-1 Convertible Preferred Stock, the holders of such shares of the Series B-1 Convertible Preferred Stock shall be entitled to receive, out of funds legally available therefore, dividends at the rate per annum equal to 6% of the Series B-1 Original Issue Price . . .

5. Are any of the series "Participating Preferred"? This is usually found at the end of the liquidation preference clause. You will note that you

won't necessarily see it explicitly stated as "participating preferred" in the certificate, although you will generally see it referred to such in a term sheet. For that reason, the keyword combination to look for is "remaining" or "remaining assets," since that generally precedes the explanation of what happens to proceeds after liquidation preferences are paid. If "remaining assets" are said to be distributed to common stock, with no mention of preferred stock, then the preferred is probably not participating preferred. If remaining assets are said to be distributed to both common stock and preferred stock, then it's some variety of participating preferred (either capped on uncapped). Examples of certificates that have capped and uncapped participating preferred are at the companion Web site referred to earlier. The excerpt that follows from Kayak.com's certificate shows its preferred to be non-participating preferred.

Upon any Liquidation Event, immediately after the holders of Convertible Preferred Stock shall have been paid in full the Liquidation Preference Payments, the remaining net assets of the Corporation available for distribution shall be distributed ratably among the holders of the then outstanding shares of Common Stock in proportion to the number of shares of Common Stock held by each holder on the date of such Liquidation Event.

6. What's the original issue price for each series? As you've seen from the preceding items, the original issue price per share plays a key role in how dividends are accrued, if applicable, how much is paid out per share as a liquidation preference, and perhaps most important, in many cases, how many shares of common stock will be reserved to enable conversion of the preferred stock to satisfy the conversion ratio in effect at the time of a liquidity event. To better understand how this relates to any given company, one has to look at the adjusted price per share, conversion price per share, and anti-dilution-related clauses.

7. What's the conversion price for each series? The important thing to remember with respect to conversion price for each series is that deemed original issue price/adjusted conversion price = conversion ratio (in most cases). The lower the conversion price, as a percentage of the original issue price, the higher the conversion ratio and therefore the greater dilution to owners of other series or classes not benefiting from the adjustment. The primary reason for an adjustment to the conversion price is a dilutive issuance, such as a "down round." A dilutive issuance is an issuance of securities at a price per share less than the adjusted conversion price in effect at that time (in most cases). The clause below relates to the mechanics of adjusting the price (weighted average broad

anti-dilution), whereas additional clauses in the copy at the companion website reference how and when the adjustment is triggered.

Adjustment of Applicable Conversion Price Upon Issuance of Common Stock. Except as provided in subparagraphs 5E and 5F, if and whenever the Corporation shall issue or sell, or is, in accordance with subparagraphs 5D(1) through 5D(7), deemed to have issued or sold, any shares of Common Stock for a consideration per share less than an Applicable Conversion Price in effect immediately prior to the time of such issue or sale, then, forthwith upon such issue or sale, such Applicable Conversion Price shall be reduced to the price determined by dividing (a) an amount equal to the sum of (i) the number of shares of Common Stock outstanding immediately prior to such issue or sale (including, for this purpose, (i) shares of Common Stock issuable upon conversion of the Convertible Preferred Stock and (ii) shares of Common Stock issuable upon the exercise of outstanding Options (excluding unvested Options)) multiplied by such Applicable Conversion Price in effect immediately prior to such adjustment and (ii) the consideration, if any, received by the Corporation upon such issue or sale, by (b) an amount equal to the sum of (i) the total number of shares of Common Stock outstanding immediately prior to such issue or sale (including, for this purpose, (i) shares of Common Stock issuable upon conversion of the Convertible Preferred Stock and (ii) shares of Common Stock issuable upon the exercise of outstanding Options (excluding unvested Options)) and (ii) the total number of shares of Common Stock issuable in such issue or sale. For purposes of this subparagraph 5D, the following subparagraphs 5D(1) through 5D(7) shall also be applicable:

Finding Profit Opportunities without a Formal Cap Table At the beginning of this case, you were able to estimate that the earliest optionees received grants that were overvalued by as much as 900%. You were able to do this without a capitalization table, without access to the company's income statement, and, for the most part, without even using a calculator. If the parties receiving the overvalued, or in this case overpriced, grants applied the same very basic techniques, would they have made different decisions? That's not clear; every situation is different and different parties have varying degrees of bargaining power as an enterprise moves from startup to a thriving concern. One thing is clear already, simply from our analysis of the pricing activity. Had those parties been granted options at a fair price, they would have gains of millions more.

The next parts of our analysis of this case apply more specific measurements to turn the "millions" into amounts per share. After that, the analysis goes even further and compares the conclusions reached by investors and valuation professionals to those you were able to reach by applying the techniques previously covered in this book.

Applying the Carver Deal Term Test to Kayak.com   You can quickly get a more specific idea of relative values for the different securities a venture-backed company has issued by applying the Carver Deal Term Test. As part of the name implies, you have to have some knowledge of the deal terms in order to draw meaningful conclusions from the test. However, one of the most important valuation variables for venture-backed companies, as we've mentioned time and time again, is the amount raised, or size of each financing round. The analysis that follows verifies this point again by applying the Deal Term Test to Kayak using the raw Crunchbase data without using the inputs from the Kayak Certificate of Incorporation. Then it compares those outcomes to the Carver Deal Term Test results we generate after getting the Kayak certificate. If you're skeptical of the potential results, which you should be, keep in mind that this test has uncovered millions in value without even looking at the company's Certificate of Incorporation.

The defaults used in the deal term test based solely on Crunchbase reported data were that the most recent round of financing was senior to the prior, and so forth (no pari passu liquidation preferences). The defaults here also assume 1.0X liquidation preferences and no cumulative dividends. These are the West Coast defaults, but for many East Coast deals in the Internet space they tend to be close. See Exhibit 7.6.

The 1.5X multiple liquidation preference, which is not the typical deal term, results in a sizable difference in the claims to Kayak's proceeds under an M&A scenario. Similarly, Kayak's Certificate of Incorporation indicated cumulative dividends at a rate of 6% per year for the Series A, A-1, B, B-1, C, and D. This means that a portion of the preferred claim grows each and every year, meaning that the hurdle rate for common stock to participate in any sale proceeds also grows. If the hurdle rate for common stock participation grows, the relative value of common stock decreases a bit from what it would have otherwise been if the company were acquired or merged, as opposed to going public.

To get a feel for the relative values of the different classes of stock under an M&A scenario, we put those variables into the Carver Deal Term Test for both the raw Crunchbase data and the data we got from Kayak.com's certificate and built some charts to allow further comparisons of the respective conclusions. Exhibit 7.7 shows the raw Crunchbase data with the amount raised and date closed only; no certificate data from 12/31/2010.

EXHIBIT 7.6 Crunchbase Default Assumptions versus Details from Kayak.com Articles

My Defaults with Crunchbase Data (Not Incorporating Actual Certificate)

	Amount Raised	Rank/Seniority	Liquidation Preference	Participation	Participation Cap	Dividends
Series A	$8,500,000	4th	x1.00	No	N/A	No
Series B	$7,000,000	3rd	x1.00	No	N/A	No
Series C	$11,500,000	2nd	x1.00	No	N/A	No
Series D	$196,000,000	1st	x1.00	No	N/A	No

Terms from Actual Certificate of Incorporation

	Amount Raised	Rank/Seniority	Liquidation Preference	Participation	Participation Cap	Dividends
Series A	$6,600,000	6th	x1.50	No	N/A	6.00%
Series A-1	$1,650,000	5th	x1.50	No	N/A	6.00%
Series B	$6,999,999	4th	x1.50	No	N/A	6.00%
Series B-1	$3,000,000	3rd	x1.50	No	N/A	6.00%
Series C	$11,625,002	2nd	x1.50	No	N/A	6.00%
Series D	$167,384,329	1st	x1.50	No	N/A	6.00%

Source: Liquid Scenarios, Inc., Crunchbase API, SEC Filings.

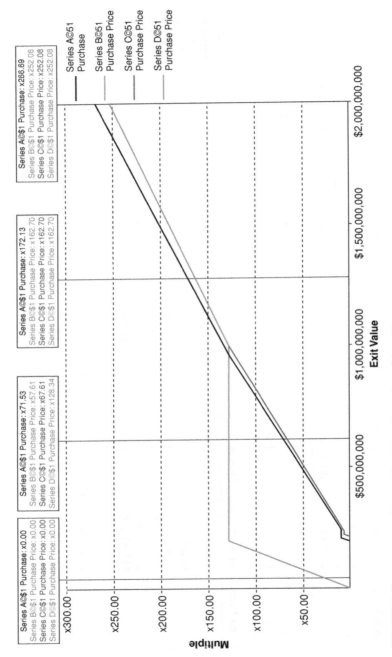

EXHIBIT 7.7 Carver Deal Term Test Using Raw Crunchbase Data
Source: Liquid Scenarios, Inc.

As you might expect with a $196 million dollar round of financing, which of course is rare for venture-funded companies, the last round is the most valuable to a purchaser that can acquire any series at a price of $1 per share, which is an assumption of the Carver Deal Term Test. The more surprising outcome here is that the Series A financing is the second most valuable security under an M&A scenario. Based on amounts raised, our default formula assumed a down round occurred, based on relative round sizes somewhere between Series A and Series C, and triggered anti-dilution provisions. The adjusted conversion price that accompanies the anti-dilution protection means that additional proceeds, on a per share basis, would be realized at amounts above the liquidation preference, which here we assumed to be 1X as a default. Exhibit 7.8 shows adjusted Crunchbase data, improved with certificate data from December 31, 2010.

Adding data from the certificate of incorporation on the companion Web site gives us the payout diagram in Exhibit 7.8 for each of our $1 per share purchases of Series A, Series B, Series C, Series D, assuming we don't adjust the series names to match the certificate.

Using Blind (No Capitalization Table, No Detailed Information) Deal Term Test Results
Despite the obvious benefit of being able to tell how different classes of securities fare at different exit values, as a return multiple on an equal investment at an equal purchase price per share, there are additional questions that remain. These questions include:

1. What additional information did we get from deal term test versus the list of transaction prices over time?
2. What additional information did we get from the certificate versus the list of prices?
3. How does this put us in a better position to increase gains/minimize losses?

In order to address the first question, we need to go back to our financial hammer metaphor of the discount formula. Assume that we built a perfect discount rate that was matched exactly to the risks of Kayak at the point of our analysis, based on future period expected benefits. Our financial hammer only works if we have nails, the benefit stream, which are most often some kind of future expected cash flows of course. Were there any explicit benefit streams in the list of transaction prices we presented in Exhibit 7.3?

So, if we assume that each of the transaction prices represents an increase in at least some security's value and most likely an increase in the total equity value of the company, then yes, this is a benefit stream we could apply a discount rate to and get a result. The better question, however, is

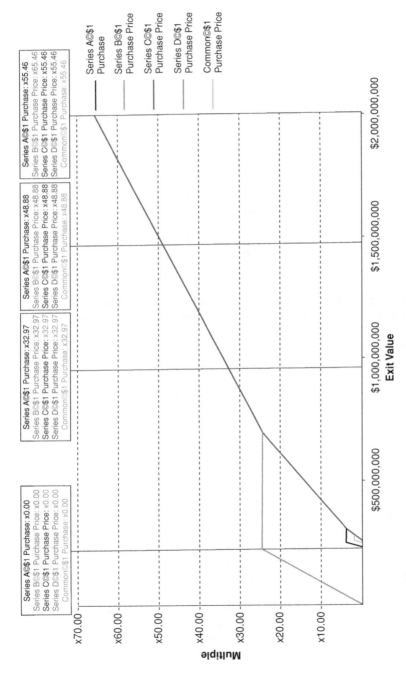

Series A@$1 Purchase: x0.00	Series A@$1 Purchase: x32.97	Series A@$1 Purchase: x48.88	Series A@$1 Purchase: x55.46
Series B@$1 Purchase Price: x0.00	Series B@$1 Purchase Price: x32.97	Series B@$1 Purchase Price: x48.88	Series B@$1 Purchase Price: x65.46
Series C@$1 Purchase Price: x0.00	Series C@$1 Purchase Price: x32.97	Series C@$1 Purchase Price: x48.88	Series C@$1 Purchase Price: x55.46
Series D@$1 Purchase Price: x0.00	Series D@$1 Purchase Price: x32.97	Series D@$1 Purchase Price: x48.88	Series D@$1 Purchase Price: x55.46
Common@$1 Purchase: x0.00	Common@$1 Purchase: x32.97	Common@$1 Purchase: x48.88	Common@$1 Purchase: x55.46

Series A@$1
Purchase

Series B@$1
Purchase Price

Series C@$1
Purchase Price

Series D@$1
Purchase Price

Common@$1
Purchase Price

Multiple

x70.00
x60.00
x50.00
x40.00
x30.00
x20.00
x10.00

$500,000,000 $1,000,000,000 $1,500,000,000 $2,000,000,000

Exit Value

EXHIBIT 7.8 Carver Deal Term Test Using Adjusted Crunchbase Data
Source: Liquid Scenarios, Inc.

the quality of the results we get. Let's assume that you receive the options at $1.00 per share that we identified as being overpriced even without applying the Carver Deal Term Test. We could simply ignore the grant price for a moment and apply our financial hammer to one of the future transaction prices, for instance the May 2006 Series C original issue price of $2.98 per share (the assumed benefit stream), discounting back to the date the options were granted (March 2004, so about 2.167 years) to give us a present value. Assume that the perfect discount rate of 40% has been determined, taking into account the risk-free rate, equity risk premium, industry risk premium, size premium, and company-specific risk premiums. This gives us a present value of approximately $1.44 per share, calculated as follows:

$$(1 + r)\hat{}- t^*C = PV$$

$$(1 + 40\%)\hat{}- 2.167^*\$2.98 = \$1.44$$

Now, if we instead apply the same "perfect" discount rate to actual cash flow per share the common stock would get if the preferred stock, any of the preferred stock, was entitled to $2.98 per share in proceeds, we end up with zero, or $0.

If Series X Preferred Stock Proceeds = $2.98, Then Common Proceeds = $0

We can't get this information from a simple list of pricing from period to period across different classes of stock. We need some kind of a waterfall. Even an approximate waterfall will give us a better value indication.

Generating a Waterfall and the Black-Scholes Model So if we could have seen the future perfectly on March 2004 and envisioned a scenario where Kayak.com would sell for a price that generated $2.98 per share for preferred stockholders, no "rational" or reasonable investor, other than a preferred stockholder, would pay $0.00001 for Kayak.com common. If, instead, we agreed that $2.98 was one potential value per share the preferred stockholders could realize by May 2006, $6.00 per share was another potential value, and $1.00 per share was yet another, it's possible that at $6.00 per share common stock gets some proceeds. If there's a possibility that the common stock will get some of the proceeds in an acquisition generating $6.00 per share in proceeds, then it's also possible (depending on the option strike price) that the options will get some of the proceeds.

With the Carver Deal Term Test, which is a simplified way of generating an easy-to-use waterfall, we can get answers to some of these questions. Simply looking at the list of prices doesn't give us specific information about relative cash flow rights for different classes of stock, largely because we don't know the amounts that were raised and other details about the different series. Without information about the range of possibilities for each security we want to value, it's impossible to make a credible estimate as to what those possibilities are worth today. The same basic information we end up with, which is a pretty good approximation of breakpoints, or company sale/proceed values at which the slope or behavior of a security's payout line changes, can be used to measure the cost or value of uncertainty. One way of doing this, as we've mentioned before, is using an option-pricing method, as we've done with the Black-Scholes models throughout this book, including in Chapters 1, 4, 5, and 6.

The Black-Scholes formula, like other approaches that assume a standard normal (symmetrical) distribution of prices, has been criticized by many in favor of skewed (asymmetrical) distributions. However, it's important to keep in mind that inputs to the formula begin with a lognormal distribution of returns, which reflect the reality that in most venture investments, the amount at risk is limited to the amount that's investment. Other perceived shortcomings of using Black-Scholes include the failure to account for a greater frequency of extreme observations (kurtosis) as noted earlier.

Despite these challenges, Black-Scholes represents a simple, verifiable, and relatively objective way to reflect uncertainty while looking for clues, or indications, of today's value for a venture-backed company security. Since reality is that in almost every case the exact price a company will fetch in an acquisition is unknown until the date it sells, you can attempt to reflect that risk with a higher discount rate, an option-pricing model (with an appropriate input for volatility) or a combination of those (as done with the CWERM models previously). In fact, in some cases the exact proceeds sellers will realize remain unknown even after the company has been sold, due to earnouts or contingent consideration. These same techniques are appropriate when tempering expectations by modeling uncertainty for earnouts.

Since these relationships are a lot for us to think about simultaneously, and only intuitive for statisticians or others that deal with the calculations regularly, Exhibits 7.9 and 7.10 show a few of the illustrations used to convey these concepts.

Keeping in mind that volatility, for our purposes, is equal to sigma, then the higher our volatility input, the more possible values we can expect in the future for our shares, enterprise value, or other underlying "asset" we are trying to get a value indication for. Since the first breakpoint is almost always $0 to some number less than the first liquidation preference, or debt obligation, the value we end up with for N(d1) and N(d2) should

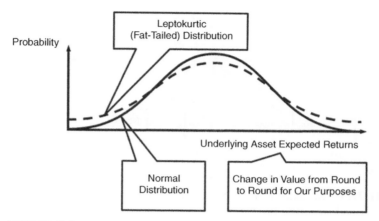

EXHIBIT 7.9 Fat-Tailed Distributions versus Standard Normal Distributions
Source: Liquid Scenarios, Inc.

almost always be one (1). I say almost because if the time horizon, t, is equal to zero we will of course get a value of 0.50 for both N(d1) and N(d2), since we have a standard normal distribution with absolutely no time value.

This characteristic, N(d1) and N(d2) being equal to one (1) for the first breakpoint, $0, should occur whether we use the ubiquitously low volatilities you see in most 409A valuations and MD&A disclosures, or

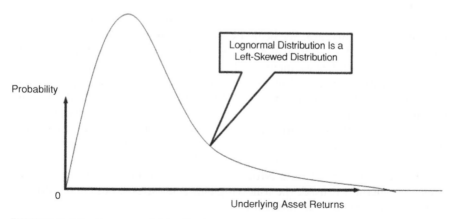

EXHIBIT 7.10 Lognormal Distribution
Source: Liquid Scenarios, Inc.

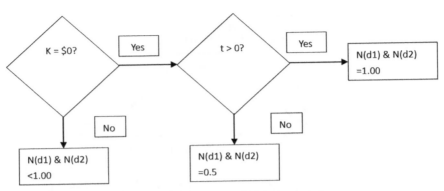

EXHIBIT 7.11   Kayak.com N(d1) N(d2) OPM Characteristics
Source: Liquid Scenarios, Inc.

if we use volatilities that are more consistent with actual venture-funded companies, either using historical averages (as Cochrane 2005, Michael Ewing 2010, and others have) of around 109% or improved observations of venture-funded companies (which is closer to some of the ranges we've proposed in other cases in this book). Exhibit 7.11 shows key N(d1) and N(d2) characteristics for the first breakpoint where the strike price is $0.

This relationship is illustrated by doing a backsolve for the $2.98 Series C price. Another way to explain the backsolve method is as matching the Series C price paid on May 2006 for Kayak.com preferred to an equal OPM value for Kayak.com that implies an overall enterprise value (that our formulas solve for) composed of the sum of each securities value based on rights to proceeds, adjusted for uncertainty using an option pricing model, Black-Scholes in this case. We begin by using a volatility in the range of what companies were disclosing around 2006, then the 110% volatility observed by others in the studies we mentioned, followed by the 2X disclosed volatility shortcut mentioned and finally a volatility buildup is also suggested as an alternative means of objectively building up an appropriate volatility in the absence of data or time. Initially, we assume a time horizon (t) of five (5) years for each of the volatilities and apply a capitalization date as of December 31, 2010, assuming no future rounds of financing. The least influential variable, the risk-free rate, has been set at 3%.

In addition to N(d1) and N(d2) always being equal to 1, assuming the backsolve method is used, the following characteristics should generally be present in the first breakpoint call value:

$$K * e\,\hat{}\,rt = \$0$$

This makes sense, since the strike price of the first breakpoint is almost always $0. Also, it's important to recall that K*e^rt can be thought of in the following ways if it helps you remember the role it plays in helping us take uncertainty into account when generating a value indication. K*e^rt is effectively getting the present value of a zero coupon bond with a face value equal to the first breakpoint (the strike price, K).

The constant e (approximately 2.1775) to the r (risk-free rate in this case) * t (time or term, in years for this example) should bear similarity to the financial hammer mentioned throughout the book, since that's what it is. This term discounts the cash needed to exercise the option (an option on the first breakpoint for Kayak.com with a strike price of $0) at the continuously compounded risk-free rate. Although it's obvious to almost everyone that regardless of what rate we discount at, if the strike price is $0, the present value of the $0 we will need to exercise is also $0. However, if you use this formula in practice, or someone that works with or for you uses it, you can easily check whether the model is internally consistent by plugging different EV, volatility, or other values into the first breakpoint. The other reason this is of importance is because it speaks to the assumptions concerning return and price distributions and how they relate to the implied probabilities that will determine value indications this technique generates.

We care about N(d2) because it tells us the chance, or probability based on the formula, that C (the call option, in this case, the $0 call on the first breakpoint of Kayak.com) will be in the money and, therefore, exercised. If we don't have to pay a penny to exercise the option on the first call option on Kayak's equity, we will of course exercise, so there's a 100% chance that option is in the money, since the underlying asset (the first breakpoint) can't be worth anything less than zero. If we've included some straight debt in our Kayak.com model, then we might be looking at a call on both the equity and the debt, with the debt generally representing the first breakpoint. The important elements of N(d2), again, are as follows (see Exhibit 7.12):

1. We can't solve for (d2) until we've solved for (d1).
2. Once we've solved for (d1), solving for (d2) is easy:
   a. Just multiply the square root of t (our time horizon) by volatility (sigma or standard deviation)
   b. Subtract the result (a) from d1 to get d2. That's it.
   c. Since were subtracting the square root of t * volatility, we will end up with negative outcomes for some of our breakpoints, or call options. This is fine, since when we apply a standard normal distribution (N) to (d2) we end up with a positive number less than 1, of course.

In this iteration, we used the same backsolved total equity value, approximately $60.2 million. This total equity value indication was arrived at

EXHIBIT 7.12   Kayak.com OPM Model Version One

	Series C Liq. Pref.	Series C Liq. Pref.	Series C Liq. Pref.	Series C Liq. Pref.
	@60%	@120%	@109%	@ 1.81X 60%
Breakpoints	Breakpoint 1	Breakpoint 1	Breakpoint 1	Breakpoint 1
Strike Price (K)	$0	$0	$0	$0
BEV Estimate (S)	$60,231,839	$60,231,839	$60,231,839	$60,231,839
Breakpoint Call Value	$12,321,154	$4,983,471	$6,107,971	$6,107,971
Call Value at Floor	$60,231,839	$60,231,839	$60,231,839	$60,231,839
Term in Years (t)	5.00	5.00	5.00	5.00
Risk-Free Rate (r)	3.00%	3.00%	3.00%	3.00%
Volatility	60.00%	120.00%	109.00%	109.00%
d1	21.00	11.51	12.41	12.41
d2	19.66	8.82	9.97	9.97
N(d1)	1.00	1.00	1.00	1.00
N(d2)	1.00	1.00	1.00	1.00
S * N(d1)	$60,231,839	$60,231,839	$60,231,839	$60,231,839
K * e^-rt	$0	$0	$0	$0
Times N(d2)	$0	$0	$0	$0
C Value at Ceiling	$47,910,685	$55,248,368	$54,123,868	$54,123,868

Source: Liquid Scenarios, Inc.

by using the $2.98 Series C price with a volatility factor of 120%. As you can see in Exhibit 7.12, with the same assumed total equity value, N(d1) and N(d2) both equal one (1), suggesting a 100% risk-adjusted probability that the present value (discounted at the risk-free, or risk-neutral, rate) of S, with S equal to the total equity value of $60.2MM in this case, will be greater than the strike price K ($0) for this breakpoint between now and the time horizon t (5 years) or expiration of the option.

However, notice that despite equal N(d1) and N(d2) for each scenario above, the differences in volatility result in a different value for the same breakpoint. At the lowest volatility input in Exhibit 7.12, 60%, we end up with the highest value for the first breakpoint, approximately $12.5 million, or around 20% of the total indicated equity value. At the highest volatility input in the table, 120% volatility, we end up with the lowest value for the first breakpoint at just under $5 million, or about 8% of total equity value we input. Finally, the middle value of the three volatilities, 109% volatility, coincidently matches the risk-adjusted volatility from our volatility build up. It allocated around 10% of the $60.2 million, or approximately $6.1 million, to Kayak's first breakpoint. This exercise would appear to suggest that the higher the volatility input, the lower the value of the first breakpoint for a venture-backed company. Before getting into that further, we can easily test that theory by backsolving for the Series C price of $2.98 for each of the respective volatilities, as opposed to just using the same backsolved indicated value we generated with the 60% volatility that was often cited by similar companies in 2006.

So naturally, the ability of our discount rate to indicate a present value is only as good as the quality of our projected benefit stream, or future cash flows to investors. In most of our cases, the most important future cash flows are in the form of capital appreciation, as opposed to periodic earnings that could be distributed to holders as a cash dividend, which you can see if you look back at Exhibit 7.3.

The likelihood, risk, or probability of realizing those future cash flows can be reflected in our discount rate, with a higher discount rate for a lower probability of realizing the cash flow and a lower discount rate for a higher perceived likelihood of realizing the cash flows. As previously mentioned, the relationship between higher perceived risk and higher required return is intuitive not only to business people but to anyone who's tried to accomplish something, such as trying to break a record in a long-distance race or investing heavily in an ad campaign or capital outlay for a small business. The risk increases the moment you decide you want better results or returns.

We can also assign, or otherwise generate, probability estimates for a limited number of scenarios and weight each potential outcome to arrive at a future benefit stream to discount back to today. Variations of this approach are referred to as the probability weighted return method (PWERM), risk-adjusted net present value (rNPV or eNPV). Even the Chicago or so-called VC methods of valuation involve applying probabilities to scenarios and weighting the outcome to arrive at a present value.

But going back to the reality that we don't know exactly what price a company will sell at, or even the exact price a company's next round of financing will command without a means of quickly and verifiably distributing the potential outcomes around some kind of an average, we would have to create a large number of discrete scenarios in order to reflect every possible future benefit stream around a mean. The option-pricing method is an efficient means to acquire this perspective and insight, without the cost (and additional subjectivity) of modeling hundreds or thousands of DCF scenarios explicitly or applying a Monte Carlo analysis that's better suited for other finance problems than venture payoff scenarios.

Reconciling with the Mandelbaum Factors   Now that we've briefly examined the calculation of a discount for lack of marketability, DLOM, based on the protective put, we should reconcile that with the Mandelbaum factors if we are going to use the results for a 409A valuation. The criteria are the following:

- Private versus public sales of the company's stock (public sales decrease discount)
- Financial statement analysis (stronger the position, lower the marketability discount rate, in general)
- Dividend policy (if there is one, then you would end up with a lower marketability discount)
- Nature of the company, history, position in the industry, and its economic outlook (better it is, the lower the marketability discount should be, in theory)
- Management team (stronger it is, the lower the marketability discount should be, relatively)
- Amount of control in the transferred shares (shareholder rights agreements giving little if any rights to common holders, for instance, would justify an increased marketability discount)
- Restrictions on transferability of stock (more restrictive, higher discount for lack of marketability)

Unless you include Christopher Columbus backers, King Ferdinand and Queen Isabella of Spain, the theory regarding discounts for lack of control predates the first real venture-capital fund in the United States, which would be ARD, founded after World War II, as we discussed earlier in this book. The *Cravens v. Welch* 1935 case most cited to explain why a minority discount, or "discount for lack of control" (or DLOC, for short), is applicable, includes the following wisdom: "Minority stock interests in a 'closed' corporation are usually worth much less than the proportionate share of the assets which they attract."

Like Mandelbaum, this case and quote are often cited in valuations of privately held companies. However, often in valuation reports for venture-backed companies (either for 409A/FAS123R [Topic 820] or for FAS 157 [Topic 820]), it's rarely encountered. This firsthand experience is reinforced by both the venture-backed IPO cases in this book and the overwhelming majority of venture-backed IPOs that have occurred since stock-based compensation MD&A disclosures concerning 409A/FAS123R valuations started. There's a variety of explanations for why DLOCs are absent from the venture-backed company valuation analysis, but before discussing some of those with valuation experts in Chapter 8 and 9, be forewarned that they can easily become internally inconsistent and complicated.

IMPORTANT QUESTIONS TO ASK

For readers who are skipping around in this book, or readers who simply need a refresher on certain topics, some of my notes follow regarding the first case in this section, which was pulled from Kayak.com's MD&A section. As noted before, without a detailed capitalization table, it can be difficult to get an exact breakdown of "who." As in previous examples, let's use three free sources where this data can be gathered:

1. Crunchbase
2. Press releases and RSS feeds
3. Web sites of investors/funds

Asking "Who?"

Exhibit 7.13 illustrates the strong background of Kayak.com's founding management team. For a traditional business, these advantages would most often be reflected in a lower company-specific risk premium. As discussed previously, if we were to build a volatility rate, similar to the way a traditional valuation analysis would call for building a discount rate, we would actually increase the volatility based on the strength of management, since that would likely result in subsequent increases in round-to-round pricing.

Daniel Stephen Hafner Co-Founder – CEO (January 2004)	Paul M. English Co-Founder – CTO (January 2004)	Terrell B. Jones – Chairman of The Board (March 2004)
Co-Founder Orbitz, Former VP Consumer	Former VP Technology Intuit	Former CEO Travelocity
Consultant, Boston Consulting Group	Cofounded Boston Light Software Corp. – it was acquired by Intuit Inc.	SABRE

Public: Shareholder Rights Agreement

Private: Certificate of Incorporation

	Vintage						
General Catalyst Group II, L.P.	2001	25,000,000	23,375,000	16,349,957	33,168,188	6.8%	1.40x
General Catalyst Group, LLC	2000	3,975,000	3,875,625	3,875,609	4,001,038	0.6%	1.00x

EXHIBIT 7.13 Kayak.com Management Team Highlights and Volatility Buildup

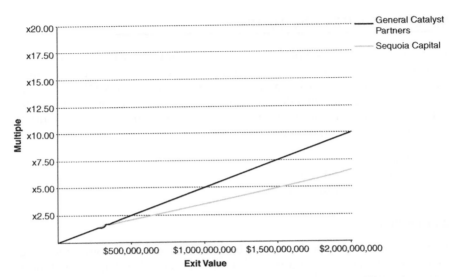

EXHIBIT 7.14   Kayak.com Estimated Payouts to GCP and Sequoia Assuming M&A

Source: Liquid Scenarios, Inc.

General Catalyst co-founding partner George Bell, who, in addition to being an Emmy award winner was the CEO of Excite@Home, at one point had an opportunity to purchase Google. Recalling the impact of "who" in these transactions, Vinod Khosla, as you may recall from the Google and Excite cases on the Wiley Web site, was responsible for the initial funding (directly and indirectly) of Excite. According to press reports, it was Mr. Khosla, at the time a partner with Kleiner, who proposed that Excite acquire Google transaction to Excite@Home.

General Catalyst co-founder and Kayak.com Board member Joel E. Cutler was also on the board of General Catalyst portfolio company ITA Software, sold to Google in June 2010 for $700MM. Sequoia also invested in ITA's $100MM.

Exhibit 7.14 illustrates the power of a first-round investment when things go well. The dark gray line is the payout multiple, under a variety of M&A scenarios, for General Catalyst and the light gray line is the payout multiple, under a variety of M&A scenarios, for Sequoia Capital. In the range of $1 billion to $2 billion, you can see how there's a substantial difference in the slope of General Catalyst's payout line and Sequoia's, with General Catalyst getting a 10X return at $2 billion and while Sequoia Capital gets a 6.6X multiple at the same exit value of $2 billion. Why is this important to know as a current or prospective investor in a venture-backed company? If an M&A scenario is a possibility (it almost always is), then knowing the relative return possibilities of the key investors is critical to understanding the "takeover value" of the company.

The extracts that follow are from the Kayak.com Web site and show how the investors in Kayak.com describe themselves.

> *Battery Ventures is a leading venture capital firm with $4 billion under management, and focuses on investing in technology companies at all stages of growth.*
>
> *With $4 billion under management, this is a fund that has the bandwidth (management fees to compensate personnel and, ideally, investable funds), to follow through on investments.*
>
> *General Catalyst Partners is a venture capital firm that invests in exceptional entrepreneurs who are building the technology-based companies that will lead innovation and transform industries. The firm has approximately $1.8 billion under management.*
>
> *PAR Investment Partners, a private partnership with a focus on companies related to and operating in the travel industry, has over $2 billion in assets.*
>
> *Sequoia Capital provides venture capital funding to founders of startups who want to turn business ideas into enduring companies. As the "Entrepreneurs behind the Entrepreneurs", Sequoia Capital's Partners have worked with accomplished innovators who build great franchises such as Apple, Cisco, Google, Oracle, Yahoo, and YouTube.*

If you had never heard the name "Sequoia" before, simply seeing the list of companies it has listed in this brief excerpt tells you it has been a successful investor. Successful investors have successful networks that can, generally, act faster than and more efficiently than their competitors. From a valuation perspective, consider two companies that are identical in almost every way and close a Series A financing round for $5 million, at the same pre-money valuation. The only difference is that one company receives the $5 million from Sequoia and the other receives the $5 million from Lorenzo Partners, and it's Lorenzo Partners first investment ever. You don't need a calculator to conclude that the total company equity value for Sequoia investment is worth more on that day than the Lorenzo Partners portfolio company's total equity value, even though both were for $5 million and both were at the same pre-money and post-money valuations. Obviously, you can't simply write down the investment by Lorenzo Partners on day one. However, you can make adjustments to the inputs to valuation methods so that the value given to the common shares and options is lower than if Sequoia was the lead investor. The easiest way to do this is to decrease the term (modeling to the next round of financing, not the ultimate liquidity event) and adjusting the volatility used in an OPM backsolve, for example.

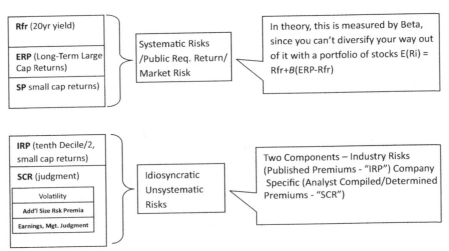

EXHIBIT 7.15   How Volatility and Who Investors Are (Track Record) Can Fit into Traditional Discount Rate Build Ups.
Note: Rfr is risk free rate, ERP is equity risk premium, and SP is size premium. Unfortunately, Betas for private companies are sometimes taken from public "peers" that have linear earnings prospects. In theory, an analyst could increase the company specific risk (SCR) to account for differences in expected volatility based on capital structure and who the investors are (track records).

Spectrum Equity Investors manages approximately $4 billion in equity capital and invests exclusively in established, profitable companies in the information services, media, and communications industries.

Asking "Why?"

If the MD&A section of a prospectus, notes to financial statements for a fund or LP, 409A valuation report, or any other documents says that a "discount rate of X%" was used, multiplying X% or its discount factor by the future rewards indicated in the report will rarely put you in a better position of understanding that valuation, other than being comfortable that a math check was performed. Instead, remembering that for publicly traded companies, most of the discount rate used is set by an active market for three items. Treasuries (the Rfr or risk-free rate), long-term stock yields, such as the S&P 500 (Rm, or market risk), and the dispersion (volatility) of a stock's prices over a given period of time compared to the dispersion (volatility) of the market's prices over that same period of time (B, or Beta). In this book we've taken a much closer look at idiosyncratic risk, also referred to as company-specific risk, which accounts for the lion share of expected returns (and losses) for venture-backed companies. One way to quickly and accurately model this risk, or uncertainty, is by using an appropriate assumption concerning expected volatility of the company's value and the value of the company's securities.

In the case of a private company, not just a venture-funded private company but any privately held company that's not about to be liquidated, the percentage of systematic risk (risk you can't run away from simply by diversifying holdings in the same investment class) should be the same as what's used in the discount rate. If that's the case, then you know that the discount rate should almost always be higher for the private company than the discount rate used for the public equity market. If it's a venture-backed private company, the discount rate should be substantially higher than that.

Before concluding this chapter, an examination of some of the disclosures in Kayak.com's registration statement as it relates to valuation, compared to the analysis we just did, allows you to reflect on the differences we've highlighted throughout this book.

Common Stock Valuations per Kayak.com MD&A

From Kayak.com MD&A:

> *To make our estimates, we utilize guidance set forth in the 2004 AICPA Practice Aid,* Valuation of Privately-Held Company Equity Securities Issued as Compensation, *or the AICPA Guide. We recognize that the value of our stock changes between valuations and, as such, consider other factors when determining the fair value of our stock for the purposes of determining stock compensation expense, such as:*
>
> - Sales of our Common Stock: *Sales of our common stock can be a strong indicator of the value of our stock, but do not necessarily determine the value. We consider the volume of shares sold in the transaction, the circumstances of the sale and the sophistication and independence of the buyer in order to determine whether or not the sale indicates a new fair value of our common stock.*
> - Sales of our Convertible Preferred Stock. *Sales of our convertible preferred stock can assist in estimating the fair value of our common stock. In order to determine the fair value of common stock after a sale of convertible preferred stock, we consider the volume of shares sold, circumstances of the sale, independence of*

the buyers and the value of the preferential rights associated with the class of convertible preferred stock sold.

- Specific Events at KAYAK: *In addition to the above factors, we consider significant events at KAYAK that may have impacted our value, such as launch of a new product, signing a significant new customer, significant change in management team, etc.*

Observations based on the above disclosures by Kayak.com in its MD&A include:

1. Emphasis of Market Approach: Kayak points out reliance on recent sales of both common stock (secondary sales) and preferred stock (original issue securities)
2. This MD&A disclosure is closer to how valuations are actually performed for these companies, versus strictly and simply acknowledging the use of AICPA Practice Aid *Valuation of Privately-Held Company Equity Securities Issued as Compensation.* As a result, it's also more closely aligned with the disclosure recommended in Chapter 5 of this book.

Exhibit 7.16 set forth the option grants over the last two years and discuss the methodology to determine the fair value of our common stock at each grant date. In 2009, options to purchase shares of common stock at the following exercise prices were issued.

From Kayak.com MD&A Disclosure:

In February 2009, the board of directors determined the fair value of our common stock to be $15.50 based on the last sale of 626,664 shares of our common stock to an independent third party in April 2008. The purchaser of the stock was a sophisticated investor with no previous ownership in our company and which performed

EXHIBIT 7.16 Equity Grants, Fair Values, and Intrinsic Values—Kayak.com

Grant Date	Options Granted	Exercise Price	Fair Value of Common Stock	Intrinsic Value
February 26, 2009	265,000	$15.50	$7.50	$—
May 19, 2009	535,000	$7.50	$7.50	$—
July 7, 2009	2,044,000	$7.50	$7.50	$—
July 22, 2009	170,000	$7.50	$7.50	$—
November 13, 2009	255,000	$7.50	$11.29	$3.79

Source: Kayak.com SEC Filings.

adequate due diligence to determine a fair value of $15.50 per share. There were no other significant transactions in our stock from April 2008 to February 2009 and as a result, the board of directors believed that this sale best represented the fair value of our common stock on that date. There was no significant change in our operating results or forecasts during this time period.

Note that this is an example of a market approach in which 100% of the fair value conclusion (essentially the fair market value in accordance with tax law, or Revenue Ruling 59-60) was determined to be the price paid by the independent third party on April 2008. Based on what you've read in this book, even if you only glanced at the first couple of chapters, does that seem reasonable? In addition to the largest financial crisis in recent history, or more accurately as a result of it, the vast majority of guideline public companies (comps) had their price to revenue multiples cut by double digits, with Expedia seeing its multiple cut by 90% and even Google trading at a fraction of its 2007 multiple. While I don't believe that private company values vary one to one with their public peers, as I've noted already, we all do live in the same economy. So if $15.50 per share was in fact fair market value for one share of Kayak.com common stock in April of 2008, it is highly unlikely that it was also the fair market value of one share of Kayak.com common stock on February of 2009, when equity markets around the world rapidly breached new lows.

Thereafter, Kayak.com took a more rigorous look at the fair value at which it was granting options and adjusted the price to $7.50 share, or less than 50% of the $15.50 the February options were granted at. These adjustments were said to be based on weighting (a) 50% of the value indications arrived at through the income approach (DFC) and (b) 50% of the value indications arrived at using the market approach (comps). Those amounts were allocated using the OPM (like we did earlier in this chapter several times), with volatility of 80% and a marketability discount of 20% (far less than what we derived in our rough calculations earlier).

On a positive note, it did use market multiples based on revenue, but naturally those multiples would have been substantially less during December 31, 2008, which explains part of the reduction in the fair value conclusion per share Kayak.com came up with. Here's an excerpt from the portion of the Kayak.com MD&A section that references those valuations:

In early 2009, we estimated the fair value of our common stock as of December 31, 2008 using the market approach and the income approach, in order to assist the board of directors in assigning an exercise price to future stock grants. We believe both of these approaches were appropriate methodologies given our stage of development at that time. For the market approach, we utilized the guideline company method by analyzing a population of comparable companies and selected those technology companies that we considered to be the most comparable to us in terms of product offerings, revenues, margins and growth. We then used these guideline companies to develop relevant market multiples and ratios, which were applied to our corresponding financial metrics to estimate our total enterprise value. We relied on the following key assumptions for the market approach:

- *our projected revenues determined as of the valuation date based on our estimates; and*
- *multiples of market value to expected future revenues, determined as of the valuation date, based on a group of comparable public companies.*

For the income approach, we performed discounted cash flow analyses which utilized projected cash flows as well as a residual value, which were then discounted to the present value in order to arrive at our current equity value to arrive at an enterprise value. We relied on the following key assumptions for the income approach in addition to the management projections discussed above:

- *discount rate applied to forecasted future cash flows to calculate the present value of those cash flows; and*
- *terminal value multiple applied to our last year of forecasted cash flows to calculate the residual value of our future cash flows.*

In determining our enterprise value, we applied equal weighting to market and income approaches, as the indicated equity value under the scenarios was reasonably similar. In allocating the total enterprise value between preferred and common stock, we considered the liquidation preferences of the preferred stockholders and utilized the option-pricing method, or OPM, for calculating a range of values for the common stock, based on the likelihood of various liquidity scenarios. The OPM utilized a volatility factor of 80% based on the peer group above and applied a lack of marketability discount of 20%. We assumed a 30% likelihood of an initial public offering within one year, 10% likelihood of a strategic sale and 60% likelihood of remaining as a private company, which produced an indicated value of our common stock of $6.50–$8.48. We then chose the midpoint of the range to arrive at a common stock value of $7.50. This value was significantly lower than our last indicated value due to an overall decrease in public company *comparable multiples of 50%, as well as to our lowered forecasted revenues and cash flows as a result of the poor econ.*

Based on the results of the appraisal, the board of directors determined that the fair value of our common stock was $7.50 per share. There were no significant transactions involving our common stock or convertible preferred stock during 2009.

During the fourth quarter of 2009, we increased our forecasted revenue and cash flows due to a strengthening in our results. Accordingly, we performed an updated valuation of our company as of October 31, 2009. This valuation again calculated an overall enterprise value, but relied on the income approach to calculate the value, as we believed that it best considered our expected high growth and profitability. The market approach was used to validate the results of the income approach, but no weight was assigned to it. In performing our calculations, we relied upon the methodologies described above as of October 31, 2009, however, with respect to our application of the market approach we used a multiple of projected EBITDA instead of revenues due to our recent demonstration of profitability.

The enterprise value was then allocated to the various classes of our stock using the OPM and applying a 70% volatility factor and 40% likelihood of an initial public offering within 12 months. We then applied a 20% discount to the value due to lack of marketability to arrive at an estimated fair value of our common stock of $11.29, which the board used to determine the exercise price of future stock option grants.

In 2010, we issued options to purchase shares of our common stock at the following exercise prices (see Exhibit 7.17).

EXHIBIT 7.17 Kayak.com Detail Option Grants from SEC Filing

Grant Date	Options Granted	Exercise Price	Fair Value of Common Stock	Intrinsic Value
February 11, 2010	315,000	$11.29	$11.29	$—
April 29, 2010	1,075,000	$13.00	$13.00	$—
July 22, 2010	205,000	$13.00	$14.82	$1.82
October 7, 2010	140,000	$14.82	$17.60	$2.78
October 20, 2010	2,079,590	$14.82	$17.60	$2.78
October 21, 2010	40,000	$15.50	$17.60	$2.10
November 15, 2010	110,000	$16.50	$17.60	$1.10
December 8, 2010	235,000	$16.50	$17.60	$1.10

Source: Kayak.com SEC filings.

Probability Assigned	40%	30%	30%
DLOM	17%	3%	33%
PV Factor (@22%)	86% (Rounded)	55% (Estimate)	55% (Estimate)
Indicated Value/Sh.	$18.42 Net of DLOM	$14.72 Net of DLOM	$10.11 Net of DLOM
Probability Adjusted	40%*$18.42 = $7.37	30%*$14.72 = $4.42	30%*$10.11 = $3.03
☐ Prob. Weighted	$14.82 per Common Share Value Conclusion @ 7/31/2010		

Year	40%	50%	60%	70%	80%	90%
1	15%	19%	23%	27%	31%	34%
2	21%	27%	32%	37%	42%	46%
3	26%	**32%**	38%	44%	49%	55%
4	29%	36%	43%	49%	55%	61%
5	32%	40%	49%	54%	60%	65%

EXHIBIT 7.18   Volatility Card

On March 22, 2010, an independent third-party investor purchased 769,230 shares of common stock (2.32% of outstanding
common equivalents at that time) from existing investors at a price
of $13.00 per share. The investor is an institutional investor who
previously had no shares in Kayak and who conducted appropriate
due diligence. There were no other significant transactions involving
common stock or convertible preferred stock or significant changes
to our business between March 22, 2010, and July 22, 2010. The
board of directors concluded that this transaction established the
fair value of common stock which was the best representation of
common stock value at April 29, 2010. See Exhibit 7.18.

The volatility card in Exhibit 7.18 shows 33% discount (rounded) at
50% volatility in three years, which is pretty close to the 48.68% volatility
and 33% discount disclosed in Kayak's MD&A for the July 31, 2010,
valuation. As a result, we assume a discount factor based on a three-year
forecast.

SUMMARY

Note that without doing very rigorous calculations, you can now determine the reasonableness of many value conclusions regarding venture-backed companies, such as Kayak.com. As a result, you can also see how many parties could have made more money as a result of understanding these basic concepts, as we illustrated in the Facebook case and every other case in this book.

In Chapter 8, you get the first of several perspectives from actual valuation parties that have to not only judge the reasonableness of value indications and conclusions but must do so in accordance with the value standards we've discussed, the auditor demands, the client demands, and the investor demands. Based on those firsthand accounts, you should get a better appreciation for the environment both causing and curing the issues we discussed concerning venture-backed company valuations such as those related to Kayak.com.

CHAPTER 8

Don't Hate the Appraiser
(Blame the Auditor Instead)

"... it may be inappropriate to use discounted cash flows for valuing an equity investment in a start-up enterprise if there are no current revenues on which to base the forecast of future earnings or cash flows."
—Auditing Fair Value Measurements and Disclosures,
Statement on Auditing Standards No. 101

I've had the pleasure of working with a wide variety of appraisers almost exclusively with respect to the work they do valuing venture-backed companies to fulfill either financial reporting or tax compliance requirements. In this field, one often hears that "valuation is more of an art than a science." In fact, I have a memory peg for that, which is included in this chapter. But despite the saying, if you've spent time with any of these valuation professionals, you realize that they are truly dedicated to what they do, take the opinions they issue very personally, and are constantly making an effort to remain current in the latest technology and techniques to reach more meaningful and appropriate value conclusions.

This chapter offers a candid interview with Jeff Faust, an Accredited Valuation Analyst whose practice expertise has focused on 409A valuations. Following the interview with Jeff in this chapter, Chapter 9 then offers a group discussion including two other valuation professionals who have focused primarily on 409A and Topic 820 valuations for venture-backed companies and venture funds since the regulations became effective. However, unlike this chapter, which leans more toward the experiences of a single analyst with respect to 409A valuations, Chapter 9 is focused on linking the interactions with valuation professionals, auditors, and the rules they follow with the needs of company founders, CFOs of portfolio companies, and CFOs of venture funds.

INTERVIEW WITH JEFF FAUST, AVA

The first interview is Jeff Faust, AVA, Senior Manager of Business Valuations for Berger Lewis in San Jose, CA. I met Jeff through my National Association of Certified Valuation Professionals course titled "Five Mistakes Your Auditor Made," which was partially on some of the topics we discuss in the interview. In addition to being a valuation professional, Jeff was also a co-founder of a Bay Area technology company that makes online option tracking and accounting solutions used by some of the most popular publicly traded technology companies.

Be Flexible With VCs (Partners) and Valuators

LORENZO: Jeff, could you give a background on how you got into valuation?

JEFF: Sure. I've been doing valuation for over 15 years. I got into valuations when I was hired by an ESOP consulting firm to learn the overall product from an installation and implementation perspective. Once I had that down, I got moved over to the valuation group and kind of learned valuations from the ground up through employee stock ownership plan design and valuation.

I got into valuations for venture-backed companies because I rolled one of my valuation practices into a CPA firm in 2006, and the CPA firm I'm at now focuses heavily on venture-funded companies and entrepreneurs working through complicated tax situations. Because of that I do a lot of venture-funded company valuations now.

LORENZO: In your experience in dealing with venture-backed, early-stage companies, is there one thing that sticks out as so important that you would want people running those companies or CFOs of those companies to know about valuation?

JEFF: I think the biggest focus is to be flexible. Valuations are determined in a lot of different ways and incorporate a variety of measurements. So I think that being flexible and being open to other views is the biggest message I would want to get across. I believe that's the biggest thing, to be flexible. I think too many CFOs or owners of companies have a preconceived notion of value when they go into negotiations with VCs. But they might be better off if they threw those preconceptions out the window and were open for discussions. The same should apply to third-party valuations.

Another thing I would say along those lines is don't expect too much [of the company], be willing to give up a big chunk of it, understanding that venture firms can bring a lot more than the dollar amount they invest. I think that's another thing founders and management don't always take into perspective. VCs have typically invested in lots of companies and have access to a lot of networking opportunities. So if an owner thinks, "Wow, I'm giving up 40% of my company" as opposed to thinking, "I'm gaining a partner." The owner is adding a partner, not just someone delivering the funds. So that power they bring, if you get the right VC, overwhelmingly exceeds the 40% ownership founders give up (see Chapter 5).

The "Pre-Money Myth" Revisited

LORENZO: That's a great point. I actually have something along those lines that we've been working on for a while for descriptive purposes. On this whole concept of the definition of pre-money value and how that's different than actual company value (see Chapter 1), I think it would be helpful for both entrepreneurs and investing partners to understand the limits of the current definition. So this is one of the most popular versions of the definition you'll see, which is "Pre-money value equals the company value prior to financing." So the problem is that when a financing round closes, people think, "Well, that means my company is worth the pre-money value plus the amount of cash we raised and my percentage ownership times that amount is what my stake is worth."

- VCs invest $5 million at $5 million pre money (50%)
- Entrepreneur/Founders own 30%
- Option pool reserve is 20%
  - Founder (Board) grants 1% of shares to key hire

Founder perceives value of grant on common stock as 1% X $10 million ($100,000), despite having far fewer rights and protections than if the 1% was granted in shares of the preferred stock purchased by VCs.

That, of course, is not the case, since they (the founders) got something different than these people (the VCs) have. So really what pre-money and post-money "value" are describing, or reconciling, is the fully diluted percentage of the company that's been sold in the most recent round of financing. As a result, I think it would be beneficial to revise the part of the definition that refers "pre-money value" as the "value of the company immediately before the next round of financing." Do you have any thoughts on that?

JEFF: That's correct and I would agree. Your suggestion hits on the whole issue of share dilution and preferences not being taken into consideration with respect to true pricing. At the end of the day, either the math has to agree or you have to change the definition as you've suggested. So conceptually and practically I understand that there has to be a way to test the math for share prices paid in a new round. But to call that a valuation of the entire company is problematic, because it does not take into account the preferences and priorities. So your classic Boolean logic doesn't quite get factored in here if you consider the rights.

The problem you have that this relates to is the whole standards of value (see Chapter 1) and definitions of value (see Chapter 5). I mean is it fair market value or is it investment value? Technically speaking, all of this is investment value, but then you have to flip over the coin for compliance and treat it as if it's a fair market value transaction and it's not. Also, allocation that is so critical to fair market value concepts for venture-backed companies (see Chapters 3 and 5) is not in the traditional formula or definition for pre-money value or post-money value.

So as long as people realize that these concepts are disconnected, they can continue to use the formula. Modifying the definition could help to make it clear to people that they are not the same concept. Investment value is not fair market value. It's kind of an interesting thing when you roll it over and start doing 409A valuations and after-the-fact concepts where you're using these post-money valuations as a guideline and see people crisscrossing standards of value. In that case, your investment value and your fair market value will be split, and people who have invested in these rounds could be looking at that as a measurement of their investment and saying, "Wait a minute, I got ripped off" and that's not the case.

For that reason I think it's very critical to establish a definition of what those are [pre-money value, post-money value, investment value, and fair market value]. The limitations of what this implies and the ramifications represent a gap that needs to be bridged in the definition of pre-money value.

LORENZO: That's similar to what I've heard from some active investing partners when discussing adjusting the definition of pre-money value as I've suggested here. They said, yes, I agree with that completely but when we are negotiating with founders they can be motivated by getting a certain "valuation" based on the existing definition. In reality, the numbers would stay the same; the terminology (pre-money value, post-money value) would stay the same. The only change would be in the definition.

Also, when you look at some of the companies that got financing in late 2008, at the height of uncertainty with respect to financial crisis, there were fair amounts of up rounds for promising venture-backed companies. In those deal transactions were no aggressive (lopsided) deal terms because funds wanted to get in on the transactions. With a substantial up round and founder-friendly deal terms, pre-money value according to the existing definition and company fair market value start to come together. But of course, some of that depends on industry also.

JEFF: Yes, absolutely.

LORENZO: So if you're dealing with a biotech deal, there tend to be much longer term bets than an Internet company, and the deal terms reflect that added risk, with things like cumulative dividends and more complex redemption provisions for instance. If you're dealing with a hardware company it might depend on whether the deal's on the East Coast or Bay Area.

JEFF: Yes, and that's the other thing that I don't think people understand is the whole hype cycle in pre-money valuations where people say, "Well, Facebook got an X amount valuation," and founders ask, "How do I get that hype on my valuation?" But there may be something to that from a portfolio valuation perspective. If you have a VC that's invested in a ton of social media companies, it may not have a need in its portfolio for another, whereas if you're talking to a VC that was late to that game, you might end up giving up a little less of the company.

LORENZO: Now we've talked a bit about valuations from the new round of financing perspective, and you've done a lot of work around 409A valuations and tax compliance work.

JEFF: That's correct.

LORENZO: A lot of the valuation practices are now being applied for financial reporting purposes are actually from the tax world, correct?

JEFF: Yes.

LORENZO: So I'm kind of curious, in that space, when you do the 409A valuations, and you come up with a fair market value for the common stock, it seems like you have to balance the requirements for tax compliance with the demands of auditors that will be reviewing your work from a financial reporting perspective.

JEFF: Right.

Why Don't Users Read the 409A Valuations?

LORENZO: What percentage of the management teams when they get that report actually understand what's in it?

JEFF: VERY LITTLE, and that's the sad part.

There's an e-mail I recently got that said that price is still the major factor for decision making for 409A analysis. But there are so many 409A valuations that are done wrong, auditors are so picky on them that they throw them out frequently, that I'm surprised quality is still not in their minds (see Chapter 5).

Cost is still the primary issue. So my experience plus that drives to me that these people they don't understand at all what they're getting. That's troubling to me because it's important for management to understand the disconnect between the investment value stated in financing transaction, the fair market value of their common stock, and more important, what's a buyer going to consider down the road? Perhaps more important to them as founders, what happens to them when they get acquired. I mean I literally had to walk a CFO through why the company had to sell for $50 million before any of the management team was entitled to a penny. He had no idea and got real angry and was furious with me, because he didn't know what he was getting into when he got his funding.

LORENZO: Right.

JEFF: That's so critical, and that of course is an extreme case. But all along the way they have to understand valuation. IPOs can be a different situation, but even some of those have thresholds that should be considered and the 409A valuation gives a good glimpse into that.

LORENZO: Applying more rigorous valuation methods to venture-backed companies started with 409A for portfolio companies but quickly started to follow, in theory anyway, to venture funds as a result of FAS 157, which became Topic 820. When discussing Black-Scholes and OPM models with venture-fund CFOs and analysts, one of the questions we would often get asked at Liquid Scenarios is "Where do we get the variables from to input into the model?" My response was you just paid, indirectly, for a thoroughly researched set of risk-free rates matched to time, volatilities, and comparables in the 409A valuations for your companies. Those are really artful and time-consuming processes, so grabbing a template that may be six- to nine-months old can still quickly get you up to speed. Depending on your ownership percentage and shareholder rights agreements, most companies will send you a copy if you ask nicely.

JEFF: Absolutely.

LORENZO: But the answer we generally get is, well, we sometimes might take it into consideration, but we don't want to be forced to base our valuations on it. My reply has generally been that the standards of value are different, so an auditor can't really hold you to what's in the 409A valuation. However, to take it into consideration, you might want to look at the variables that apply both to the fair market value and the value to you as an investor. With volatility, risk-free rates and comps right at your fingertips, that's going to save you time and get you indications of value quicker regardless of what the standard of value is.

JEFF: Yes, exactly, that is a lot of work. Also, auditors are super picky about consistency and you know sometimes if you arrive at odd conclusions but use consistent methodology they are more likely to work with you.

Deriving Discounts for Lack of Marketability

LORENZO: Along those same lines, one of the other things I want to address is on the various types of discounts applied to arrive at fair market value for a minority interest. This is something that I believe will become more important as parties getting these reports or relying on them start to ask how was that arrived at, what are you really doing with those discounts, are you just trying to get to a certain number?

Perhaps briefly you could just share some of your experience in terms of when you apply a marketability discount and what percentage of the time you use a quantitative model versus some of the other methodologies.

JEFF: Sure, we run quantitative models on all of our companies. They don't always produce numbers that are relevant necessarily, so in those cases we have to switch over to more qualitative models. We run a lot of them, so we do the protective put, the QMDM, and we've implemented the Rand Curtiss, where you answer a bunch of questions and it recalculates based on your starting point, which is your classic Mandelbaum criteria (see Chapter 1, "Court Rulings"). So we'll run a bunch of models, get a gut feel, cross-check them, and see which is most applicable to the company.

It's kind of like the trend of running both the Duffs & Phelps and the Ibbotson Buildup method for the required rate of return. You do them both to see how they compare and end up with a more defensible argument. The challenge that we have in all of that is that the competition, primarily firms relying on overseas analysts, is getting fierce. There are foreign competitors coming in, undercutting everyone, and for us to do all of that and still remain competitive for a Series A or B company is almost impossible for us here in the Bay Area. That's the difficulty, auditors keep requiring more and more and clients want to pay less and less. If someone goes down the road and shops your rate, they may face problems a year later but by then there's no benefit to our firm.

Still, we try to use as many methods as possible because we know the auditors are not going to like the one we choose. So if we do all of them, we can just present the ones they feel are better quickly.

LORENZO: [Laughing] Yes, that appears to be the consensus approach.

The Auditor versus the Valuation Professional

JEFF: And it's funny because before we do a valuation we meet with every company's auditors, especially if they are Big 4 auditors, and discuss what are you looking for, are we heading down the right path with our plan, by the way there's judgments, and are you OK with that? But then when we're done with all of the work, we still have to go through this process where they ask for something that's not in our report. Then we say, well you told us that was OK when we started, and they say well we want to see a fact-based judgment. Our position is, isn't all of this a fact-based judgment or opinion? Don't misunderstand me, I understand that they want to see an audit trail for why various comps may have been rejected, for instance, so using judgment based on something statistical. I get that; that's what we do as valuation professionals, but at the end of the day it's a judgment call.

So I think the key thing for me is that rather than noting it as a judgment, we say, here's what we did to get to that answer. That can allow us to walk the auditors through our logic and that gets them to a place where they can say, OK we're good.

LORENZO: And they have to ask a lot of those questions to satisfy their SAS101 requirements, so providing a logical flow they can test is helpful.

JEFF: Exactly. But in order to keep your fees down, you have to not only do the best work, but also have an idea of what to expect from an auditor during a given season. At this point we have to prepare clients for the auditors and we simply have to charge for auditors who keep asking questions that don't relate to the work we've done. To address that, we've gone through the process of discussing with clients what to expect from the auditors, and that's something they tend to be grateful for.

We had one set of auditors telling us that each scenario in a PWERM had to contain the same specific individual risk. The next auditors were, like, no they all have to be the same. So we changed it so that they all had the same risk. The next year, we get another auditor saying, no they all have to be the same. But then, I realized, they don't have their valuation person consulting on this engagement, because there's been times when auditors have gotten together without understanding the impact of things. They need to get the perspective from the valuation community. So I really think there needs to be the valuation community and the audit community in a room talking about these things.

What are we allowed to do, according to the auditor's perspective, what are the variations? What's logical and figure it out. Otherwise we're all getting frustrated as one auditor bashes you and you make an adjustment, only to get a completely conflicting demand from another auditor. That's the most challenging for us valuation folks. But you may have hit it early on in suggesting that some smaller clients feel they are trapped in a billing machine. The 409A valuation is viewed as a having a fixed price range, within reason, whereas the audit simply has to get done so if extra work is spent, that's going to be reflected in the audit bill at some point.

I've spent an agonizing amount of time with an auditor discussing a client's valuation and going, wow, that was tough, but at least next year we can give them exactly what they want. We give them exactly what they want and now it's a whole other set of problems and you are like "why?"

LORENZO: Is there a continuity in audit personnel, though, because often they represent very small jobs and staff are of course transitioning?

JEFF: In this particular case [details taken out] there was, in a lot of cases there's not continuity, and that's what causes the problem. Of course, as appraisers, we completely understand that they [the auditors] have to remain skeptical. It's a big part of their job. So we shouldn't get offended. But they need to be reasonable with their requests as opposed to saying, "Well, we asked these 10 questions last year, so let's just find 10 other questions to ask this year." Or, if there's a reason for asking totally different questions, then explain that in the context of the engagement, and we can all get further more successfully to serve the client, as opposed to creating work just to be that way. I think there's got to be a fine line; understanding that we appreciate it's their job to question our work, within reason.

LORENZO: I think one of the things along those lines that some of the valuation professionals we worked with when 409A was expected to become effective is that a lot of the audit personnel assisting with developing tests were from Big 4, at the time accounting firms were valuation teams focused on Wall Street–type analysis for publicly trading firms with earnings or at least some revenue. Obviously, in those cases someone has already solved for "S" the value of the stock and that someone has been the market of buyers and sellers. So anything after that is a very different type of analysis that comes up with a value for a security that no third party has ever paid cash for in an arms-length transaction.

The issues aren't the same. There's many acceptable ways to approach some of the variables, but with so many other variables that are unique to each particular situation, there's a different type of expertise that has to be applied.

JEFF: Yes, yes, that's absolutely right. Also, it's worth noting that with respect to actually doing the valuations, the audit firms could never afford to actually perform them because no startup could pay 30 grand for a 409A valuation. Period. So I've asked time and time again to auditors, "Have you ever done a 409A valuation?" and I'm told, "No, but we look at a lot of them" To which I respond, well, understand that in order for me to do all of the additional analysis you are requesting, that's 30 grand. I can't charge a client that. I can only charge 20% to 30% of that. In that scope, I'm going to have to choose the most important elements.

Even the practice aid talks about the cost-benefit relationship of these analyses; there's a whole paragraph that talks about it. They [auditors] love to quote that whole book as a bible to them except that one page, "Oh, I don't want to talk about that." You can spend 800 hours on a brand new Series A venture-funded startup and be no better off than grabbing a percent of its recent round and being done. Was it really worth spending thousands of dollars? Absolutely not. So there's a fine line for startups where it's very hypothetical. You can apply a lot of science to a hypothetical situation. At the end of the day it's still hypothetical.

So that's all a valid point I don't think auditors always consider and that's a valuable lesson for owners to understand that this is going to go on. That may give owners and founders better perspective when they are raising a new round of funding as to some of the factors at play.

LORENZO: That's interesting what you mention about the practice aid, about the cost-benefit analysis, because prior to 409A there used to be another practice aid on valuing private companies, and it more or less explicitly states that for most early-stage companies, their resources are better spent creating value than measuring it. So if it wasn't for the tax law and then the revisions to FAS123 for financial reporting, then none of this would really be getting done. But there's always been a recognition that for early-stage companies there's a cost benefit to be considered. This is very similar to how auditors approach control procedures for these companies. How many people should a startup hire to put financial controls in place? Well, in most cases it should not hire anyone just for that, and auditors are used to just assuming that control risk is at its maximum and test appropriately to make sure that things have been properly.

What 409A Valuation Professionals Actually Do

LORENZO: Along those same lines, this is kind of an attempt to simplify what valuation professionals do in a manner that anyone can understand. I'd just like to get your opinion if you think this is fair. It's kind of consistent I think with what we've discussed . . .

You basically gather some data
You apply some kind of a formula
And then you make a judgment
So based on where that all lines up you may start all over again.

JEFF: Yes, I think that's exactly what it is. I'd probably put the arrows back in the other direction. Sometimes you teeter between the three all along the way. It's kind of like putting a plane on autopilot or making small corrections all along the way. The more you learn, the more you make adjustments and you start pinpointing and then when you realize no additional information is going to change your opinion you realize, "OK, it's done." So that's a great way to describe valuation absolutely.

LORENZO: Great. So this then would be the qualifiers of where you go through the different stages. Is there anything you would add to these with respect to valuation standards or would you say that this covers it? My intention was to create a mnemonic to assist CEOs, CFOs, founders, and venture-capital investing professionals in remembering it, since it's said that valuation tends to be more art than science, so we have "art": accuracy, relevance, and timeliness.

JEFF: Absolutely. That's a perfect way to describe it because so much of the data we get is all about transactions. But then we have to ask how many are recent—are the older ones actually more relevant—and none of these factors is ever set in stone. For instance, another appraiser called to confirm that I never use transactions that are over five years old and I said yes, unless there's one that's a primary competitor, the only deal that's gone on in the same space forever and appears to be a perfect match. So like you say, it's an issue of relevance.

LORENZO: Before I wrap up, is there anything you'd like to point out to a CFO or your fellow valuation professionals to increase the quality of understanding or the quality of the profession?

JEFF: I guess the biggest thing I would say is just share information. I'm surprised by appraisers that when they figure something out, they don't want to share it as if they've discovered this huge thing that's going to make them competitively better than the rest. The challenge is that because of that behavior not a lot of people are going to embrace sharing new ideas or discoveries. If it's of use, it still won't benefit them or the profession if they are so secretive about it that no one gets a chance to convince the auditors that it's sound. I think there needs to be a certain amount of collaboration among the appraisal community. I think we can be more powerful in delivering our message. That could be a function of too many appraisal societies or because people get so guarded about their work. When the practice aid came, we figured it out quickly at one of my firms, and they were very guarded about it. I thought that was kind of silly because I know other appraisers that are doing it wrong. They're talking to auditors, and we need to start sharing.

I personally started collaborating with fellow appraisers proactively and I believe it's improved all of our services. I've learned from them and when I started sharing, someone would modify my model to make it better.

Reviewing the Carver Deal Term Test

LORENZO: Oh, thanks for reminding me. I wanted to share a technique I've been recommending to some valuation professionals, as well as venture-fund CFOs and some angel investors for the past few years. I call it the Carver Deal Term Test.

The basic idea is that you take each security that a company has and you assume that it's possible to do a secondary purchase of each of those securities for the same price per share, let's say $1. So, for example, you could buy 100,000 Series A for $100,000, 100,000 Series B for $100,000, 100,000 Series C for $100,000, 100,000 Common Shares for $100,000, just as an example. This is basically leveling out the amount paid across rounds. Next, across the breakpoints you show what the multiple would have been, or the price per share, or the percentage of proceeds would be for each of the securities you purchased side by side.

JEFF: So you do that after you've built in all the preferences, right?

LORENZO: Yes, absolutely. I've found this to be much more effective in getting across the relative value of securities, especially when speaking to venture-capital fund finance teams and certain founders that have more than a couple of rounds of financing behind their venture. Instead of diving right into the Black-Scholes model and sorting through why the Series A got allocated more of the company value than the Series C, they can easily grasp the relative rights to sale or exit proceeds assuming each investment was made for the exact same price.

Well, Jeff, thanks a lot for taking the time to share some of your insights for founders, CFOs, CEOs, angels, auditors, VCs, and other valuation professionals.

JEFF: Thank you, Lorenzo.

SUMMARY

The interview in this chapter shows how some of the methods and cases discussed previously in this book relate directly to every venture-backed company that either intends to get another round of financing or plans to comply with 409A.

In Chapter 9, I combine snippets from one of a series of interviews I did with some of these valuation professionals who were willing to go on the record with their opinions, despite the frankness with which they express their positions, with some of the illustrations used in the book to convey the context of practitioners in this particular area. Auditors, company CFOs, fund CFOs, and perhaps others can certainly get a better idea of what goes into some of the analysis explained, and challenged, within this book.

CHAPTER 9

Don't Blame the Auditors (Blame the Practice Aid Instead)

409A Valuation Professionals Discussing Topic 820 (FAS 157) with VC CFOs

In preparation for this book, I held a conference with three valuation experts I know have focused almost exclusively on venture-backed company valuations and done so at difference firms. The goal of the conference was to give venture-fund CFOs and finance teams an idea of trends taking place with 409A as a result of Topic 718 audits, as those same audit firms would likely be applying some of the same requirements on Topic 820 related audit work they conducted when auditing venture funds.

I was surprised by several things that became clear immediately after the meeting. First, the venture-fund CFOs and finance teams, all of whom were extremely well versed in finance and especially well versed in VC transactions, felt like much of the conversation from the valuation experts was a foreign language. I anticipated there would be some points of disconnected terminology and experience but hoped to bridge that gap with real-world examples from venture-backed companies that went public. While there was great appreciation on both sides, the venture-fund finance teams generally felt it was too much technical information to take in given the time constraints. The next thing I realized was the degree to which auditors might, potentially, be influencing the value conclusions reached by otherwise unrelated valuation professionals. Each of the experts on the panel is clearly independent, but as the discussion proceeded, it became clear that the auditor "requests" or preferences for various approaches in these valuations might in some ways indirectly be placing the responsibility for the value conclusions reached on the auditors. This could have long-term implications, not just with respect to valuations but also with respect to the independence of auditors, who are by definition not supposed to be making the value estimates, but rather testing them in accordance with GAAS and GAAP.

During the conference we also tried to highlight the IPO disclosures. However, it was hard for CFOs and finance teams to interpret the valuation speak while also looking at interactive PWERM models, OPM models, and illustrations demonstrating how the figures in the MD&A section started as many of the basic calculations we've reviewed in this book thus far. To improve upon that, I've broken the comments from the panelists, as well as my questions to those panelists, into sections here. After each major section, I present a relevant MD&A valuation disclosure along with some competing valuation inputs, where applicable, to emphasize the status quo in the valuation industry, the prevailing auditor recommendations, and the recommended deviations from those methods by me.

INTRODUCTION TO THE EXPERT PANELISTS

The first panelist you will hear from is Joe Orlando, AM, MBA, a venture-capital valuation expert with over 20 years of experience. In addition to being an accredited member of the American Society of Appraisers and participating on thousands of valuation, Joe was an investment banker, working on M&A and corporate finance.

Josh Cashman, JD, MBA, ASA, has been performing 409A valuations for venture-backed companies since the regulation first went into effect. Before that, he was regional VP and director of a national trust company, specializing in investment management and securities analysis. Josh is an accredited senior appraiser.

Jeff Faust, AVA, introduced in Chapter 8, has been performing valuations for high-growth ventures for more than 15 years.

LORENZO: Good morning, this is Lorenzo Carver from Liquid Scenarios and we're getting ready to start Topic 820 2/20—VC Fund YE 2010 Insights from Valuation Experts. We're very fortunate to have some bona fide valuation experts, each of whom has been known for some time now. Combined they have some 500 audited valuations of high-growth venture-backed companies behind them.

The techniques and insights that they'll be sharing today are directly applicable to every finance team of every venture-capital fund or private equity group for this year's upcoming audit.

So one of things we'll be doing is actually looking at companies that have gone public this year, since there have been so many that were venture backed, looking at their disclosures, and trying to tie that back to how you can use the 409A valuation work that was done by experts like those that you're going to hear from today to better prepare yourself for your audits in the coming year and to better prepare the documentation for your funds on your portfolio companies.

I wanted to start by going through several items as we introduce the participants and put them into a context for valuing your portfolio in the new year and also going through some of the Liquid Scenarios models for those companies.

THE AUDITOR'S VALUATION "BIBLE"

LORENZO: One of the most consistent references you'll see in the MD&A sections of registration statements for venture-funded company IPO is to the AICPA's Technical Practice Aid for Valuing Private Companies, officially titled *Valuation of Privately-Held-Company Equity Securities Issued as Compensation.*

Joe, how heavily do auditors rely on this Practice Aid when reviewing your valuation work as part of an audit?

JOE: Sure, as a valuation expert we consider this Practice Aid to be sort of our bible in terms of methodologies not only in terms of valuing the enterprise but in terms of allocating the value. I think the biggest focus that auditors zero in on is the appropriate allocation methodology, in terms of allocating value in terms of what is most likely an option pricing model based on the stage of development of the company. The three allocation values that they look at, a current value approach and a probability weighted expected return [PWERM] certainly have their place, based on the stage of development of the companies. For the later-stage companies that are about to go public, the PWERM is appropriate, but most of the attention seems to be on the option pricing method (OPM) for early-stage companies.

I think the updated Practice Aid, which should be coming out for public consumption in the next month or so, goes through some more models in terms of some hybrid models and so forth.

LORENZO: Great. Jeff, could you follow through on Joe's point on how this Practice Aid has evolved over time? As I recall, when it first came out, it was so far from the way that actual venture-capital deals are done that some of the suggestions in it weren't applicable. But obviously it's improved a bit as auditors, venture-fund finance teams, and CFOs of the portfolio companies, along with valuation professionals such as yourself, have tried to work together to make it more relevant.

AICPA Practice Aid Cap Tables	Real-World Cap Tables
Preferred	Preferred
Common Stock	Common Stock

Warrants on Preferred
Warrants on Common
Options on Common
Various Exercise/Strike Prices
Various Sensitivities to Time

Complexity Gap When Applying Option Pricing
Model, Probability Weighted Expected Return,
and Even Current Value Method

(See Chapter 6, "Why You Should "D.O.W.T."
(Doubt) Venture Capital Returns")

EXHIBIT 9.1   On the Complexity Gap between the Practice Aid and the Real
World of Venture-Capital Valuations
Source: Liquid Scenarios, Inc.

JEFF: Sure, it's interesting that while the Practice Aid has become the
409A bible as Joe points out, and I agree, but back when it first came out,
409A valuations were essentially box check reports for auditors. Auditors
would ask, "Have you done one?" and then check a box. Also, a lot of
the allocation methods presented in the Practice Aid are so simplistic that
they didn't apply, because none of the companies I've ever dealt with have
cap tables that are that simple. So it was hard to apply those simplified
models to companies that were always more complex. It was not used early
on for complex models until the AICPA published more detail later on its
interpretation of how to apply the option pricing method (OPM) in greater
detail. This allowed analysts to engineer their models and programs much
better. (See Exhibit 9.1.)

SAS101 TESTS, PWERMS, AND OPMs

LORENZO: Excellent. Josh, I'd like you to continue along those same lines,
regarding the applicability, in terms of auditors reacting to the models you
create versus the test models they create. Also, if you could, discuss how
auditor perceptions of when it's applicable to use the different allocation
methods mentioned in the Practice Aid have changed over the past several
years since the Practice Aid first came out.

JOSH: Sure, Lorenzo. Joe talked a little about the current value approach
and the PWERM, but the OPM is typically what we're finding most auditors

prefer, and I think the reason for that is that with fair value accounting, that's perceived to be the least subjective. So, most of the judgment is perceived to be taken away from the valuation analyst and there's a certain amount of auditor subjectivity that goes in, but a lot of that has to do with market data. In that way, I think the OPM is viewed as a variation of a market approach. So what we're looking at is the most recent round of financing and establishing the implied equity value of the company based on the capital structure of the company, so effectively a waterfall analysis. In cases where a current value method may be relevant, the Practice Aid is fairly clear as to when the current value approach is appropriate. That's simply looking at the traditional valuation approach, and that's what we did four or five years ago before we saw the OPM taking over.

I think, and I'll let Joe and Jeff correct me here, but I think it's less clear certainly in the Practice Aid when the PWERM is most relevant. I think we all know as practitioners that a probability-weighted expected return method is (and more recently we've also recently heard it called a "Power Method"), to me, less clear when they think it's appropriate. But to me the PWERM seems more like a real options approach. Like Joe said, we typically have requests for it by auditors when a company has engaged an underwriter for an exit, and to me in my view that seems pretty late along the line. So we see the current value method applicable where there haven't been any rounds of financing, where the company is underperforming, or hasn't been meeting its objectives and may not even continue as a going concern. Then you have this huge space in between where the option pricing model is appropriate. That's what auditors seem to want to see these days.

JEFF: Josh, if I could pipe in here, one of the things we've started to see in the last year ago or so, not for companies that are in the early stage because it's a waste of time and money, but we started running all three allocations for every company that got funding. My theory was that these methods need to jibe and work together, and the stage of the company should drive the allocation approach, but at what point should you be switching allocation? When we started running all three in tandem, we started noticing a significant relationship between the methods and we've made some hard stances because of that analysis as to when the company should be switching methods. The typical rule we arrived at was at stage Series A you just do a waterfall, as a company matures you do the option pricing method, and when you get close to an exit then you start incorporating the PWERM. When an actual transaction is imminent, then of course you do the actual waterfall for the liquidity event, so you more or less go full-circle back to the waterfall for fair value. So we'll try to do more quantitative and qualitative analysis on that to try to get more data behind our theory and how they relate.

JOE: Yes, I can chime in also. From the reports that I've seen, as a resource to our audit group at Frank Rimmerman, I've seen a lot of different uses of the PWERM, which Josh mentioned. I think the PWERM is appropriate when there is data for specific industries, life science in particular. I do think that some valuation firms are looking at the PWERM as a multiple or a return on invested capital, based on some proprietary data. In those cases it's an interesting application of the PWERM for very early-stage companies and even those that are maturing where an option pricing model may be used. I have seen what Jeff mentioned, using all three methods and reconciling those methods. There is a school of thought that says the PWERM should reconcile with the OPM in many respects, given what the PWERM's looking at in terms of specific scenarios versus the normal distribution of an option pricing model. But I do think that all of that information is a good reconciliation for a valuation expert to come up with a final conclusion.

JOSH: Lorenzo, just to beat this dead horse a little more, this is Josh Cashman again with Intrinsic. What we have been asked to do a few times is to do a variation on the PWERM and the OPM. This is in the space where the company is entertaining an exit but hasn't necessarily locked in a date or an underwriting. In cases like that you can run a variation on the IPO, acquisition, or OPM along with a PWERM.

LORENZO: Great, that's ton of information and a good place to link that to some of the fund managers, finance teams, and accounting teams on this call, because one of things we experienced early on, as I'm sure you are all aware of, is that auditors would focus on creating waterfalls manually and a lot of those waterfalls had errors in them. They just weren't accurate. When they were doing it with the valuation professionals, they were billing the client, but the valuation professional in a lot of those early cases had to eat the cost of showing the auditor how the auditors' test model was incorrect. However, it seems like now as things have become more sophisticated, we see a much higher quality of questions from the auditors and with that the auditor requirements for those valuations.

Part of the motivation for this conference was anticipating that some of the trends we've seen in 409A valuation audits might start to move over to venture-fund audits. So, for instance, last year (2009), most auditors when reviewing venture fund valuations of portfolio companies would pretty much ask for just a waterfall, or current method analysis, for most portfolio companies. The exceptions tended to be ones that were more sensitive, in which cases they might dig into whether a PWERM or comps would be more appropriate. Going forward, it appears that the standard may be increasing, so the documentation and the use of multiple methods may start to get more substantial.

So, based on that, one of the comments you made earlier, Joe, was with respect to life-science, or biotech companies, for instance, and how you've seen the PWERM used there. Is that accurate?

PWERMS AND rNPV/eNPV MODELS

JOE: Yes, I think that industry lends itself given the phase of development and defined growth periods based on FDA approval. There's a lot more data out there about probability and success.

LORENZO: Right. This is why even the terminology in calling it the PWERM is kind of interesting. Are any of you familiar with the expected net present value method (eNPV) also known as the risk-adjusted net present value method (rNPV)? Because it's pretty similar to the PWERM. You see it used a for life science and biotech companies a lot, and looks a lot like the PWERM where they apply a probability for each phase, so pre-clinical, Phase 1, Phase 2, Phase 3, and then assign a probability and adjust the expected cash flows based on the reduced risk as the company moves from one stage to another.

JOE: Yes, I've definitely seen that before. You're absolutely right—it [rNPV] does lend itself toward that fundamental methodology of probability weighting some expected scenarios.

LORENZO: But the difference appears to be that in the biotech space when they apply a probability, like you said the risks are kind of defined because there's a large population where they can say this is the percentage of leads, candidates, or new drugs that apply at this stage and this is how many get through. So, based on a large sample size, this is the probability that a new drug candidate will get to the next stage. That compares to one of the criticisms of the PWERM that I'd like all of you to perhaps give your opinion on, which is that it tends to be more subjective. I realize there are techniques that valuation professionals use to attempt to quantify the probabilities that are assigned if possible, but even the Practice Aid suggested that these are target returns that should be used by stage. Similarly, other people have suggested these are guideline probabilities that might be assigned by the venture-backed company stage in a given industry. Perhaps each of you could speak to how you address subjectivity when using a PWERM in your valuations.

SUBJECTIVITY AND THE PWERM (OR "POWER") METHOD

Management teams, VCs, and even valuation professionals appear to prefer creating PWERMS in part because they allow the opinions of management to come through in the form of a model of various scenarios. For this reason, some have started to refer to the method as the "Power" method. But this may be fading, as auditors have begun to rely on models that backsolve for the PWERM values in an attempt to objectively measure the reasonableness of probabilities and weightings. The discussion that follows reflects the experience of the valuation professionals we interviewed in this regard.

JEFF: Typically, what we do is we work with clients pretty significantly in terms of what sort of opportunity they have at present, what's going on in their space, what sort of acquisitions are going on. That helps us support the probability of certain events. The same thing applies to IPOs: If they're in a space that hasn't had any IPOs for a while, that could limit their probabilities if the time horizon is shorter, but it depends on how far out they go. It's not only your probability of a specific event, but at what time frame. You could be 10% probability of an IPO, but that could be five years from now and that could keep your values down.

Again, when we started running all three allocations and shifting from an option pricing method, we have to make sure the PWERM is not coming with a lower value than the option pricing method from a prior year in some cases. So proper weighting of the probabilities should help to take care of that. We have to be careful, because a lot of times entrepreneurs are optimistic and will in cases give you the optimistic hope of an IPO timeline for the PWERM. But that's not what we want to use, because putting 40% probability on an IPO for an early-stage company would of course spike the price per share you arrive at. We have to be realistic because as a company starts moving from one stage of development to another, we are remeasuring how far away it is from an acquisition. We typically work very specifically with clients when working with their models, trying to identify when certain exit events will occur.

JOE: Coming from the audit side, which Jeff comes from as well, it's not something that's defined in Webster's as auditable, but certainly the PWERM has audit risk in terms of the subjectivity you mentioned. The only time we would have more objective measurements would be, like you said, in cases of the life sciences or drug companies. I think the PWERM is really two numbers, taking an outcome and then assigning a probability to that outcome. Both of those generally have very subjective components to them, and I think the valuation expert's job is to get an understanding from the client and to get as defensible a position as possible for those inputs, making sure that methodology is as sound as possible.

JEFF: I wanted to comment on how many people in companies don't value the 409A valuation—they think it's a commodity or a box check where they have to pay this price and that's it. Really, I think companies need to start changing attitudes on that. The 409A valuation can give significant insights into capital structures, waterfalls, and possible exits for the company. Companies should understand that not only is all of that valuable information but, as Lorenzo alluded to earlier, these methods are going to start working themselves over to the other side of the valuation for VC funds. So when venture funds are dealing with their auditors, they're going to have to start understanding these methodologies, which is of course a good reason for those funds to start paying a lot more attention to the 409A analysis. There's a lot of great information in there's that I think both the companies can use and the VC firms can use as well.

FINDING INPUTS FOR THE OPM MODEL

LORENZO: Maybe that's a good place to start moving into some of the sample companies that we have, so for instance, in the 409A valuation reports, you will notice that there are a number of methods used and the MD&A section of a registration statement will show how an appraiser applied a weighting to each of them. So one of the things we've talked to different venture funds about is how they can use some of those variables to create their own models. Even if they're not going to use that model as an input they present to the auditor, but rather simply for running an alternative OPM analysis, they might go to the 409A valuation report and see what would happen if they use the volatility estimate the analyst used. We've suggested that they can go to the 409A valuation and perhaps have a record of how one version of comps were arrived at or how the risk-free rate was matched to a given time horizon, or the marketability discount was applied to the common stock. So perhaps we could talk through how a venture fund might repurpose a couple of those variables for a quick comparison to its own models and the process each of you goes through when you select those variables. The hope is that some of the venture-fund CFOs and finance teams on the line can use those resources from reports they've already paid for to populate some of their models.

As an example, Josh, could you share with the CFOs how you go about finding an appropriate risk-free rate to use for an OPM analysis?

JOSH: What I'm typically looking at, depending on how far out we're going—in other words, in an option-pricing method, I can either use the Black-Scholes method or the binomial option pricing model. Typically, I use Black-Scholes, in which case one of the variables is theta, or time to expiration. Time to expiration in these models is generally the point in time that you expect an exit, and I'm usually looking at a three- to five-year window, but certainly nothing in excess of five years. But I'm also interesting in learning what Joe and Jeff use in terms of their theta (time) in their option-pricing models. But what happens if you go too far out in time is that the value of those options increases, which is kind of the inverse of what you'd anticipate because in a privately held company where you're holding that company for a longer period of time, in fact the value of those securities would decrease. Because without the liquidity or marketability, having to hold onto those securities longer would have an inverse effect of what a Black-Scholes model would imply. So what I'm normally looking at is the time to expiration.

So if it's a three-year time period, I'm looking at three-year Treasuries for my risk-free rate. Typically in finance, you're looking at a 10-year Treasury as the risk-free rate. But again, in the Practice Aid there's this suggestion that you're using consistent time periods both looking backwards and forward. For instance, vega, or volatility, another one of the variables in the option pricing model, is based on the time to expiration. So if you are looking out three years, we calculate volatility by looking back three years. Again, all of that is meant to be as consistent as possible.

JOE: I would confirm that relative to matching the risk-free rate to the term that's used [if it's a three-year time period, for instance, a three-year treasury will be used]. I think, like Josh said, the issue with the option-pricing model is the higher the term, the greater the value of the option. I think that really flows into the normal distribution in terms of the basis for the Black-Scholes methodology.

To deal with the term, what we will do if the company is expected to remain private for a long period of time is to look at the different expected scenarios for a company and apply a probability to each of those. Weighting the time periods from those scenarios using the same probabilities, we can arrive at a probability-weighted term.

ENTERPRISE VALUES VERSUS ALLOCATIONS

LORENZO: Great. So I guess it would be helpful for some of the venture-fund CFOs and finance teams to get an understanding of how you come up with an enterprise value versus an allocation and how those act as a test for each other. I think it sometimes gets confusing even for people when they're practicing, having a discussion, or just digesting a valuation report that they've received in terms of understanding the difference between how you allocated the value versus what the enterprise value conclusion is. It can get even more difficult in certain circumstances when you're using the allocation to confirm what you came up with for the enterprise value. Does that question make sense?

JOSH: I think it's an interesting question, and I think it's something we've all talked about. I know Joe and I are part of the Fair Value Forum and I know it's been up there before. I think traditionally in finance, equity value has been based on enterprise value. So I think all of our calculations are first targeting the enterprise value and thereafter distilling in the equity value, and thereafter for these types of companies establishing the common stock value based on the capital structure. Those are the steps, and I think those steps are based on principles of finance established by Modigliani and Miller. Those are the steps involved in each of our valuation approaches.

JOE: Yes, I agree with Josh. I think what you're talking about, Lorenzo, is the backsolve of the enterprise value from the recent equity round of financing and basically going from the bottom up to the enterprise value and then allocating back down using the option pricing model to get the value of the common stock. I agree, it's a rub sometimes for CEOs who have done a very good job of negotiating terms for a VC round of financing where there's no participation and the pre-money value of the company is very high. But what happens is the value of the common stock is a reflection of those negotiations, so the value of the common stock is actually higher than what they would normally see or normally want.

JEFF: Despite popular belief, 10% of preferred is not always the value of the common stock, even in the early stage. That's a great point by Joe, since the non-participation causes common to be worth more earlier than you would want, especially in the earlier stage.

LORENZO: I'd like you all to expound on that a little to tailor it to the cases of the venture funds. In the case of the venture funds, pre-money or post-money value isn't that reflective of the most recent round of financing in a lot of cases, because of the way that it's expressed versus the definition. In a lot of cases, like you've said, when the founders say this is the pre- or post-money value of the company and compare that to the common stock value you arrive at, they just multiply that by the fully diluted shares and get confused or even upset because the number they arrive at is lower than their perceived value of the company. Is that essentially what you guys are saying?

JOE: Yes, exactly. I think if you were to look at it very simplistically, pre- and post-money would assume that the value of the common and the preferred are equal, and we know that's not correct based on the rights and the preferences of the preferred over the common. So you're right. I If you were to go to the extreme, the opposite direction, and based on an option-pricing model, and multiply the value of the common by the number of fully diluted shares, you'd be saying the value of the preferences associated with the preferred stock are worth nothing. So the answer is somewhere in between, and the hard part is really reconciling with the CEOs, the CFOs, and the board members how our value of equity from an enterprise value is different from the pre- and post-money.

JEFF: Let's also be clear, too, and I get kind of frustrated about this when I get auditors who are focused on a particular close or round when it's strategic—that's not fair market value. 409A is clear that our job is to establish fair market value. When these rounds are closed, I question whether these are fair value because a lot of times when VCs invest in these companies, they are paying an intrinsic value, or attempting to peg what it could potentially be worth in the future. So the pricing for these rounds is essentially backed into often. If I'm putting in 2 million and getting 25% of the company, then all of a sudden the company's worth $8MM? But that doesn't necessarily mean that's fair market value. So when you run allocations on the pre of $8MM or the post $10MM, you already may know that there's no way that $8MM or $10MM is fair value and therein lies some of the frustration.

JOE: Coming from the audit side, when we see a fact patter like that, from a creation perspective we'll make sure we reconcile with a discounted cash flow approach. From an audit perspective, we'll make sure to ask the valuation expert what he's done to reconcile that value and whether there are some strategic inputs that went into the pricing of the round. In fair value parlance, it's a level two input, not a level one input, so you're not really looking at the sale value of common, you're looking at the implied value of common based on the sale of preferred. But you certainly want to incorporate that data point, regardless of whether it's strategic, and make sure that you reconcile.

NEXT ROUND PRICING AND TOPIC 820

LORENZO: Directly in the context of what we are talking about today, most of the venture funds are faced with supporting the values they have for preferred stock. As you've mentioned, that's often opposite of some of the issues that are at play when valuing the common, although in theory all of these approaches should fit together with some consistency. One of the reasons I believe they don't tend to fit together is because different parties tend to count the shares differently.

So, for instance, if the company is doing an IPO, then the underwriters generally consider (or deem) only shares that are actually outstanding as issued when they arrive at a capitalization for the company. This is the opposite of how the pre-/post-money capitalization is being arrived at for purposes of a venture-capital investment round, then of course it's fully diluted and you're counting as many shares as possible. To just apply a market cap approach, where you say price per share times number of fully diluted shares equals enterprise value, you know right off the bat that the implied enterprise value will be overstated at least by the amount of the reserved options pool, especially if it's a seed or very early-stage company. However, down the road, as the company gets closer to an exit, the post-money values and enterprise values start to become closer, but even then there's a difference between that and the implied pre-money market capitalization since both granted and unissued reserve shares will be excluded from the IPO calculation.

Do any of you have comments or insights on that?

JOSH: There's no doubt that when you're looking at the traditional post-money capitalization on a VC financing round, you're looking at all issued shares and all authorized options, whereas in our calculations we're not necessarily looking at all authorized options. Though those options may represent earmarked common stock to be issued in the future, they are not outstanding as of the issue date, so in our calculations we're looking at all outstanding options. That's an area I've heard some disparity or some disagreement on that subject.

JOE: Yeah, the only other issue that I'd bring up is to make sure that if you're going to use that method (of including the options), that you are taking into account the cash that's going to be generated from the exercise of those options. We tend to use the treasury method when we're looking at the options and allocating and just making sure that we don't need to skew the cash generated by the exercises by using the treasury method to get to a net option count.

LORENZO: That' s also an issue we've seen for venture-fund fair value calculations [Topic 820 (FAS 157)] and also the 409A valuation side, which is where a company has a cap table and so much of the pool is reserved. So regarding the timing of the exit, Joe and Josh, you mentioned going out three to five years for the variables in the OPM models. Do you adjust the capital structure based on the valuation date of shares outstanding or the expected capital structure three to five years from the valuation date?

JOSH: That's an interesting point, Lorenzo, and I'm sure there may be cases where (and maybe this is something where Jeff brought up earlier) a VC's initial investment in a company is not likely to be its only investment in a company. That investor may participate in additional rounds of financing over the course of a number of years, in which case the capital structure of the company would change, and that would be a way of capturing any adjustment based on fair market for the foreseeable future. That's a fairly rigorous study, but it's something that can be done, and it's certainly something anyone on this call who's a valuation professional has had to do, to capture the fact that a VC is not necessarily going to make one investment in a company, but rather that VCs are setting the stage to make a series of investments.

JEFF: I've been told by auditors, especially when looking at cash flow, that we can't take into consideration cash coming in from future rounds or cap structure, so it's an interesting discussion, but we typically don't try to factor that in.

But, Lorenzo, you bring up an interesting issue. My personal thought is that in the option pricing method, the pricing term should try to estimate when and how long the company can go until the next round. I know the prevailing practice is to measure until the assumed exit, but really, if you're close enough to see an exit, you should be using a PWERM. So my opinion is that the option pricing method's term should be until the next round so that you're taking into consideration the capital structure, since I know the company's not going to make it unless it gets another round. So why are we estimating exits in that specific cap structure? Now, it's hard to estimate what the possible future capital structure will look like, but I think we need to be looking at shorter pricing (OPM) terms to take that into consideration.

JOE: Yes, but I think the difficulty in modeling that out has led us not to include future rounds in the allocation using the option pricing model. But we have looked at technology to more easily model those future financing scenarios and incorporate them reasonably into our models. Because otherwise, as Josh mentioned, figuring out what's the potential future pricing for those rounds, their terms, the size, how the cash will be used, and so forth is a tedious and time-consuming task. So I think the biggest thing you want to look at in terms of coming to a conclusion of value is what the least wrong number is.

DIFFERENT WAYS OF TREATING GRANTED, UNVESTED, AND RESERVED OPTIONS

LORENZO: One of the other questions that's come up that we've actually seen with venture funds, especially for larger holdings that they have, provides us with a great opportunity to reconcile what the venture funds might see on a 409A valuation versus what they encounter with their auditors, with respect to a waterfall. This has to do with the dilutive impact of future option grants on the value of the preferred. That tends to have not as much to do with additional rounds of financing, but simply relates to the passage of time. In most years when I've looked at auditor comments, I've noticed they are not taking in to account future grants of stock options. Is that consistent with what you've seen recently?

JEFF: For the most part, yes, that's true. But in some cases, particularly recently, I've seen times when auditors have insisted that the future grants be taken into consideration, particularly when it's anticipated that a large number of grants will be happening after the round currently being negotiated.

JOE: Yeah, and I've had that question before, and we look at it as a sensitivity analysis. So we'll look at the outstanding option pool, and we will initially not take it into account. But if we are asked to look at it and allocate those future grants, we'll assume that it's iterative and that all the options get priced at the final conclusion of value for the common stock in our analysis.

LORENZO: That's great to know, because we see a different between how auditors approach for purposes of 409A and how they approach it for venture funds. It has seemed to not be applied consistently.

So, we've pulled out some of the MD&A notes from some of the filings of venture-backed companies that went public in 2010, and I thought we'd go through those terms with you valuation experts so some of the fund CFOs can get more familiar with some of the terms that are being used with respect to fair value and how that terminology has evolved.

Two related terms you see a lot in the MD&A sections are claims on the company's assets and allocation. So, allocation between debt and other equity classes, I believe that used to be referred to in the context of the OPM as a contingent claims mode. Do you recall that?

JOE: I'm not sure what the previous terminology was, but I think there was initially a huge discussion among the Big 4 as to whether debt should be used as the first breakpoint of an option pricing analysis in terms of that contingency because there was a thought that the allocation using the option pricing model in this context should start with an equity value versus a capital value. But that would assume that the value of the debt was equal to its face value, whereas when you run the OPM analysis, it's possible that the value of the debt can be less. Josh and Jeff, have you seen that evolve over time as well?

JEFF: I have, but you know my preference is to go from enterprise value down to equity, taking out the debt, and then running that through the model. But you're right, it does raise an issue I asked one of my analysts the other day about whether we think this debt is worth what it's being shown at to allow us to make that comment. But that's something that I think is interesting to analyze as certain liquidity issues come up with companies where maybe the value of debt is not its face value dollar for dollar. We don't do that now but we are doing it now.

JOE: That's one of the biggest comments we get: If you use debt as the first breakpoint, you will always get a value of debt that's lower than the face value based on a normal distribution that assumes a value of zero as the starting point in the lowest extreme. We've been asked whether our allocation methodology using an option pricing scheme is in fact deriving a fair market value for the debt, and I think that's a big topic that's being discussed at the AICPA relative to this update of the Practice Aid.

JOSH: Well there have been times where we've had just round after round of convertible debt into a future round that hasn't been issued. Have you seen that before?

JOE: Definitely. We've seen debt used as that first breakpoint, and we use it as our first breakpoint because we assume there's a possibility it can go to zero. That's why we have a dissolution scenario in there and value the debt as at risk if a dissolution scenario occurs. Granted, they have the first right, but that's why they're the first breakpoint.

JEFF: I think the characteristics of the debt will drive some of that also. Are they convertible, are they event convertible, are they convertible based upon a vote of all the other equity holders? There are a lot of variations to the debt. You have to be aware of them and make decisions that are appropriate to each in your model.

VALUING WARRANTS IN VENTURE-BACKED COMPANIES

LORENZO: Yes, that's something we saw a lot of in late 2008 and early 2009. There were a lot of convertible notes issued in response to the financial crisis. A lot of those convertible notes had multiple liquidation preferences on them. Instead of having a 1X liquidation preference, which ordinary debt generally has, these issues could have a 2X or even a 4X liquidation preference. So when you do a Black-Scholes on it, you actually end up with an indicated value for the debt that's higher than its fair value, because of the optionality.

JOE: Right, and that doesn't take into account the value of the warrants that they were issued as well.

LORENZO: Yes, and that's right because another issue that comes up is the valuation of the warrants. A lot of these deals have warrants, so you can allocate some of the equity value to the warrants using the option pricing method, but then you still have to adjust that value based on the expected life of the warrants, or the contract life of the warrants. One of the things we see is that sometimes there's a difference in how you account for the warrants if the underlying stock is redeemable preferred versus preferred stock that's not redeemable. Have any of you come across that at all?

JOE: We've come across some warrants that have a put feature, but usually when we see a warrant it's simply a straight. I've actually done the valuation of a warrant portfolio for a large bank, and we've seen the vast majority of those [warrants] on preferred but also some on common. It's a creative instrument for the banks, but depends on whether they want more warrant coverage or greater liquidation preference.

JOSH: I haven't seen that relationship between warrants and redeemable preferred, but we have seen the anti-dilution provisions that have to be measured on redeemable preferred as a contingent liability. But we haven't seen an impact on the redeemable preferred and the warrants.

LORENZO: I asked because we see instances where a portfolio company has to have an outside valuation professional calculate the fair value of the warrants on redeemable preferred to arrive at a discount, because of the account accounting rules around beneficial conversion features. The accounting rules sometimes require that if the preferred is redeemable, you have to book the warrants as interest expense. So to do so, you have to first come up with the fair value first. Have any of you been involved in those engagements?

JOE: We have not been engaged to come up with the interest, but we have been asked to value the underlying preferred so that the company can do its own valuation using Black-Scholes for that exact reason. So we don't really value the warrants, we give them a value for the underlying [security] so they have the tools to value the warrants.

LORENZO: One of the other reasons that I asked is because I'm wondering if that's going to impact the way that the funds are required to value their warrants. In certain circumstances, you'll see the value of the common stock used to extrapolate the value of a preferred warrant, and in other cases we've seen where the warrants aren't included at all because when they're issued with the preferred, there's the question of how much value goes to the preferred that I purchased and how much value, if any, goes to the warrants I received for leading the round. So you can see how that becomes its own allocation exercise.

QUANTIFYING QUALITATIVE INPUTS TO VALUE CONCLUSIONS FOR VC-FUNDED COMPANIES

LORENZO: One of the items that I thought would be worth reviewing are some of the less quantifiable disclosures we see regarding how people value these companies: for instance, important developments regarding the company's line of business, the company's stage of development, how the company meets any financial milestones, where a company is compared to its business strategy, and how complete its management team is. Can you go over, perhaps at a high level, how you incorporate some of these factors into your conclusions and how they relate to any quantifiable inputs into the models or enterprise values that you arrive at?

JEFF: What we typically do in those situations is try to assess what stage the company is in. The practice guide outlines six stages of development for a startup and addresses things like each of those aspects you've mentioned. Each of those aspects helps identify what stage a company is in and then corresponds to which allocation method is appropriate.

So if it's in the middle stage, it might have made some progress on its business model, not have the management team completely built but hired a few key roles. It could be generating some revenue but isn't profitable. Each of those things would suggest to me that this company is a middle stage company, so I would argue that using anything other than an option pricing method in that case would be hard to argue, especially if the company has closed a recent round. So I think each of those characteristics helps me determine which stage a company is in.

JOSH: Yes, I'd agree with Jeff. The six stages that are outlined in the Practice Aid help us map a correlation to the level of the enterprise, whether it's seed or early stage, first stage, and so forth. So we're able to integrate that into our income model in our discounted cash flow model to an appropriate discount rate based on VC hurdle rates. The various stages of development are a big part of how we go about selecting an appropriate discount rate and aligning it as closely as we can.

JOE: I agree with both Jeff and Josh. We certainly do look at it in terms of the stage of development. Where a company is in the development stage has a large influence on what allocation method we use. We certainly take into account those risks and opportunities, which are the less quantifiable lists that you mentioned as our adjustment to the discount rate in terms of the company's specific risk premium. But we also take these less quantifiable inputs and work them into our probabilities used for a probability-weighted return, the probability of an exit scenario, or determining the term of the option pricing model.

DISCOUNTS FOR LACK OF MARKETABILITY (DLOM) AND VENTURE-FUND PORTFOLIOS

LORENZO: The other area that we suspect might become more important for venture-capital funds going forward is the various discounts applied for lack of liquidity, lack of marketability, or lack of control that you see applied in traditional valuations of private company securities. In the case of your valuations of common stock for venture-capital-financed companies, you always apply a discount for lack of marketability to the common stock. On the other hand, there's of course a prevailing theory that such discounts are incorporated into the price of the preferred already, since a knowledgeable party made the purchase fully aware of the relatively illiquid security he or she was buying. I think it would be helpful if each of you could walk the venture-fund CFOs and finance teams, at a high level, through what goes into the discount for lack of marketability and how you might envision some of the venture funds or private equity funds applying that to various securities that they encounter in their valuation efforts.

JOE: I think we could probably spend a full day talking about discounts for a lack of marketability. It's the one single topic in valuation where you see a passionate disagreement in terms of how you look at it, how you calculate it. I think the best way that we look at marketability when it comes to a round of financing is that we would assume that the preferred round is marketable and that common by definition has a semi-marketable component to it if you arrive at an enterprise value that backsolves using the last round of preferred. Because there's a market component of willing buyer and willing seller for that last round of financing, we're assuming that the preferred is marketable. A lot of this discount for lack of marketability in terms of what you use and how you use it is really based on the starting point for the enterprise value.

If I do a discounted cash flow analysis as my starting point for my option pricing model, I'm assuming that has a minority component to it but that it's a marketable minority value. If I apply a market approach, using guideline public companies, because I'm starting using minority value in terms of per share value, from which a market capitalization was arrived at, I'm also assuming a marketable minority value. But if I use transaction analysis, there's a control component in there, so I'd assume the value I'm getting for the enterprise from the transaction analysis is the control marketable value. When I apply my discounts, I have to take into account both the discount for lack of control as well as the discount for a lack of marketability. So I think the starting point for the enterprise value is really the jumping off point for the discussion of discounts for lack of marketability.

Do you agree with that, Josh and Jeff?

JOSH: Absolutely. But first let me say that I'm glad that you had to answer that question first, Joe. I've seen a lot of work done on this particular area, including work done by Joe, and a lot has changed just over the last several years. If we looked at fair market value just a few years ago, fair market value discounts for lack of marketability were in that context in the tax realm; they were based on empirical studies. You would use databases that had restricted stock studies or others comparing restricted stock purchases of publicly traded companies to prices paid for their publicly traded counterparts, or pre-IPO studies that looked at transactions in shares of companies that were about to go public and evaluated the impact that had on the marketability of their shares. More recently in the context of fair value, and I think what's generally promoted these days, also in the context of fair market value or tax, are quantitative studies. Quantitative studies look at a protective put, or similar methods that rely more on calculations. I think that over the next few years we're going to see even more developments in terms of applying real discounts for lack of marketability based on the secondary market for restricted stock. We're seeing different venues such as auction sites where restricted stock in privately held companies can be sold, and it'll be interesting to see what discounts are implied by those transactions as well.

So the discount for lack of marketability is something that's evolving. I think it's something that we're all getting a lot of guidance on and, like I've said, Joe's done a lot of work in this area, and it's a space where there's still a lot of work to be done. This includes further understanding both the discount for lack of marketability and the discount for lack of liquidity.

They are, at least theoretically, discrete. But, Joe, I'd be interested, I know this is something you've talked about before, if you wouldn't mind elaborating on the relationship you generally see in terms of what you've been asked by most auditors as the maximum discount on common as it relates to the most recent round of preferred, when applying a discount for lack of marketability. I know you've talked about that before, but just talk about the relationship between common, the price for common, the price for preferred in the most recent round of financing.

JOE: Yes, I think the most conservative approach in terms of a discount for the lack of marketability when you're solving for the last round of preferred is to assume that the preferred has some kind of market component to it so it's a semi-marketable enterprise value being derived. So what we'd do in that case is take an incremental discount for lack of marketability based on what we think the implied discount for lack of marketability built into the preferred round is, less what we think the total lack for discount of marketability is. So, for example, if the last round of financing were priced and we thought there was a 15% lack of marketability built into that pricing, that implies the buyer was making the purchase assuming there was some kind of discount associated with that. In that case, the incremental discount for lack of marketability on the common may be 5% because the total discount for lack of marketability was 20%, but 15% of that was thought to be allocable to the preferred. We believe that considering an incremental discount for lack of marketability attributable to the common versus the preferred is a conservative approach. I think that there are situations where you can push for a discount for lack of marketability that's higher than that, and that subjective component is based on the rights and preferences of the preferred compared to the common. So, if I have a preferred that's a non-participating preferred that in many ways except for the liquidation preference looks like common and has a high probability of being converted to common because it's a later stage company, that discount for lack of marketability for the preferred may be very similar to the discount for lack of marketability attributable to the common. It all depends on those rights and preferences associated with the preferred at the last round financing and what the implied discount for lack of marketability is for that preferred.

JEFF: Great. I got off free for both of those. I don't want to go too much further into it because I think you guys did a great job. But I did want to quickly add that I personally think that discount for lack of liquidity is not the same as the discount for a lack of marketability; I think they're drastically two different things. While each one of them can have a little bit of a component of the other, I think they are completely different and they should be applied carefully and you have to make sure that you are applying it to the right asset. I wouldn't just blindly apply a discount for lack of liquidity unless I know that that asset has liquidity issues versus marketability issues.

JOE: Yes, and I think that's a very good point because the discount for lack of liquidity is really more in terms of a tax realm, where gaining liquidity is expected to have some costs associated with it in terms of realizing proceeds. That's certainly not the same basis by which determining fair value looks at marketability.

LORENZO: In a practical context then, it sounds like in most cases anyway there's not a strong argument in a lot of these cases for applying a discount for lack of control to any of the preferred stock in your opinions. I know it's hard to make generalizations, but is that a fair assumption?

JOE: Well, it depends on what percentage ownership the last round has and whether that has a control component to it. If it does, then you may want to look at a discount for a lack of control relative to the other securities. But normally we don't see that, so when we look at a marketability discount, we're assuming that control is taken into account at the starting point of the enterprise value. Most likely we'll use a discounted cash flow method or a guideline public company approach, which assume a minority ownership to start with. If you're backsolving for a round of preferred that has a minority component associated with it, you're going to get a minority value as well. So usually that control is taken out of the equation based on the methodology that's used. But like I said, if we used a transactions approach, which we do when we value a winery, for instance, where there's good data that looks at actual transactions, we'll take a discount for lack of control before we take a discount for lack of marketability.

JEFF: I think that's the key point here; there are a lot of discounts floating around here, a lot of issues that we're discussing. The key thing is that you don't apply them in all situations. Every method shouldn't have a discount for lack of marketability or a discount for lack of control, because as Joe alluded to, there are times when you're comparing it to control transactions. The key is to make sure you are consistent with the enterprise value assumptions and apply the appropriate discount for that situation.

SHARESPOST, SECONDMARKET AS MARKET INPUTS

LORENZO: Josh, one of the other items that you had mentioned was regarding secondary sales. As you've pointed out, these have become more popular, especially for some of the Internet and social media companies, and it's starting to expand to other types of companies as well through some of the marketplaces like SecondMarket or Sharespost, for instance. In addition to that, we've also seen, because of the long road to liquidity during the first decade of this century, more stock repurchases, where you have a stock repurchase financed by a venture fund. So essentially a venture fund comes in and buys Series D stock, for instance, and then the company will use some of those proceeds to repurchase common stock from people who have left the company or people who have been there for a certain period of time. Obviously, those transactions have multiple implications with respect to the value of the common stock and also with respect to the value of the preferred stock to a certain degree. I was wondering if any of you would like to comment on those as separate pieces. First, looking at secondary transactions in some of these marketplaces where parties, not necessarily in coordination with the company, buy and sell shares of a venture-funded company. How would that impact your valuation analysis, if at all, today?

JEFF: I'll take this one since you guys hit the last one. I take into consideration all transactions. I get calls all the time asking, "What happens if we have a sale out here, are you going to take that into consideration? How much is that going to impact the value?" My general answer is that I am absolutely going to take it into consideration and it really depends on the details as to how it might impact the value. I think you have to look at the details of some of these transactions and the block of stock we're looking at. So in the example you've presented, in that situation you have a lot of people being able to buy stock or being able to sell stock and I think that's a pretty good indication of value. I think it's important for you to look at those blocks of shares. I had a client disclose a transaction to me, and I said I would probably weight that a pretty good amount of the transaction. The client tried to argue his way out of putting weight on it because it was significantly higher than what we were coming up with on a separate standalone basis. The more he talked, the worst it got, as we came to find out it was more than one transaction but a very large purchaser buying shares from lots of shareholders. Then we discovered it wasn't just a onetime transaction, but that those sales had taken place throughout the year, so I ended up putting 100% weighting on those transactions. Since these were significant investors, very well informed about what was going on, paying this price, versus the company's argument that these were a bunch of rich guys that didn't know what they were paying. My position was, I don't think so. People don't generally get rich in this space by making poor decisions around valuation. They must know something. So I do think these transactions are very important, although I'm a little concerned about what these marketplaces are going to do to private company price per shares and how are they going to be paralleling the 409A. As I said before, I think people consider 409A as too much of a commodity, whereas there's a lot of value in those analyses that should be taken into consideration when people go to the secondary markets. Otherwise, you can end up with a big problem down the road, a big disconnect.

JOSH: You know, I think this is a fascinating area. It's one that's just now growing up and I'm not sure we fully understand it, and by "we" I mean me. We've had a number of cases where we've dealt with Big 4 audit groups and they've said, no, no, no, that most recent transaction isn't relevant. Exclude it entirely, and we've done our best to defend our 409A value or Topic 718 value for fair value on the basis of what the market is shown to bear based on transactions in the secondary market. I will say that from a tax perspective, Revenue Ruling 59-60 implies that an isolated transaction goes to Jeff's point, in that you have to look at who's involved in that transaction. Is it an arm's length transaction? Is it simply an isolated transaction where you have executives disposing of shares? If that's true, then, and you can't necessarily factor in blockage discounts in that transaction. These may be sophisticated investors that don't consider it. So I think all of those factors are relevant in deciding whether to use that transaction in a secondary market as a data point. I think you could make a compelling case one way or another depending on the facts and circumstance of each particular case on whether you're going to weight that transaction. This is an area that I think we're going to see a whole lot of change in as the secondary market matures.

JOE: This topic came up twice over the last couple of weeks: once at the Fair Value Summit in San Francisco when the founder of SecondMarket spoke at that summit and once at a followup at our Fair Value Forum meeting in terms of just bringing up the topic. The question I asked at the Fair Value Summit of the founder of SecondMarket was for a company like Facebook, which is traded on the SecondMarket, is does it even require a 409A valuation because the SecondMarket value is a Level 1 input according to Fair Value terminology? His answer was yes, the client still does have to get a 409A valuation done and that is used to reconcile with what's being traded on the open market. But for Facebook, which has a significant volume attached to it because it is the single highest volume company for SecondMarket in terms of private company trading, it has to be looked at and it has to be taken into consideration.

Now the flipside is at the Fair Value Forum where I brought the same topic up, there were two people in the room from the Big 4, and both had varying degrees of opinion. One said that you have to look at it, and if anything you have to look at it as a primary indication if there are more than three to five sales. If it's an isolated single sale, then you may want to look at it with a little less weight. But when you have three, five, 10, or even a hundred sales, you have to look at what that trending price is in terms of reconciling value, since by definition a willing buyer and willing seller, third party, is the most pure input for determining value. The other Big 4 participants said, well you have to look at who's buying and why are they buying it. Are they buying it as a marketable product or are they buying because they just want to say "I love Facebook and I want to own Facebook, no matter what the price is"? Also a lot of that has to do with the amount of information they have available to them to price the market. The 409A valuation certainly looks into all of the data with full disclosures of financials, forecasts, and access to management, whereas a SecondMarket transaction generally doesn't have any of that data association with it because there are no information rights associated with the ownership of that stock.

So it's something, like Josh said, that's growing up over time and growing up before our eyes. I don't think investors will have the available information they need to make a sound judgment as to what these companies are worth unless a research model develops around these companies. So you have to take it as it is as a transaction, but maybe not a transaction that's done at a fair market value based on the fundamentals. But I come from an investment banking background, and when I was working on IPOs in 1999 and 2000 at Credit Suisse, fundamental value never played a part in pricing an IPO. The fair value is what a buyer is willing to pay for it.

LORENZO: Exactly.

JOE: When you're dealing with companies that have no revenue or you're valuing it based on eyeballs or page views back in the late 1990s it's tough to throw a fundamental approach to it.

LORENZO: Great. So what I have up here is the University of Texas report on IRRs for funds, which I'm sure everyone's seen. Obviously, one of the biggest components now for fund performance is the unrealized value, which is heavily dependent on how different funds estimate value from period to period.

From a valuation perspective, obviously this has some of an impact on the value of the fund stock. But also the secondary sale of common stock in these marketplaces has some impact on the marketability of all shares. So a lot of what we have been discussing is with respect to using transactions as a data point. But what I'm curious about is how do you adjust your marketability discounts to reflect that fact that there's obviously a venue to liquidate common interests in some of these companies? Does that make the value of everyone's stock worth more, depending on the enterprise value you took, since the preferred shareholders, if they wanted to, could either convert to common and effect a sale or more likely sell the more desirable preferred shares they have in a secondary transaction?

JEFF: Yes, I definitely think so. I've done a lot of ESOP work, and the existence of a put option for your ESOP lowers the marketability discount, and the same theory should apply here. Granted, most of those companies trade a very limited volume, so it wouldn't eliminate the discount, but it could lower it. Now, obviously, this is a growing industry so it will take time for us to get data that says what kind of reduction to the marketability discount is needed when the secondary market exists. Is there a trading window? What kind of volume is there? All of those things will have to be taken into account.

JOE: Yes, I've looked at the possibility of adjusting the lack of marketability based on the bid-ask spread, and I think you can learn a lot in the secondary markets, not by the prices where sales occur, but rather by the bid-ask spread. So I would assume that if you have full access to a market as a common stockholder and you have a transaction that occurred at a price, you take the same approach you take when looking at restricted stock for a publicly traded company or an option to own those shares. We all end up with a smaller discount for a lack of marketability when looking at that methodology.

JOSH: To continue on Joe's point, it's kind of a continuum. On the one hand, you have a liquid market, and that liquid market would be measured by a narrow bid-ask spread or by significant trading volume regularly, as well as adequate breadth and depth of trading volume. On the other end of the spectrum, you have a privately held company for which there is absolutely no market. So a zero discount applies to the liquid market, and 100% of the available discount applies to the privately held company without a market for its stock. You'd have to make an argument based on your judgment as to where a given company on SecondMarket falls on that continuum. Thus far, I haven't seen any evidence that this is truly a liquid market, yet. I would continue applying discounts for lack of marketability. It [secondary market transactions] would lie somewhere on that continuum that we've all described.

JOE: Yes, I agree. I think that Facebook would be an outlier here, because Facebook represents the highest percentage of volume, so in that case the discount for lack of marketability would be the lowest, if not zero. But it's still not by definition a fully liquid market.

LORENZO: We could easily take this just one step further. Suppose we move beyond the secondary markets and move on to the repurchases of stock. For instance, in addition to Facebook, Groupon had a similar significant transaction with DST where DST would acquire a significant portion of common stock as part of its investment in the company. You saw the same thing with Zynga, where a substantial portion of the common stock would be acquired as part of the investment. Obviously, that creates liquidity for everyone immediately and sets the price for the common stock as well as all the other securities. So each of your comments, as well as the techniques we've discussed, supports approaches to addressing the issue of both market inputs (market approaches to valuation) and marketability discounts (the continuum you've referred to). Thanks for those insights.

SUMMARY

In this chapter many of the techniques that were introduced and covered throughout this book were discussed with expert valuation practitioners who use them daily in their work for venture-capital-financed companies. The shortcuts presented earlier, as well as the methods for identifying weaknesses in value conclusions to enhance profits, can be applied quickly in most cases. However, the techniques these professionals apply, and the way in which they present their analyses and conclusions, can determine if auditors, tax authorities, and securities regulators approve of their reports. In an ideal situation, all of these elements would converge and find equilibrium at a similar value conclusion, adjusted for differences in standards of value. In the real world, sometimes simply having a better understanding of how and why different parties reach their respective conclusions can allow you to more effectively close that gap with your own insights, intuition, and analysis.

In Chapter 10, we will quickly review some of the techniques and keys to remember to avoid losing your share of the millions foregone daily in the world of venture-backed companies due to failure to understand "value."

Now That You Understand Venture Capital Valuation, Share It

"Rising prices are a narcotic that affect the reasoning power up and down the line.... Isaac Newton participated in the South Sea bubble. Originally got out. And then he couldn't stand prices going up any longer and so he went back in and got cleaned. And this was a fellow who was generally regarded as being pretty bright."
—From Warren Buffett's testimony in front of the Financial Crisis Inquiry Commission

If you read even the first chapter of this book, you've effectively transitioned from the 99.9% of decision makers involved in a venture-capital-backed company who are losing money because they don't understand valuation. As illustrated in our very first case of valuation issues—Facebook v. ConnectU—you don't always need complicated math to bridge the gap between different standards of value. All you need is to know that there is a difference in value standards, understand what the assumptions are for those standards, and then apply a little multiplication, division, or subtraction to figure out how one value indication compares to another. This can make valuations for venture-backed and angel-funded companies easier than they are for traditional private companies and public companies. Knowing the track records, strategic motivations, and exit horizons of the parties in control is also an advantage one has when turning value indications or clues for these companies into meaningful value conclusions.

In the capital markets, price appreciation can be addictive, as Warren Buffett noted in his testimony to Congress after being subpoenaed to offer insights on what he referred to as "the granddaddy of all bubbles, it affected an asset class of $22 trillion." Although venture-capital- and angel-backed companies are made up of humans, and naturally susceptible to the lure of rapid capital appreciation, I believe there's a big difference between how rising prices, or values, work in these companies versus how they work on Wall Street. The vast majority of people involved in venture-capital- and angel-backed companies are employees who have chosen to work for small companies with negative earnings (on an accounting basis) and no meaningful operating cash flow. These employees include the founders themselves, who envisioned the businesses, key hires who share that vision, and entrepreneurial managers who see a way to execute it. These people are, by and large, motivated by the opportunity to create something that's going to make a difference. But without price appreciation for the funds and angels that invest in those ventures, most of these companies will be sorted by natural selection, just like the evolving markets they are pursuing. In this environment, rising valuations are less of a narcotic and more of an antibiotic, fighting off the chances that everything goes to zero and the enterprise gets shut down. This environment, however, creates more volatility than most of the firms bailed out in the financial crisis ever experienced, even during the height of the crisis, and that's a good thing for these same employees, if it's reflected in the models that determine a key component of their compensation.

Unlike trading options on an exchange, or even buying or selling equity or debt in the open market, venture-funded companies almost always require collaboration and teamwork with parties that may get more than their pro-rata share of proceeds when the company is acquired or goes public. Understanding what the different parties hold and how those values are interconnected can only help foster better alignment of efforts when things get really tough, when things go extremely well, and even when a company appears to be going sideways. Each of these scenarios can apply to a high-velocity company multiple times during its young history and each, of course, has profound and distinct impacts on valuation.

So now that you are able to make better venture-backed company valuation decisions than the experts advising ConnectU, who should you share that information with? Share it with everyone. Starting with your friends and the people you trust. They may not agree with your insights immediately, but as they encounter these transactions more often, their perspectives will change and they will no longer see a "valuation" as a single point estimate, but rather as a "what if" expression subject to certain assumptions. Those assumptions are often far more important than the single point (or value conclusion) presented. For instance, if they know, as you now do, that the volatility assumption being used is too low, which we've demonstrated is the case with almost each and every venture-backed company valuation, then how does that impact their investment? Perhaps more importantly, consider how that single assumption might impact the ability of each of the following parties to make or lose money:

- Founders, CEOs, CFOs, and investors in biotech, clean tech, Internet, IT, and other high-growth private companies.
  - Founders, CEOs, and CFOs would effectively be granting options at a higher strike price for most a company's life with volatility estimates too low, as shown throughout this book. When the company value gets quite high, the impact would decrease with respect to the estimated total company value, but would persist in the absence of secondary markets such as Sharespost and SecondMarket.
- Venture fund analysts and investing partners, angel investors, secondary purchasers, and journalists covering private equity, venture capital, biotech, clean tech, Internet, and IT.
  - Venture-fund analysts at some funds routinely build waterfalls, but hardly ever apply volatility to the cash flows of those waterfalls as of the date this book is being published. As a result, the range of possible payouts is often limited to a handful of possible outcomes, as opposed to an "infinite" amount of payouts, as would be the case by simply applying Black-Scholes in an option pricing model (OPM) as demonstrated throughout this book. Venture-fund analysts are generally hired from top schools and tend to have far more time to do these analyses than your typical angel and far more inclination to want to do the analyses than your typical investing partner. If they are not measuring investing cash flow potential in a way that explicitly considers volatility, then almost no one in a venture is except the valuation professionals and the auditors, whom the investment decision makers tend to see as sources of compliance-related expenses, not sources of investment insights.
  - Secondary purchasers on SecondMarket and Sharespost, if they are not VCs, generally have access to very little information concerning a company other than one critical piece of data: perceived growth trajectory. These investors are especially counting on volatility, yet few of them model it explicitly as a discounting factor when making their purchase decisions. That may be appropriate when private companies are valued in the billions, like Facebook, Zynga, or LinkedIn, but what about the other 7,000 or so companies? A little analysis using volatility as an input can go a long way toward realizing venture-like returns for secondary purchasers who aren't VCs.

- Chief Investment Officers and analysts at limited partners, such as insurance companies, pension funds, and endowments.
  - Some limited partners literally spend millions attempting to understand where their alternative asset portfolio is heading so they can meet future obligations. However, few if any are applying the simple volatility inputs we've discussed to their holdings to better refine those estimates and potentially benefit by increasing direct interest in winners through secondary purchases based on volatility. Although detailed analysis of fund holdings is not generally available, we've shown that for most companies, you can generate models that would be superior to what these limited partners generally have to work with today simply by using a certificate of incorporation from SecondMarket or Sharespost combined with some data from the Crunchbase API. With so much at stake, hiring a young analyst at $80K to $100K per year just to do this type of analysis could yield billions (yes, billions), simply using the techniques we've demonstrated in this book.
- Auditors, valuation professionals, legal counsel, and other advisors to the VC ecosystem.
  - Trusted advisors want to deliver the best advice and insights. But sometimes, it's hard to change from the status quo without an incentive. If an auditor were to say in 2008, "100% of the volatility inputs to Black-Scholes for equity compensation calculations are too low for our venture-backed clients," that person had better have a big title and a collection of clients who care. Since very few financial statement notes are even read, the connection between a company's equity compensation disclosures and the value to the employees of the company's option grants is not something most companies are aware of. By working together, attorneys, valuation professionals, and auditors make an understanding of the basic valuation inputs and methods we've discussed in this book as widely understood by their clients as net income or cash on hand is.

The next time someone says the "pre-money value" of a company was a certain amount, realize that in most cases, that's just an expression of the percentage ownership acquired in the most recent round and the resulting price paid per share for the new round. You know that unless the company is worth many times more than the capital it has received to date, which means the pre-money value immediately before the financing plus the cash received (the traditional "post-money" value definition) does not equal the fair market value of the company. You also realize, however, the takeover value for the company immediately following the financing round may in fact be much higher than the post-money valuation.

Unlike thousands of private company investors and fund limited partners, you should no longer have to simply dismiss the amounts on fund balance sheets as "estimates," or rely solely on actual cash-on-cash returns as convincing evidence of interim IRRs. Unlike millions of venture-capital- and angel-capital-backed company employees, you will no longer have to view your options as "worthless" and hope for the best. And as a founder or officer of one of these companies, you can better align the actions of your advisors with the needs of your stakeholders and thereby serve your employees and investors better by stopping parties from losing money before it's too late to do anything about it and understanding how "value" changes their rights to cash flow at every stage of a company's evolution.

About the Author

Lorenzo Carver, MS, MBA, CVA, CPA, is CEO of Liquid Scenarios, a technology-based financial business intelligence solution company that provides software and services to investors, practitioners, and entrepreneurs at high-growth private companies.

Carver has a 20-year track record of helping thousands of investors, practitioners, and entrepreneurs measure and realize high-growth venture value. He is the author and developer of *BallPark Business Valuation*, the number one selling, award-winning small business valuation solution software covered by *Business Week, Inc. Magazine, Entrepreneur, CPA Software News, Kim Komando,* and business journals worldwide, as well as the author of the first software applications designed to automatically value venture-capital investments and stock options in accordance with IRC §409A. He was issued a patent on his venture-capital valuation technology, has developed over 200 strategic plans for information technology and life sciences companies, and participated in over $1 billion in private financing rounds as an advisor and planner and a comparable amount of debt financing transactions. Lorenzo's *Carver Import Algorithm* enables importing financial reports in seconds, without data tagging or manual data entry, and converting them into interactive models anyone can use immediately. He has worked on numerous IPOs and successfully rebutted SEC fair value and impairment-related accounting inquiries.

Index

Printed and bound by CPI Group (UK) Ltd, Croydon, CR0 4YY

23/04/2025

14660924-0003